Concepts of

Personal Financial Planning

Ben T. Bernacchi, CFP®
and
Eleanor B. Bernacchi, CFP®

Copyright © 2001 by Ben T. Bernacchi

Published by   Bernacchi Financial Services
                4748 Sardis Road
                Murrysville, PA 15668
                (724) 327-7470
                Fax: (724) 325-2740
                e-mail: btb72123@nb.net
                www.mysecurityfinancial.com

ISBN 0-9716262-0-0

Source for the following charts and tables: *Stocks, Bonds, Bills & Inflation, 2000 Yearbook*™, © Ibbotson Associates, Chicago, IL. Used with permission. All rights reserved.

Charts: 3-1, 3-2, 3-4

Tables: 3-1, 3-2, 3-3, 4-11, 6-1, 9-13

This book is designed to provide as accurate and current information as possible, as of the date of publication. It is presented with the understanding that the author offers no legal, tax or accounting services, nor does he sell any financial products or manage clients' money. If such professional services are required, the reader is urged to seek the services of a competent professional person.

The author apologizes for any errors or omissions of information that may have occurred, inadvertently or due to changes in legislation or otherwise.

Revised: October, 2002
Printed in the United States of America

INTRODUCTION

An incredible amount of money and human energy are expended in the interest of achieving financial security, and yet, most people still do not have a good understanding of the intricacies of the financial planning process.

The primary objective of this book is to provide a conceptual understanding of the *personal financial planning process*, and the planning tools and strategies used in the development of a comprehensive financial plan.

The basic building blocks of a comprehensive financial plan include the following.

- Protection against catastrophic or unexpected events, such as disability, premature death, etc.

- The accumulation of savings to fund specific goals, such as college funding, retirement, etc.

- The management of investment assets; that is, having an understanding of the return and risk characteristics of investment securities, the development of an diversified investment portfolio that will participate in the up markets and provide protection in down markets, etc.

- Tax planning, for which the primary objective is to minimize the tax liability using strategies such as deferral of taxation, regular IRA's, 401-k plans, etc., and/or tax-free investment securities (i.e. Roth IRA's, municipal bonds, etc.), and to maximize the use of allowable deductions, tax credits, etc.

- Estate planning, for which the primary objective is the transfer of accumulated assets to chosen beneficiaries while minimizing estate taxes. Estate planning comprehends the use of legal documents such as wills, trusts, durable powers of attorney, etc.

The basic *initial steps* required in the development of a personal financial plan are as follows.

Step 1. The calculation of your current *net worth*; that is, the current total assets minus the current total liabilities. The calculation of the net worth provides a financial picture of what your financial position is at a point in time.

Step 2. The driving forces behind a financial plan are the various financial goals that you establish, such as retirement, college funding, purchase of a new home, etc.

Not only is it necessary to identify the financial goals, but they must be quantified and prioritized.

Step 3. The integration of your incomes and expenses, that is, a *cash flow analysis*, projected over a defined planning period, such as 5, 10 or more years.

The financial planning process is an *iterative process* , in that changes in your cash flow analysis, such as a change of job, life events such as a marriage or divorce, an addition to the family, pre-mature death, etc., all require the updating of the financial plan.

Over the last decade, the trend has been to replace employer retirement pensions with tax-deferred savings plans, where the participant is responsible for the decisions as to how much to contribute and the selection of how to invest, both of which may be limited by options available within the plan.

The investor's responsibility for making investment decisions may, in the future, also apply to a portion of his/her social security contributions.

The internet provides extensive financial information relating to stocks, mutual funds, etc. However, this universe of information may complicate an individual's decision making capability, in that *information* is not *knowledge*. With a proper understanding of the basic *concepts of personal financial planning*, the internet information may be processed in an orderly fashion into knowledge.

Over the last decade and a half, it has been our observation that the learning curve of individuals, as it pertains to financial planning, has improved significantly.

The level of presentation in this book is designed to bring added value to this learning curve.

It is the author's belief that, if the financial planning concepts are truly understood, then the transformation of information into knowledge, using realistic assumptions and the application of the planning tools, will produce results which can be interpreted with a high level of confidence.

ABOUT THE AUTHORS...

Ben T. Bernacchi–Mr. Bernacchi has a degree in Chemical Engineering from Purdue University and a Masters degree in Industrial Engineering from the University of Pittsburgh. By the time he was 29 he was Director of Engineering for a firm that managed a munitions factory for the U.S. government. Later he joined a major international corporation, and over a 25-year career worked his way up to the position of Director of Strategic Planning and Industrial Engineering.

Eleanor B. Bernacchi–Mrs. Bernacchi also has a degree in Chemical Engineering from Purdue University, but focused her early years on the raising of their three daughters, each of whom is successful in their chosen field. Mrs. Bernacchi has been interested for many years in the education and nurturing of handicapped children and has been active, as a volunteer, in many community activities in this area. Mr. Bernacchi has shared this interest and, together they have served many years in community service and on the Advisory Board of a private school for the handicapped.

As Mr. Bernacchi approached retirement he looked for financial advice for themselves. In his search he learned about the *College for Financial Planning* in Denver, Colorado. They received their designations as Certified Financial Planners, CFP™, in 1984 and 1985, respectively.

Mr. Bernacchi is a *Registered Investment Advisor*, Mrs. Bernacchi is a registered representative associate and both Mr. And Mrs. Bernacchi are licensees with the *Certified Financial Planner Board of Standards*.

They decided to use the knowledge gained to share with and educate others who might also be seeking personal financial planning services. They formed *Bernacchi Financial Services, Inc.* in 1986, which provides financial planning consulting services only and is not involved in selling any financial products or managing money. Over the years Bernacchi Financial Services, Inc. has successfully served hundreds of clients. Mr. Bernacchi has also taught courses in personal financial planning at the local community college, and participated in corporate sponsored pre-retirement seminars for employees of many major corporations.

A primary focus of their financial consulting service is that of educating their clients, in that a knowledgeable client will have a higher level of confidence in attaining his/her goals.

With the same intent, it is hoped that everyone reading this book will feel more informed and more comfortable from knowledge gained, when dealing with their own personal financial planning and/or their financial planning advisor.

HOW TO USE THIS BOOK...

You don't need to start at Chapter 1 and read through the whole book sequentially to the end, just go directly to the section of the book that discusses the personal financial planning topic of particular interest.

The Personal Financial Planning issues of interest will depend on the reader's age, family and career status. For example, for a single individual just entering the work force, the personal financial planning issues of interest would be different than those for a middle career individual with a family, or for an individual already in retirement.

The table below provides some general guidelines for prioritizing the chapters of greatest interest, based on the reader's career status, age, etc. Priorities have been assigned to five chapters for each of the respective career stages, with '1' being of the highest priority or interest and '5' being of the lowest priority for that career stage. However, it should be pointed out that all of the chapters have something of interest for every reader.

		PERSONAL FINANCIAL PRIORITIES			
		--------CARREER STATUS--------			
CHAPTER	CONTENTS	EARLY	MID	PRE-RETR	RETIRED
1	FINANCIAL PLANNING PROCESS	1	3		
2	FINANCIAL. POSTION, GOAL SETTING ,CASH FLOW	2	2		
3	INVESTMENT MANAGEMENT, RISK & DIVERSIFICATION	4	1	1	1
4	INVESTMENT MANAGEMENT, MEASUREMENT OF PERFORMANCE	5	4	4	5
5	INVESTMENT MANAGEMENT ,BONDS			5	4
6	RETIREMENT PLANNING		5	2	3
7	RISK MANAGEMENT	3			
8	ESTATE PLANNING			3	2
9	TIME VALUE MONEY				

It should be noted that Chapter 9, **Time Value of Money,** has not been prioritized for any career stage in the above table.

This is because the computational procedures used in the various chapters are all based on time value of money concepts. If the reader is serious about understanding his/her personal financial plan management, this is a *'must read'* chapter.

–Table of Contents–

—FINANCIAL PLANNING PROCESS—

Overview

Personal financial planning is not something a person does only once. It is an ongoing process involving all of the activities of his/her life. It involves projections and assumptions, which may need to be modified from time to time, as situations change and the planning period progresses.

The personal financial planning process may be defined as the application of planning tools and techniques to the development and implementation of a total coordinated plan, such that personal financial goals are realized on a timely basis within the constraints of time and available financial resources.

Personal financial planning should be viewed as similar to a business entity. If a business enterprise is to be profitable, its earnings must be positive; that is, its net revenues must exceed its total operating costs.

If a personal financial plan is to achieve its goals, the incomes must exceed the expenditures, such that discretionary savings are available to fund the various financial goals, such as retirement, college funding, etc.

If a business enterprise is not profitable, it is necessary to increase revenues or reduce operating costs, or both.

If the discretionary savings of a personal financial plan are minimal or negative, similar measures must be taken. The opportunity to increase income may be limited; in which case, the expenditures must be reduced.

It has been our experience, after many years of developing comprehensive financial plans for many clients, that clients' knowledge of how their income is allocated to the various items of expense, such as food, housing, utilities, transportation, recreation, etc., represents one of the *weakest* links in the planning process.

Knowledge of expenditures is essential if they are to be controlled.

The basic building blocks of a comprehensive personal financial plan are as follows:

- Present security
- Future security
- Investment management
- Tax planning
- Estate planning

In the development of a comprehensive personal financial plan the *use* of financial resources must be balanced against *available* financial resources.

The inflows and outflows of financial resources are *integrated* through the development of a *cash flow* analysis over a designated planning period.

The financial planning process is an iterative process, in that *changes* in the inflows and outflows of financial resources, over time, need to be integrated into the planning process. In other words, the plan must be updated to comprehend changes.

Today's computer software and the financial information and planning tools available on the internet can provide the platform for the development of a comprehensive personal financial plan.

However, without proper understanding of the basic planning concepts, and if unrealistic assumptions are made, the use of computer software may create more problems than it solves.

Confronted with the unlimited financial information and planning tools available, an individual may be overwhelmed by terms such as *asset allocation, risk/return, portfolio optimization, time value of money, inflation adjusted income, simulation modeling,* etc.

These financial planning terms represent complex mathematical procedures; however, it is not necessary to learn the mathematics, just the basic concepts. If concepts are truly understood, then, with the application of financial planning techniques and using realistic assumptions and inputs, the resulting plan may be viewed with a high level of confidence.

The following is a brief overview of the basic building blocks of a comprehensive personal financial plan.

The respective financial planning building blocks will be described in great detail in this book. Where applicable, worksheet examples and templates are provided at the end of the respective chapters for the benefit of the reader.

Present Security

The personal financial planning building block, *present security*, also called the management of risk, should be given the highest priority.

The basic goal of risk management is protection against financial problems arising from catastrophic or unexpected events: such as, disability resulting in loss of earnings; major medical expenses; property losses; pre-mature death, etc.

The primary investment vehicles used to provide present security are various insurance products, such as...

- Life insurance
- Health insurance
- Disability insurance
- Home-owner/renter insurance
- Auto insurance
- Long term care insurance

Life insurance and disability insurance protect against loss of income. Home-owner and auto insurance protect against loss of property. Health insurance and long term care insurance insure against loss of wealth.

Insurance such as life insurance is required in the early years, to buy time during the period in which we are accumulating wealth, and the need for life insurance is the greatest. In later years, as wealth is accumulated, the need for life insurance decreases.

In contrast, the need for other types of insurance coverage increases with age, such as health insurance and long term care insurance.

Home-owners insurance and auto insurance are necessary as long as you own a home, other property, or a car.

Future Security

The personal financial planning objective, *future security*, involves the funding of such goals as...

- Retirement
- College funding
- Purchase of a home
- Purchase of a new car
- Accumulation of wealth

The various goals must be prioritized and be realistic in terms of your ability to fund such goals.

The required periodic savings needed to achieve a stated goal are a function of the total sum of money required, the time available for accumulation and investment rates of return. The Chapter 9, **Time Value of Money**, provides an in-depth discussion of the time-value-of-money concepts.

Over the last decade the trend relating to retirement savings has been away from defined benefit pension plans and toward tax-deferred savings plans.

Tax-deferred savings plans, such as 401-k plans, 403-b plans, IRA's, etc., require the individual employee to be responsible for making investment decisions on how to invest his/her savings for retirement.

The investor's responsibility for making investment decisions may, in the future, also apply to a portion of his/her social security contributions.

Retirement planning comprehends two phases:

- Pre-retirement
- Post-retirement

Pre-retirement planning requires the calculation of the annual savings needed during the years prior to retirement such that the amount of savings required at the start of retirement are achieved.

The calculation of the savings required at the start of retirement is a function of the following.

- Other retirement resources, such as pensions, social security, etc.
- Projected expenditures, such as living expenses, taxes, etc.
- Life expectancy
- Investment rates of return
- Inflation rate
- Etc.

Post-retirement planning requires the calculation of the retirement life style that can be supported by the *actual* savings accumulated at the start of retirement. If the actual retirement savings are less than the target savings, then adjustments to the retirement life style is required.

Investment Management

The funding of future goals and the accumulation of wealth projections are based on the assumption that the savings will realize some expected investment rate of return over the holding period.

The expected rate of return is an average rate of return, in that, from one time period to another during the holding period, the actual return will deviate from the expected rate of return. The deviation, or volatility, of investment returns is correlated with the investment portfolio risk.

The return on an investment portfolio is directly correlated with risk, that is, the higher the expected return, the higher the risk.

Investment risk may be the risk of loss of purchasing power or loss of principal, or both.

To structure an investment portfolio which will provide an expected rate of return, while minimizing risk, will require the diversification of investment dollars among various investment securities, such as cash, bonds and stocks.

The allocation of investment dollars to cash, bonds and stocks must comprehend such issues as the individual's age, the planning time horizon, risk tolerance, marginal tax rate, etc.

Pre-retirement and post-retirement both represent planning periods with long time horizons. Therefore, the projections of savings required at the start of retirement, etc., are very sensitive to the assumptions used in the planning process, such as investment rates of return, etc., in that such assumptions are not linear, but are compounded over time.

Tax Planning

In the pre-retirement years the following income sources are subject to federal income and, perhaps, employment taxes.

- Earnings/wages
- Interest/dividend income
- Capital gains

The list above is not an all inclusive list; however, it represents over 90% of the federal taxes paid in the pre-retirement years.

In the post-retirement years the following income sources are, or may be, subject to federal taxes.

- Pension income
- Distributions from tax-deferred retirement savings
- Interest/dividend income
- Social security benefits
- Capital gains
- Estate assets

In addition to the pre- and post-retirement federal taxation, and depending on the state of residence, incomes may also be subject to state and local taxes.

Over the planning horizon, the tax liability will vary. For example, the *total* of all *taxes* divided by *gross income*, in the pre-retirement years, represents 15% - 35% of the gross income, on average.

In the post-retirement years, but prior to age 70½ when an individual is required to begin minimum required distributions from tax-deferred savings, the level of taxation may be minimal.

However, after age 70½, and depending on the amount of accumulated tax-deferred retirement savings, income taxes will continue to increase over the retirement period.

The primary objective of tax planning is to minimize the tax liability through the use of one or more of the following strategies.

- *Pre-retirement contributions* to qualified retirement plans—these contributions are not reported as taxable income when made, and the future earnings are *tax-deferred*.

- *After-tax contributions to Roth IRA*—all future earnings and distributions are *tax-free*.

- *Investment in tax-free securities* such as municipal bonds.

- *Estate Planning*, that is, maximizing the use of allowable credits, charitable giving, etc.

An individual experiences widely different taxation levels through the pre-and post-retirement years, depending on ages, family status, employment status, etc. Therefore, in the development of a personal financial plan, the use of a *nominal tax rate* for the pre- and post-retirement periods will result in cash flow projections with a very low level of confidence.

The personal financial planning model must incorporate the various IRS regulations as they relate to the calculations of the various taxes, such that the cash flow projections will result in a higher level of confidence.

Estate Planning

The primary objective of estate planning is to transfer estate assets to chosen beneficiaries while minimizing estate taxes.

The level of complexity of estate planning is a function of your estate size. The estate size is your net worth modified to include life insurance death benefits, if they are not in an irrevocable trust, etc.

In the very early years, when the modified estate net worth is below the unified estate and gift tax credit, the basic estate planning should have, as a minimum, an up-to-date *will*.

Each estate is entitled to a *unified credit*, which is equal to the amount of tax generated by an estate of $1,000,000 in 2002. In other words, if the modified estate is $1,000,000 or less, there is no federal tax.

The *Growth and Tax Relief Reconciliation Act of 2001* provides for an increase in the unified credit over the next ten years. However, tax laws are always subject to change, so the need for proper estate planning will always be important.

With a proper planning, the unified credit is available in the first-to-die estate as well as the second-to-die estate.

The will controls the transfer of assets held in the decedent's name without any beneficiary designations.

In later years, as the estate net worth exceeds the unified estate and gift tax credit, estate planning requires the use of other planning techniques, such as trusts, powers of attorney, disclaimers, gifting, etc.

The following is a graphic representation of the basic building blocks, both inputs and outputs, encompassed in a comprehensive personal financial plan.

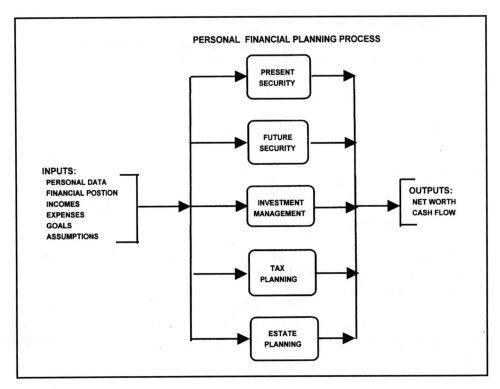

Chart 1-1

The basic planning tools of a comprehensive personal financial plan and a detailed discussion of them are as follows.

- Financial Position
- Cash Flow
- Setting Goals
- Setting Assumptions

Financial Position

The starting point for the development of a personal financial plan is the net worth statement, that is, the current financial position.

The net worth is calculated by subtracting the total current liabilities from the total current assets.

Total assets include ...

- Cash equivalents
- Investments
- Retirement savings
- Personal assets; that is, real estate (personal residence), automobiles, collectibles, etc.

Liabilities include ...

- Home mortgage and home equity loans
- Automobile loans
- Personal loans
- Other liabilities

In that the net worth is the initial starting point, assets such as a home must reflect the fair market value.

For liabilities such as home mortgages, the interest payments are adjustments to the gross income when calculating your taxable income. However, interest payments on an auto loans are not deductible; therefore, each liability must be separately detailed.

If assets exceed liabilities, the net worth is positive, whereas, if liabilities exceed assets, the net worth is negative.

The financial position, also called a balance sheet, is a dynamic instrument, constantly changing throughout the financial planning period as incomes, liabilities and assets change.

Cash Flow

The cash flow analysis integrates the incomes and outflows of financial resources for a specific planning period, such as a month, a year or multiple years.

The computational procedures for developing a personal financial plan cash flow, for a specific planning period, is schematically illustrated below.

	Total Income Sources
Less:	Living expenses
Less:	Taxes
Equals:	After-tax cash flow
Less:	Goal funding
Equals:	Discretionary cash flow

If the discretionary cash flow is negative, then adjustments to the use of the financial resources is necessary.

Because the personal financial plan is a projection over multiple years, various assumptions are required as to the changes in the income sources and expenses.

For example, a projection for an annual increase in wages is required in the pre-retirement period.

However, in the post-retirement period wages are discontinued, and the wages are replaced by a pension, distributions from 401-k's and IRA's, and social security benefits, etc.

It is very important that variable expenses, such as food, utilities, etc., be adjusted for inflation over the projected planning period.

Also, non-recurring expenses, that is, expenses which are not incurred annually, such as weddings, major home improvements or repairs, and are not being pre-funded, must be identified as to the year in which such expenditures will be incurred and the estimated dollars of expenditure.

Setting Goals

Reaching a person's financial goals in a timely manner gives the individual a sense of accomplishment and a measurement of control.

The process of goal settling requires first, the identification of the specific goals. Secondly, the specific goals must be quantified as to when the goal is to be achieved and the sum of money required. Thirdly, priorities must be established for achieving the respective goals.

The establishment of one or more financial goals, such as college funding, purchase of a new car, major home improvements or repairs, retirement, etc., must be realistic in terms of the individual's ability to fund such goals.

If the savings required to achieve the stated goals exceed the after-tax cash flow, then adjustments will be required, such as adjusting the time to achieve a stated goal, or reducing the sum the money required, perhaps purchasing a smaller car or limiting the scope of a home improvement. It may also be necessary to eliminate a specific goal.

Assumptions

The personal financial plan is very sensitive to the various assumptions used in making the cash flow projections, such as investment rates of return, inflation rates, life expectancy, income projections, etc.

Use of overly optimistic investment rates of return will result in unrealistic cash flow projections, and, perhaps not achieving a financial goal.

An understanding of historical investment rates of return will provide a benchmark in establishing realistic investment rates of return.

Why do Some People Fail?

Some people do not set their goals, some procrastinate, some fear making a mistake, some do piecemeal planning, some lack tax planning, some do not understand their employer benefits, some have outmoded wills and estate plans, some assume that their affairs are already in good order because they believe that all their assets are jointly owned. Some fail to diversify, some fail to invest regularly and some do not have a contingency plan for their families, complete with where their important papers are located so that they can find them when needed. Fewer than 5% of the people achieve financial independence by retirement! Resolve, now not to let this be **you!**

—FINANCIAL POSITION:
GOAL SETTING and CASH FLOW—

Overview: Data Input

In the development of a comprehensive financial plan, the current financial position, that is, where an individual is financially today, must be the starting point.

The primary driving forces of a financial plan are an individual's future goals, such as saving for retirement, college, etc.

When developing the personal financial plan, it is necessary to make various assumptions about future events, including such things as job continuation, investment rates of return, etc.

As we have said before, the financial planning process is an iterative process, that is, changes in inflows and outflows of the financial resources, over time, need to be integrated in the planning process as they occur.

The primary sources of quantitative data and information to be used in the development of a financial plan data base are the following documents.

- The most recent employer's savings and pension benefit statements.
- Payroll earnings and deductions statements for the last three or more pay periods.
- The most recent federal and state income tax returns, including W-2 forms and all accompanying tax schedules.
- The latest financial statements pertaining to stocks, mutual funds, annuities and other investments.
- A listing of current living expenses, i.e., a budget.
- Copies of wills and trust agreements.
- Etc.

The quantitative data and information to be extracted from the above documents, which are required in the development of the financial planning data base are...

- Insurance protection: life, disability, health, etc.
- Income resources
- Liabilities: mortgages, loans, credit card debt, etc.
- Investment assets

- Expenditures
- Estate planning status

In addition to the basic data information, a listing of a person's financial goals will be required, stating the relative importance of each of the respective goals.

For example, the following is a brief list of goals, of which one or more may be applicable to a particular financial planning process.

- Comfortable retirement
- Purchase of a new home
- College funding
- Reduction of debt
- Adequate life insurance/disability insurance, etc.
- Reduction of tax liability
- Expanded standard of living
- Accumulation of wealth
- Etc.

It is also essential that the individual make a realistic appraisal of his/her investment risk tolerance when establishing expected investment rates of return.

There is a direct correlation between expected return and risk, in other words, the higher the expected return the higher the risk. Therefore, an understanding of the historical returns and volatility for various investment securities is essential. These issues are discussed in the Chapter 3, **Investment Management, Risk and Diversification**.

At this time it is appropriate to introduce our hypothetical family, John and Mary Sample, ages 35 and 32, respectively. The Sample family has two children, Emily and John, Jr, ages 10 and 8, respectively.

John is an engineer working for a large multinational corporation, while Mary is a receptionist in a law firm.

Both have savings plans available with their respective employers.

Based on our initial *exploratory* planning meeting with the Sample family, it became apparent that they were not interested in a specific financial issue, such as investment portfolio analysis, but wanted a comprehensive view of their financial future. Therefore, the Sample family was provided with a *Data Organizer* which was to be completed prior to our next planning meeting.

The scope of the financial data required for the development of a personal financial plan is all encompassing; however, the basic information is available in such documents as previously discussed.

The *Data Organizer* provided the basis for the follow-up planning meeting.

Our financial planning organization requires complete disclosure of data and information from the client if an engagement of our services is to be provided.

The follow-up meeting, lasting several hours, established the scope of the financial services to be provided.

After the follow-up meeting, a *Letter of Agreement*, which details the specific financial services to be comprehended, such as 'investment portfolio analysis', 'college funding', retirement planning', etc., was submitted to the Sample family for their signatures.

The *Letter of Agreement* also states the exact fee to be charged for services provided and an approximate date of completion.

The signing of the *Letter of Agreement* by the Samples is required prior to the engagement of our services.

Financial Position

The current financial position, or balance sheet, documents what assets the Samples *own*, and their liabilities, that is, what they *owe*. Their net worth is then calculated by subtracting the total liabilities from the total assets.

Illustrated in Table 2-1 is a tabulation of the Sample's current total assets, total liabilities and net worth as of 1/1/2001.

Table 2-1
FINANCIAL POSITION WORKSHEET

Financial Position as of __01/_01_/2001

Assets–			Retirement Savings, Husband		
Cash Equivalents:			Regular IRA	$_____	
Checking accounts	$ 1500		Roth IRA		
Savings accounts	2500		Employer savings plan	90,000	
Money market accounts	12,300			Total	$90,000
Money market funds	_____				
Certificates of deposit	_____		**Retirement Savings, Spouse**		
US Treasury bills	_____		Regular IRA	$_____	
Cash value of life insurance	_____		Roth IRA		
Brokerage account balance	_____		Employer savings plan	8,666	
Credit union account	13,000			Total	$ 8,666
Other	_____		**Personal Assets:**		
	Total	$29,300	Residence	$200,000	
			Vacation home		
Goal Funding:			Automobiles	20,000	
College savings	$27,000		Furniture	15,000	
Other	_____		Collectibles	_____	
	Total	$27,000	Other	_____	
Investments:				Total	$235,000
Taxable Investments–					
Bonds:			**Total Assets:**	$433,881	
Municipal bonds	_____				
Tax free bond funds	_____				
Bonds, corporate	_____		**Liabilities:**		
Bonds, government	_____		Charge/Credit accounts	$_____	
Bond funds	_____		Personal loans		
Annuities, fixed	_____		Home mortgage	156,499	
Annuities, variable	_____		Home equity loans		
	Total	_____	Auto loan	15,000	
Stocks:			Other	_____	
Common stocks	$ 3,500				
Stock funds	40,415		**Total Liabilities:**	$171,499	
	Total	$43,415			
			Net Worth:	$262,382	

As shown in Table 2-1, the Sample family's net worth, as of 1/1/2001, is $262,382.

Goal Setting

Overview:

The various short and long range goals that the Sample's have established, and their order of priority, are tabulated in Table 2-2.

Table 2-2
Goal Setting

Priority #	Goals
1	Retire at age 60 for John, at age 50 for Mary
2	College funding for the two children
3	Purchase a new car by year 2010
4	Major home improvements by year 2016
5	Pre-payment of home mortgage

The Samples are currently funding both college and retirement planning. However, they have some concern relating to their future discretionary cash flows and funding the other goals.

Retirement Planning:

Retirement planning was the highest priority goal for the Samples, in that John would like to retire at age 60, and be able to support a comfortable life style, that is, at least equivalent to today's life style, over the retirement years.

Both John and Mary have 401-k plans with their respective employers. In that their employers do not provide a defined benefit pension plan, it was their objective to maximize pre-tax contributions to their respective plans.

It is also their objective to make annual contributions to Roth IRA's in the future, subject to the availability of discretionary cash flow.

The contribution parameters for their respective 401-k plans are tabulated in Table 2-3 below.

Table 2-3
Retirement Savings Assumptions

	John	Mary
Wages 2001	$65,000	$15,687
Annual wage increase	3.0%	3.0%
Current Retirement Savings	$90,000	$ 8,666
Employee pre-tax Contr, %	9.0%	10.0%
Employer Contr, %	3.0%	6.0%(1)
Retirement Age	60	50

(1) Employer contribution is 6% of employee's contribution

Their current retirement plan asset allocation is as follows.

Investment Group	% Allocation
Cash/Bonds	40%
Stocks/Stock funds	60%

In that the Samples have a long planning horizon before retirement, it was recommended that they consider a more aggressive investment portfolio asset allocation, such as 30% cash/bonds and 70% stocks/stock funds.

John, being an engineer, had made various spread sheet projections, and had established a target of $2,000,000 of tax-deferred savings by age 60, based on an 8.00% investment rate of return.

John's concern was that of investment portfolio risk, and what is the probability that his retirement goal of $2,000,000 will be realized, based on retaining his current investment portfolio asset allocation and the assumed 8.0% rate of return.

Based on the assumptions, as shown in Table 2-3, a projection of John's retirement savings at age 60 are tabulated in Table 2-4.

Table 2-4 also includes Roth IRA contributions starting in 2006, based on the projected availability of discretionary cash flow.

It was mutually agreed that the projections in Table 2-4 would be based on an assumed investment rate of return of 8.0%.

Table 2-4
John's Projected Retirement Savings

YEAR	AGE	WAGES	CONTRIBUTIONS JOHN	EMPLOYER	CUMULATIVE 401K PLAN	ROTH IRA
2001	35	$65,000	$5,850	$1,950	$105,292	
2002	36	66,950	6,026	2,009	122,051	
2003	37	68,959	6,206	2,069	140,400	
2004	38	71,027	6,392	2,131	160,475	
2005	39	73,158	6,584	2,195	182,421	
2006	40	75,353	6,782	2,261	206,397	$2,000
2007	41	77,613	6,985	2,328	232,571	4,160
2008	42	79,942	7,195	2,398	261,129	6,493
2009	43	82,340	7,411	2,470	292,271	9,012
2010	44	84,810	7,633	2,544	326,212	11,733
2011	45	87,355	7,862	2,621	363,184	14,672
2012	46	89,975	8,098	2,699	403,441	17,846
2013	47	92,674	8,341	2,780	447,254	21,273
2014	48	95,455	8,591	2,864	494,918	24,975
2015	49	98,318	8,849	2,950	546,752	28,973
2016	50	101,268	9,114	3,038	603,100	33,291
2017	51	104,306	9,388	3,129	664,334	37,954
2018	52	107,435	9,669	3,223	730,857	42,991
2019	53	110,658	9,959	3,320	803,102	48,430
2020	54	113,978	10,258	3,419	881,540	54,304
2021	55	117,397	10,566	3,522	966,679	60,649
2022	56	120,919	10,883	3,628	1,059,068	67,500
2023	57	124,547	11,209	3,736	1,159,299	74,900
2024	58	128,283	11,545	3,848	1,268,014	82,893
2025	59	132,132	11,892	3,964	1,385,906	91,524
2026	60	136,096	12,249	4,083	1,513,722	100,846

John's projected retirement savings, as tabulated in Table 2-4, are as follows:

Employer's 401-k plan $1,513,722
Roth IRA 100,846
Total $1,614,568

Table 2-5 provides a projection of Mary's retirement savings in year 2026, that is, the year that John plans to retire.

The projections of savings shown in Table 2-5 are also based on the 8.0% investment rate of return.

Table 2-5
Mary's Projected Retirement Savings

YEAR	AGE	WAGES	CONTRIBUTIONS MARY	EMPLOYER	CUMULATIVE T-D SAVINGS	ROTH IRA
2001	32	$15,687	$1,569	$94	$11,084	
2002	33	16,158	1,616	97	13,748	
2003	34	16,642	1,664	100	16,678	
2004	35	17,142	1,714	103	19,898	
2005	36	17,656	1,766	106	23,431	
2006	37	18,186	1,819	109	27,306	$2,000
2007	38	18,731	1,873	112	31,550	4,160
2008	39	19,293	1,929	116	36,196	6,493
2009	40	19,872	1,987	119	41,277	9,012
2010	41	20,468	2,047	123	46,830	11,733
2011	42	21,082	2,108	126	52,895	14,672
2012	43	21,714	2,171	130	59,514	17,846
2013	44	22,366	2,237	134	66,735	21,273
2014	45	23,037	2,304	138	74,607	24,975
2015	46	23,728	2,373	142	83,185	28,973
2016	47	24,440	2,444	147	92,528	33,291
2017	48	25,173	2,517	151	102,699	37,954
2018	49	25,928	2,593	156	113,766	42,991
2019	50	26,706	2,671	160	125,804	48,430
2020	51				135,869	54,304
2021	52				146,738	60,649
2022	53				158,477	67,500
2023	54				171,155	74,900
2024	55				184,848	82,893
2025	56				199,635	91,524
2026	57				215,606	100,846

Mary's projected retirement savings, as shown in Table 2-5, are as follows.

Employer's 401-k plan	$	215,606
Roth IRA		100,846
Total	$	316,452

Therefore, based on the above assumptions and projections, the total retirement savings available in 2026 are projected to be $1,991,020 ($1,614,568 + $316,452).

The projections in Tables 2-4 and 2-5 are based on a constant rate of return of 8.0% over the pre-retirement period from 2001 through 2026.

Chapter 3, **Investment Management, Risk and Diversification** illustrates the variation in investment rates of return that can occur from one holding period to another. The magnitude of variation is a function of investment portfolio risk. An investment portfolio return over a designated holding period is not only a function of the variation of returns, but also the sequential occurrences of the returns. For example, two investment portfolios with the same average rate of return over a given holding period may result in significant differences in the investment portfolio growth.

In response to John's inquiry as to the probability of realizing his retirement goal of $2,000,000 at retirement, a projection was evaluated using Monte Carlo simulation.

Monte Carlo simulation is a method for analyzing random variations, such as investment rates of return.

The basic concept of Monte Carlo simulation is the *random selection* of investment rates of return for each holding period. The investment rates of return are selected from a universe of returns which are representative of the expected returns for a given investment portfolio asset allocation. The Monte Carlo simulation methodology is discussed in detail in Chapter 6 **Retirement Planning**.

The results of the Monte Carlo simulation, as tabulated in Table 2-6, are based on 1000 different random simulations of the projected ending retirement savings, and, therefore, are expressed as probabilities.

These probabilities are based on a 60% stock and 40% cash/bonds investment portfolio asset allocation.

Table 2-6
Probability of Achieving Retirement Savings

Projected Retr Savings	Probability of Success
$2,000,000	95.5%
3,000,000	75.0%
3,500,000	60.0%
3,500,000	60.0%

The interpretation of Table 2-6 is as follows: there is a 95.5% probability that the $2,000,000 target retirement savings will be realized.

There is a 60% probability that the retirement savings could be as high as $3,500,000.

Based on the results of the simulation, there was a *mutual* agreement with the Samples that an 8.0% investment rate of return would be used in the development of the various goals.

In that retirement savings and college funding were considered to be their top priority goals, the scheduling of the other goals was contingent on the available discretionary cash flow, in that, the Samples also wanted to continue to have a minimum of $5000 per year of discretionary cash flow going to their taxable savings account.

Based on the above constraints, it was necessary to make various cash flow projections to establish the funding parameters for the other goals, as were detailed in Table 2-2.

The *Economic Growth and Tax Relief Reconciliation Act of 2001* gradually increases employee contribution limits to qualified retirement plans, such as 401-k plans, etc. as well as traditional and Roth IRA's.

Year	Qualified Plans	Year	IRA's
2001	$ 10,500	2001	$2000
2002	11,000	2002	3000
2003	12,000	2003	3000
2004	13,000	2004	3000
2005	14,000	2005	4000
2006	15,000	2006	4000
2007-2010	15,000 (1)	2007	4000
		2008	5000
		2009-2010	5000 (2)

(1) $15,000 plus annual inflation adjustment
(2) $5,000 plus annual inflation adjustment

College Funding:

The Samples both graduated from State Universities; therefore, the college funding was based on the assumption that the children would also attend State Universities.

In making the projections of college funding requirements, it was assumed that college costs would increase at 5.0% annually. The current annual State University tuition and living expenses are approximately $12,000 per year, in today's dollars.

Emily will start college in 2009 when the projected annual cost will be approximately $17,730, whereas John Jr will start college in 2011 when the projected annual cost will be approximately $19,550.

Their college funding target was to have adequate savings available at the *start* of college for each of the children and to provide four years of college education.

In establishing the required college funding, the Samples did not assume any direct college grants, such as the Federal Pell Grants or Supplemental Educational Opportunity Grants, which do not require any payback.

Their rationale was that if such grants were received, the basic college funding not used would be available for post-graduate studies.

The Samples currently have accumulated $15,000 of college funding for Emily and $12,000 for John Jr.

Currently the college savings are invested in taxable investment accounts. In that the Sample's current marginal tax bracket is 28%, it was recommended that the college savings should be placed in a tax-deferred savings plan.

The Sample's primary concern was to maintain control over the college savings; therefore, they had ruled out such plans as custodial accounts.

It was recommended that they consider the a *Qualified State Tuition Program,* referred to as the *Section 529* college savings plan which provides tax-deferral of earnings and control over the savings in the event that the child decides not to go to college.

Discussion with the Samples provided the following pros and cons of a Section 529 plan.

- In 1996 Congress passed new legislation authorizing *"Qualified State Tuition programs,"* QSTP, referred to also as a Section 529 plan.

- Under the Section 529 savings plan, future growth is not subject to taxation. The *Economic Growth and Tax Relief Reconciliation Act of 2001, EGTRA,* allows *tax-free* distributions for qualified educational expenses.

- The Section 529 college savings plans provide flexibility, in that money in these plans can be used to pay college expenses at any accredited post-secondary school anywhere in the country, not just in the state sponsoring it. The funds can be shifted from one child to another if one child decides not to attend college.

- Non-qualified withdrawals, that is, distributions not used for higher education expenses, are subjected to regular income tax at both the federal and state levels, plus a ten percent withdrawal penalty on the earnings.

- Section 529 college savings plans are not limited in terms of the annual contributions, as compared to an Educational IRA, which is currently limited to $500 per year. However, effective for tax years starting after 2001, the allowable annual contribution for Educational IRA's is increased to $2000 per designated beneficiary.

- QSTP's may offer several different investment options. Investment options may include fixed income, age-based, equity and balanced funds.

In as much as the Sample's marginal tax bracket is 28%, they made the decision to transfer the current savings and all future contributions to a Section 529 plan, thereby avoiding future taxation on interest and dividend income at their marginal tax rate.

The calculation of the annual contributions to the college savings plans was based on an assumed investment rate of return of 8.0%.

Table 2-7 is a projection of the required annual savings and distributions for Emily, based on the various assumptions.

Table 2-7
College Funding, Emily

YEAR	EMILY AGE	START BAL	ANNUAL SAVINGS	ANNUAL DISTRIBUTIONS	END BALANCE
2001	10	$15,000	$3,338		$19,538
2002	11	19,538	3,471		24,572
2003	12	24,572	3,610		30,148
2004	13	30,148	3,754		36,314
2005	14	36,314	3,905		43,124
2006	15	43,124	4,061		50,634
2007	16	50,634	4,223		58,908
2008	17	58,908	4,392		68,013
2009	18	68,013		$17,729	54,307
2010	19	54,307		18,616	38,546
2011	20	38,546		19,547	20,519
2012	21	20,519		20,524	

It should be noted that the contributions are not fixed at a constant annual rate, but are increased annually at 4%, corresponding to the assumed inflation rate.

Table 2-8 is a projection of the required annual savings and distributions for John Jr, based on the various assumptions stated above.

Table 2-8
College Funding, John Jr.

YEAR	JOHN Jr. AGE	START BAL	ANNUAL SAVINGS	ANNUAL DISTRIBUTIONS	END BALANCE
2001	8	$12,000	$2,893		$15,853
2002	9	15,853	3,009		20,130
2003	10	20,130	3,129		24,869
2004	11	24,869	3,254		30,112
2005	12	30,112	3,384		35,906
2006	13	35,906	3,520		42,298
2007	14	42,298	3,660		49,342
2008	15	49,342	3,807		57,096
2009	16	57,096	3,959		65,623
2010	17	65,623	4,117		74,990
2011	18	74,990		$19,547	59,878
2012	19	59,878		20,524	42,503
2013	20	42,503		21,550	22,629
2014	21	22,629		22,628	

Purchase of a New Car:

The purchase of a new car in year 2011 was based on trading in the current automobile, plus a $20,500 cash payment.

The funding for the purchase of the new car, starting in 2006, is detailed in Table 2-9. The projections in Table 2-9 are based on an investment rate of return of 8.0%.

Table 2-9
Auto Sinking Fund

YEAR	START BALANCE	SAVINGS	DISTR	END BALANCE
2001				
2002				
2003				
2004				
2005				
2006		$3,500		$3,500
2007	$3,500	3,500		7,280
2008	7,280	3,500		11,362
2009	11,362	3,500		15,771
2010	15,771	3,500		20,533
2011	20,533		$20,533	

These funds are in taxable accounts and the earnings are included as taxable income each year.

Home Improvements:

The home improvements in year 2016, of $25,000, require the funding to start in year 2011.

The home improvement funding, based on an 8.0% investment rate of return, is detailed in Table 2-10.

Table 2-10
Home Improvement Funding

YEAR	START BALANCE	SAVINGS	DISTR	SAVINGS BALANCE
2001				
2002				
2003				
2004				
2005				
2006				
2007				
2008				
2009				
2010				
2011		$4,261		$4,261
2012	$4,261	4,261		8,863
2013	8,863	4,261		13,833
2014	13,833	4,261		19,201
2015	19,201	4,261		24,998
2016	24,998		$25,000	

This funding is also assumed to be in a taxable account, as was the automobile funding.

Pre-Payment of Home Mortgage:

The current home mortgage parameters are as follows.

Mortgage date	1/1/1996
Loan principal	$165,000
Interest rate	7.75%
Monthly payments	$1182
Term, years	30

The Sample's priority of making pre-payments on the mortgage was given the lowest priority. However, they had expressed concern with the issue that the cumulative interest payments, if the loan was held for the full 30 years, were approximately $260,500, exceeding the loan principal of $165,000 by approximately 60%.

In that they were itemizing their deductions, the loss of home mortgage interest payments, resulting from pre-payments, was not an issue, in that the reduction in interest payments would more than offset the tax benefits resulting from itemizing the mortgage interest if held full term.

The use of the discretionary income to pre-pay the home mortgage would also divert these pre-payment dollars away from their taxable investment account.

In that their cash/bond funds, representing 40% of their taxable account, was earning approximately 4.0%, after taxes, and the adjusted mortgage rate was 5.6%, the decision to make the $300 per month pre-payment was warranted.

Based on the availability of discretionary cash flow, it was agreed that pre-payments of *$300 per month*, starting 1/1/2011, would be incorporated into the financial plan.

Table 2-11 provides a summary of the mortgage pre-payment benefits.

Table 2-11
Pre-Payment vs No Pre-Payment of Home Mortgage

	No Pre-Pmt	Pre-Pmt
Cumulative Intr Pmts	$260,549	$230,230
Required Number of Pmts	360	304

Table 2-12 provides the home mortgage amortization schedules for both the 'no pre-payments' and 'pre-payments' based on the above assumptions.

Table 2-12
Amortization Schedules

	HOME MORTGAGE; NO PRE-PAYMENTS					HOME MORTGAGE; PRE-PAYMENTS PRE-PMTS STARTING JAN 2011			
YEAR	INTR PMTS	PRN PMTS	ACC INTR	ACC PRN	YEAR	INTR PMTS	PRN PMTS	ACC INTR	ACC PRN
1996	$12,737	$1,448	$12,737	$1,448	1996	$12,737	$1,448	$12,737	$1,448
1997	12,620	1,564	25,357	3,013	1997	12,620	1,564	25,357	3,013
1998	12,495	1,690	37,852	4,703	1998	12,495	1,690	37,852	4,703
1999	12,359	1,826	50,211	6,529	1999	12,359	1,826	50,211	6,529
2000	12,212	1,973	62,424	8,501	2000	12,212	1,973	62,424	8,501
2001	12,054	2,131	74,478	10,632	2001	12,054	2,131	74,478	10,632
2002	11,883	2,302	86,360	12,934	2002	11,883	2,302	86,360	12,934
2003	11,698	2,487	98,058	15,421	2003	11,698	2,487	98,058	15,421
2004	11,498	2,687	109,557	18,108	2004	11,498	2,687	109,557	18,108
2005	11,282	2,902	120,839	21,010	2005	11,282	2,902	120,839	21,010
2006	11,049	3,136	131,889	24,146	2006	11,049	3,136	131,889	24,146
2007	10,798	3,387	142,686	27,533	2007	10,798	3,387	142,686	27,533
2008	10,525	3,659	153,212	31,193	2008	10,525	3,659	153,212	31,193
2009	10,232	3,953	163,443	35,146	2009	10,232	3,953	163,443	35,146
2010	9,914	4,271	173,357	39,417	2010	9,914	4,271	173,357	39,417
2011	9,571	4,614	182,928	44,031	2011	9,440	8,345	182,798	47,762
2012	9,201	4,984	192,129	49,015	2012	8,770	9,015	191,568	56,776
2013	8,800	5,385	200,929	54,400	2013	8,046	9,739	199,614	66,515
2014	8,368	5,817	209,297	60,217	2014	7,264	10,521	206,878	77,036
2015	7,901	6,284	217,197	66,502	2015	6,419	11,366	213,297	88,402
2016	7,396	6,789	224,593	73,291	2016	5,506	12,279	218,804	100,681
2017	6,851	7,334	231,444	80,625	2017	4,520	13,265	223,324	113,945
2018	6,262	7,923	237,705	88,549	2018	3,455	14,330	226,779	128,276
2019	5,625	8,560	243,330	97,109	2019	2,304	15,481	229,082	143,757
2020	4,938	9,247	248,268	106,356	2020	1,061	16,724	230,143	160,481
2021	4,195	9,990	252,463	116,346	2021	60	4,519	230,203	165,000
2022	3,393	10,792	255,856	127,138					
2023	2,526	11,659	258,382	138,797					
2024	1,590	12,595	259,971	151,393					
2025	578	13,607	260,549	165,000					

Summary–Goal Funding Schedule:

Table 2-13 is a summary of the funding for the various goals incorporated into the Sample's financial plan.

Table 2-13
Goal Funding Schedule

YEAR	COLLEGE	RETIREMENT PLANNING 401K	ROTH IRA	AUTO	HOME IMP	MTG PRE-PMT	TOTAL FUNDING
2001	$6,231	$7,419					$13,649
2002	6,480	7,641					14,121
2003	6,739	7,870					14,609
2004	7,008	8,107					15,115
2005	7,289	8,350					15,639
2006	7,580	8,600	$4,000	$3,500			23,681
2007	7,884	8,858	4,000	3,500			24,242
2008	8,199	9,124	4,000	3,500			24,823
2009	3,959	9,398	4,000	3,500			20,857
2010	4,117	9,680	4,000	3,500			21,297
2011		99,70	4,000		$4,261	$3,600	21,831
2012		10,269	4,000		4,261	3,600	22,130
2013		10,577	4,000		4,261	3,600	22,438
2014		10,895	4,000		4,261	3,600	22,756
2015		11,221	4,000		4,261	3,600	23,082
2016		11,558	4,000			3,600	19,158
2017		11,905	4,000			3,600	19,505
2018		12,262	4,000			3,600	19,862
2019		12,630	4,000			3,600	20,230
2020		10,258	4,000			3,600	17,858
2021		10,566	4,000			1,200	15,766
2022		10,883	4,000				14,883
2023		11,209	4,000				15,209
2024		11,545	4,000				15,545
2025		11,892	4,000				15,892
2026		12,249	4,000				16,249

Cash Flow Analysis

Overview:

The cash flow analysis integrates the incomes and outflows of financial resources for a specific planning period, such as a month, a year, or multiple years.

The cash flow computational procedure for a specific planning period is schematically illustrated below.

	Total Incomes:
	Wages
	Pensions/Social security
	Investments
	Etc.
Less:	Expenses:
	Living Expenses
	Taxes
Equals:	After-tax Cash Flow
Less:	Goal Funding:
	Retirement
	College Tuition
	New Home Purchase
	New Car
	Etc.
Equals:	After-tax Discretionary Cash Flow

If the discretionary cash flow is negative for any given planning period, then adjustments to the use of financial resources is required.

The adjustment to the use of financial resources may comprehend reduction in living expenses, rescheduling of goals, possible elimination of a specific goal, etc.

The development of a personal financial plan cash flow, as presented in this chapter, is based on *proprietary software programs*, as developed by Bernacchi Financial Services, Inc.

Income Resources:

The income resources for the Sample family are their respective wages and taxable investment income.

In year 2001, John's and Mary's annual wages are $65,000 and $15,687, respectively. It is assumed that their respective wages will increase at 3.0% annually.

The Sample's taxable investment assets, as of 1/1/2001, are $73,275, which are allocated 60% to stock and stock funds and 40% to cash equivalents and bonds.

The calculation of the annual interest and dividend income generated from the taxable investment assets are based on the following investment rates of return.

- The composite rate of return for cash equivalents/bonds investments is 5.5%.
- The investment rate of return for equities, that is, stocks and stock funds, is ...

Stock growth 8.0%
Dividends .... <u>1.5%</u>
Total return 9.5%

Therefore, based on the above assumptions, the interest and dividend income for year 2001 is calculated as follows:

$$\$73,275 \times .40 \times .055 = \$1612$$
$$\$73,275 \times .60 \times .015 = \$659$$

Again using the above assumptions, the projection of the Sample's total income for the 2001-2010 period is tabulated in Table 2-14.

Table 2-14
Total Income Projections, 2001-2010

Client Age:	35	36	37	38	39	40	41	42	43	44
Spouse Age:	32	33	34	35	36	37	38	39	40	41
	2001	2002	2003	2004	2005	2006	2007	2008	2009	2010
1 Salary--H	$ 65,000	$66,950	$68,959	$71,027	$73,158	$75,353	$77,613	$79,942	$82,340	$84,810
2 Salary--W	15,687	16,158	16,642	17,142	17,656	18,186	18,731	19,293	19,872	20,468
3 Interest Inc	1,612	1,861	2,136	2,434	2,759	3,111	3,400	3,709	4,038	4,490
4 Dividend Inc	659	761	874	996	1,129	1,273	1,391	1,517	1,652	1,837
	----------	----------	----------	----------	----------	----------	----------	----------	----------	----------
5 Tot Income	$ 82,957	$ 85,730	$ 88,611	$ 91,599	$ 94,702	$ 97,923	$ 101,135	$ 104,461	$107,902	$111,604

Living Expenses:

Table 2-15, the living expense worksheet, is a tabulation of the Sample family's living expenses as of 1/1/2001.

Table 2-15
Living Expense Worksheet

1. Food and Household:			**7. Insurance:**				
At home (groc store)	$ 5200		Life–				
Meals out	2600			Term Insurance		$ 520	
Total		$ 7800		Fixed term		275	
			Health--				
2. Housing:				Fixed cost			
Mortgage/Rent Pmts	$14185			Variable cost		1008	
Property taxes	2685		Disability				
Property Insurance	434			Total		$ 1783	
Repair & Maint/Yard	700						
Furnishings & Equip	200		**8. Doctor & Medical:**			$ 560	
Total		$18204	(Not covered by insurance)				
3. Utilities:		$ 3029	**9. Education:**				
			Magazines/papers/books		$ 285		
			School supplies				
4. Transportation:			Tuition				
Car Payments	$ 3500		Other				
Gas & oil	1500		Total		$ 285		
Car upkeep	300						
Car Insr/Lic/Etc.	1212		**10. Recreation/Vacation:**				
Total		$ 6512	Travel		$ 1500		
			Entertaining		200		
5. Other Debt:			Club fees		70		
Home equity loans	$		Sports, etc		500		
Installment debt			Total		$ 2270		
Personal loans							
Credit card pmts			**11. Other/Miscellaneous:**				
Other			Charity		$ 500		
Total		$	Gifts		750		
			Child support				
6. Clothing/Personal Care:			Alimony				
Clothing	$ 2000		Household help				
Personal care	1104		Prof & business exp.		500		
Other	150		Tax preparation				
Total		$ 3254	Other				
			Total		$ 1750		
			12. Total Living Expenses:			$ 45,467	
			(Sum of items 1-11).				

It should be noted that Table 2-15 does not include goal funding or taxes.

The Sample's base living expenses, starting in year 2001, are $45,467.

All variable expenses, such as food and household, utilities, etc., are increased annually at an assumed inflation rate of 4.0%. Other expenses, such as mortgage payments, are held constant, as they do not fluctuate with inflation.

Table 2-16 provides a summary of the living expenses, adjusted for inflation, for the first ten years, that is, years 2001 through 2010.

Table 2-16
Living Expenses, Inflation Adjusted

	2001	2002	2003	2004	2005	2006	2007	2008	2009	2010
Food	$7,800	$8,112	$8,436	$8,774	$9,125	$9,490	$9,869	$10,264	$10,675	$11,102
Housing	18,204	18,365	18,532	18,706	18,887	19,075	19,270	19,474	19,685	19,905
Utilities	3,029	3,150	3,276	3,407	3,544	3,685	3,833	3,986	4,145	4,311
Transportation	6,512	6,632	6,758	6,888	7,024	3,665	3,811	3,964	4,122	4,287
Clothing/Pers.	3,254	3,384	3,520	3,660	3,807	3,959	4,117	4,282	4,453	4,631
Insurance	1,803	1,864	1,928	1,994	2,063	2,134	2,208	2,286	2,366	2,450
Doctor/Medical	560	582	606	630	655	681	709	737	766	797
Education	285	296	308	321	333	347	361	375	390	406
Rec/Vacation	2,270	2,361	2,455	2,553	2,656	2,762	2,872	2,987	3,107	3,231
Other	1,750	1,800	1,852	1,906	1,962	2,021	2,082	2,145	2,211	2,279
	--------	--------	--------	--------	--------	--------	--------	--------	--------	--------
Infl Adj Budget	$45,467	$46,547	$47,671	$48,839	$50,054	$47,818	$49,132	$50,499	$51,921	$53,399

Tax Projections:

If a cash flow projection is to be used with a high level of confidence, the various IRS regulations that are applicable to wages, employment taxes (FICA), investment income, distributions from tax-deferred savings, etc., must be comprehended.

The use of a *nominal tax rate* over an extended planning period may result in cash flow projections that may be very unrealistic.

The variation in taxes over the pre-retirement and post-retirement period is illustrated graphically below in Chart 2-1.

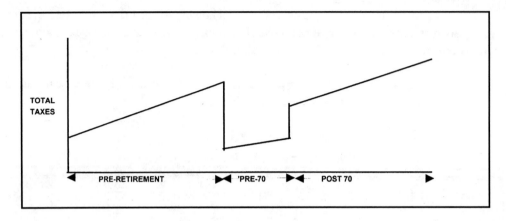

Chart 2-1

During the pre-retirement period the following taxes are comprehended.

- Federal income taxes on wages
- Federal FICA taxes on wages (employee)
- Investment income taxes, both federal and state
- Local income taxes on wages

The taxes are generally significantly lower for the pre-70½ retirement years, i.e. between retirement and age 70½, in that, taxes only on the following income resources are comprehended, when applicable.

- Pension income
- Social security benefits
- Investment income
- Distributions from tax-deferred savings required to supplement other incomes

The taxes in the retirement years after age 70½ are impacted significantly by the minimum required distributions of tax-deferred savings, which are taxed as ordinary income. The tax-deferred savings, for many individuals, may represent a significant portion of their retirement resources.

The computational procedure used to calculate the taxable income is as follows.

Total Income
Less: Pre-tax deductions
Less: Personal exemptions
Less: The greater of the (standard deduction or itemized deductions)
Equals: Taxable income

The federal tax rates applicable to taxable income, for year 2001, for single and joint filers, are tabulated in Table 2-17.

It should be noted that the taxes presented in Table 2-17 *do not* comprehend the tax law changes enacted during 2001.

Table 2-17
Federal Marginal Tax Rates, 2001

		Single		
Over–	*But Not Over–*	*The Tax Will Be--*	*Plus*	*Of the Amount Over–*
$ 0	$ 27,050	$	15%	$ 0
27,050	65,550	4,057.50 +	28%	27,050
65,550	136,700	14,837.50 +	31%	27,050
136,750	297,300	36,909.50 +	39.6%	65,550
297,300		94,707.50 +	39.65	297,300

		Married Filing Jointly or Qualifying Widow(er)		
Over–	*But Not Over–*	*The Tax Will Be–*	*Plus*	*Of the Amount Over–*
$ 0	$ 45,200	$	15%	$ 0
45,200	109,250	6,780.00 +	28%	45,200
109,250	166,450	24,714.00 +	31%	109,250
166,450	297,300	42,446.00 +	36%	166,450
297,300		89,552.00 +	39.6%	297,300

In addition to the federal income taxes, the employment taxes (FICA, Federal Insurance Contribution Act) are calculated as follows, on the assumption that the individual is not self-employed, based on year 2001 FICA tax rates.

Table 2-18
FICA Taxes, 2001

	Tax rate	Tax Base
Social security	6.2%	up to $80,000
Medicare tax	1.45%	all wages

The state and local taxes applicable to wages and investment income for the Sample's state of residence are as follows.

Table 2-19
State and Local Taxes

State Taxes	2.8% (wages + investment income)
Local Taxes	1.0% (wages only)

Based on the above assumptions, the projected taxes for the Samples, for the years 2001 through 2010 are tabulated in Table 2-20.

Table 2-20
Total Taxes

Client Age:	35	36	37	38	39	40	41	42	43	44
Spouse Age:	32	33	34	35	36	37	38	39	40	41
	2001	2002	2003	2004	2005	2006	2007	2008	2009	2010
Income:										
1 Wages/Salaries	$80687	$83108	$85601	$88169	$90814	$93539	$96344	$99235	$102212	$105278
2 Taxable Interest	1612	1861	2136	2434	2759	3111	3400	3709	4038	4490
3 Dividends	659	761	874	996	1129	1273	1422	1583	1754	1979
4 Total Taxable Inc	82957	85730	88611	91599	94702	97923	101166	104526	108004	111746
Adjustments to Income:										
401-k--Client	5850	6026	6206	6392	6584	6782	6985	7195	7411	7633
Flex-health Plan	1008	1034	1061	1089	1118	1148	1179	1212	1276	1282
401-k--Spouse	1569	1616	1664	1714	1766	1819	1873	1929	1987	2047
Total Adjustments	8427	8676	8931	9195	9468	9749	10037	10336	10674	10962
5 Adjusted Gross Income	74530	77054	79680	82404	85234	88174	91129	94190	97330	100784
6 Exemptions	11600	12000	12200	12600	13000	13400	13800	14200	14600	15000
7 Std Ded/Item Ded	18369	18353	18329	18294	18249	18191	18116	18026	17921	17801
Total Deductions	29969	30353	30529	30894	31249	31591	31916	32226	32521	32801
8 Taxable Income	44562	46701	49151	51511	53985	56583	59213	61964	64809	67984
9 Federal Tax	6684	7025	7535	8014	8518	9246	9982	10752	11549	12438
10 Marginal Tax Rate	15%	28%	28%	28%	28%	28%	28%	28%	28%	28%
11 Eff Tax Rate	19.3%	19.4%	19.7%	19.9%	20.1%	20.5%	20.9%	21.3%	21.7%	22.1%
12 FICA Taxes	6173	6358	6548	6745	6947	7156	7370	7591	7819	8054
13 State Tax	2323	2400	2481	2565	2652	2742	2832	2925	3021	3125
Local Tax	807	831	856	882	908	935	963	992	1022	1053
14 Total Taxes	15986	16614	17421	18205	19025	20079	21148	22261	23412	24669

The total taxes, line 14 in Table 2-20, range from $15,986 in year 2001 to $24,669 in year 2010, representing approximately a 54.3% increase in total taxes over the ten year period.

The effective tax rate, line 11, is calculated by dividing the total taxes, line 14, by the total taxable income, line 4. The effective tax rate in year 2001 is 19.3%, whereas in year 2010 the effective tax rate is 22.1%.

Cash Flow Projection:

The Sample family's cash flow projections for the planning period of 2001-2010 are tabulated in Table 2-21. It incorporates all income sources, all expenses and goal funding.

Table 2-21
Cash Flow Projections, 2001-2010

Client Age:	35	36	37	38	39	40	41	42	43	44
Spouse Age:	32	33	34	35	36	37	38	39	40	41
	2001	2002	2003	2004	2005	2006	2007	2008	2009	2010
1 Total Income	$82957	$85730	$88611	$91599	$94702	$97923	$101135	$104461	$107902	$ 111604
2 Less: Total Taxes	15986	16614	17421	18205	19025	20079	21148	22261	23412	24669
3 Less: Living Expense	45467	46547	47671	48839	50054	47818	49132	50499	51921	53399
4 Total Cash Flow	21504	22569	23519	24555	25623	30026	30855	31701	32569	33536
Use of Cash Flow:										
5 401k Contr–Client	5850	6026	6206	6392	6584	6782	6985	7195	7411	7633
6 401-k Contr–Wife	1569	1616	1664	1714	1766	1819	1873	1929	1987	2047
7 Educ Funding	6231	6480	6739	7008	7289	7581	7884	8199	3959	4117
8 New car savings fund						3500	3500	3500	3500	3500
9 Roth IRA contrib						4000	4000	4000	4000	4000
10 Tot Goal Funding	13650	14122	14609	15114	15639	23682	24242	24823	20857	21297
11 Discret Cash Flow	7854	8447	8910	9441	9984	6344	6613	6878	11712	12239
12 Use of Assets Use of Educ Fund									17729	18616
13 Tot Invest Assets	$236359	$277590	$322754	$372211	$426297	$489682	$556549	$630330	$691344	$756682

Discretionary Cash Flow:

The annual discretionary cash flow, line 11 in Table 2-21, exceeds the minimum savings of $5000 targeted by the Sample family.

Chart 2-2 is a graphic illustration of the annual allocations of gross income over the 2001-2010 planning period.

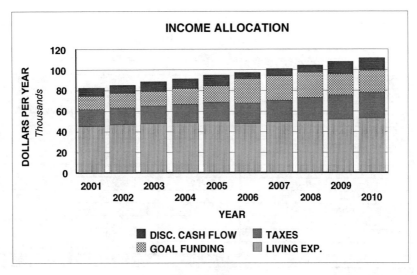

Chart 2-2

Balance Sheet:

The Sample family's balance sheet at the end of 2001, at the end of year 2010 and at retirement, the end of 2026, are tabulated in Table 2-22.

Table 2-22
Balance Sheet Profile

	2001	2010	2026
Taxable Savings:			
Cash & Bonds	$33,833	$ 90,442	$ 456,183
Stocks/Stock Fds	50,749	135,663	684,275
Total	$84,582	$ 226,105	$1,140,458
Goal Funding:			
College Funding	$35,391	$ 113,536	$ 0
Auto Funding		20,533	0
Total	$35,391	$ 134,069	$ 0
Tax-Deferred Savings:			
Employer Sav Plan–John	$105,292	$ 326,212	$1,513,722
Roth IRA–John		11,733	100,486
Employer Sav Plan–Mary	11,094	46,830	215,606
Roth IRA–Mary		11,733	100,486
Total	$116,386	$ 396,508	$1,930,300
	=========	==========	==========
Total Investment Assets:	*$236,359*	*$ 756,682*	*$3,070,758*
Personal Assets:			
Residence	$204,000	$ 243,799	$ 334,684
Home Furnishings	15,000	15,000	15,000
Auto	16,000	0	0
Total Personal Assets:	$237,000	$ 258,799	$ 349,684
	=========	==========	==========
Total Assets:	$473,359	$1,015,481	$3,420,442
Liabilities:			
Home Mortgage	$154,368	$ 125,582	$ 0
Auto Loan	12,362	0	0
	=========	==========	==========
Net Worth:	*$306,629*	*$ 889,899*	*$3,420,442*

It can be seen from the table above that the Sample's total investment assets increase from $236,359 at the end of 2001 to $3,070,758 by the end of 2026 when John retires. This represents an annual compound growth rate of 10.8% per year. Much of this growth is due to the addition of new monies to the tax-deferred savings from wages.

Comprehending their home and personal property, including total payoff of the home mortgage, their total Net Worth increases from $306,629 at the end of 2001 to $3,420,442 at the end of 2026.

Summary:

- In the development of a comprehensive financial plan, the starting basis is a balance sheet, which details the current assets, liabilities and net worth.

- The primary driving forces of a financial plan are the individual's future goals, such as retirement, college funding, etc.

  The goals must be quantified and prioritized.

- The assumptions relating to future income, investment rates of return, taxes, inflation, etc., must be realistic.

- The financial plan cash flow analysis integrates all incomes and outflows of financial resources for a specific planning period, such as a month, a year or multiple years.

- The development of the financial plan cash flow is an iterative process, in that major events, such as a change of job, marriage or divorce, an addition to the family, etc., require updating of the financial plan cash flow.

Calculation of Annual Savings Worksheet

The calculation of the savings required to achieve a stated savings goal is a function of the following variables: 1) Savings goal, dollars; 2) Years prior to the need for the savings, and 3) Investment rate of return.

The following worksheet calculates the annual savings required to achieve a stated goal.

Table A, referenced in the worksheet is found on page 43.

Worksheet Description–

Line #	Description	Example	
1	Enter on this line the savings goal	$20,000	
2	Enter on this line the years prior to the need for the savings.	10	
3	Enter the savings investment rate of return. If the savings account is a *taxable account*, enter the *after-tax* rate of return.	7.0%	
4	Choose an annual savings factor from Table A, corresponding to the years prior to the need for savings, Line 2, and the investment rate of return, Line 3.	13.8164	
5	Divide the savings goal, Line 1, by the annual savings factor, Line 4. This entry represents the annual savings required.	$1447.56	

WORKSHEET TABLE A

YRS TO GOAL	4.5%	5.0%	5.5%	6.0%	6.5%	7.0%	7.5%	8.0%	8.5%	9.0%
=====	=====	=====	=====	=====	=====	=====	=====	=====	=====	=====
1	1.0000	1.0000	1.0000	1.0000	1.0000	1.0000	1.0000	1.0000	1.0000	1.0000
2	2.0450	2.0500	2.0550	2.0600	2.0650	2.0700	2.0750	2.0800	2.0850	2.0900
3	3.1370	3.1525	3.1680	3.1836	3.1992	3.2149	3.2306	3.2464	3.2622	3.2781
4	4.2782	4.3101	4.3423	4.3746	4.4072	4.4399	4.4729	4.5061	4.5395	4.5731
5	5.4707	5.5256	5.5811	5.6371	5.6936	5.7507	5.8084	5.8666	5.9254	5.9847
6	6.7169	6.8019	6.8881	6.9753	7.0637	7.1533	7.2440	7.3359	7.4290	7.5233
7	8.0192	8.1420	8.2669	8.3938	8.5229	8.6540	8.7873	8.9228	9.0605	9.2004
8	9.3800	9.5491	9.7216	9.8975	10.0769	10.2598	10.4464	10.6366	10.8306	11.0285
9	10.8021	11.0266	11.2563	11.4913	11.7319	11.9780	12.2298	12.4876	12.7512	13.0210
10	12.2882	12.5779	12.8754	13.1808	13.4944	13.8164	14.1471	14.4866	14.8351	15.1929
11	13.8412	14.2068	14.5835	14.9716	15.3716	15.7836	16.2081	16.6455	17.0961	17.5603
12	15.4640	15.9171	16.3856	16.8699	17.3707	17.8885	18.4237	18.9771	19.5492	20.1407
13	17.1599	17.7130	18.2868	18.8821	19.4998	20.1406	20.8055	21.4953	22.2109	22.9534
14	18.9321	19.5986	20.2926	21.0151	21.7673	22.5505	23.3659	24.2149	25.0989	26.0192
15	20.7841	21.5786	22.4087	23.2760	24.1822	25.1290	26.1184	27.1521	28.2323	29.3609
16	22.7193	23.6575	24.6411	25.6725	26.7540	27.8881	29.0772	30.3243	31.6320	33.0034
17	24.7417	25.8404	26.9964	28.2129	29.4930	30.8402	32.2580	33.7502	35.3207	36.9737
18	26.8551	28.1324	29.4812	30.9057	32.4101	33.9990	35.6774	37.4502	39.3230	41.3013
19	29.0636	30.5390	32.1027	33.7600	35.5167	37.3790	39.3532	41.4463	43.6654	46.0185
20	31.3714	33.0660	34.8683	36.7856	38.8253	40.9955	43.3047	45.7620	48.3770	51.1601
21	33.7831	35.7193	37.7861	39.9927	42.3490	44.8652	47.5525	50.4229	53.4891	56.7645
22	36.3034	38.5052	40.8643	43.3923	46.1016	49.0057	52.1190	55.4568	59.0356	62.8733
23	38.9370	41.4305	44.1118	46.9958	50.0982	53.4361	57.0279	60.8933	65.0537	69.5319
24	41.6892	44.5020	47.5380	50.8156	54.3546	58.1767	62.3050	66.7648	71.5832	76.7898
25	44.5652	47.7271	51.1526	54.8645	58.8877	63.2490	67.9779	73.1059	78.6678	84.7009
26	47.5706	51.1135	54.9660	59.1564	63.7154	68.6765	74.0762	79.9544	86.3546	93.3240
27	50.7113	54.6691	58.9891	63.7058	68.8569	74.4838	80.6319	87.3508	94.6947	102.7231
28	53.9933	58.4026	63.2335	68.5281	74.3326	80.6977	87.6793	95.3388	103.7437	112.9682
29	57.4230	62.3227	67.7114	73.6398	80.1642	87.3465	95.2553	103.9659	113.5620	124.1354
30	61.0071	66.4388	72.4355	79.0582	86.3749	94.4608	103.3994	113.2832	124.2147	136.3075

ANNUAL SAVINGS FACTOR

--INVESTMENT MANAGEMENT--
RISK AND DIVERSIFICATION

Overview

Over the last decade the trend relating to retirement savings has been away from defined benefit retirement plans and toward tax-deferred savings plans.

Tax-deferred savings plans require the individual employee to be responsible for making investment decisions on how to invest his/her savings for retirement.

The investor's responsibility for making investment decisions may, in the future, also apply to a portion of his/her social security contributions.

The basic investment categories, or asset classes, are cash equivalents, bonds and stocks.

The cash equivalents category includes investments for which the dollar value is fixed, such as money markets, certificates of deposit, Treasury bills, etc.

The bond investment category includes investments that provide a fixed income over a designated time period. The market value of a bond, however, may deviate from the par value, face amount, over time due to interest rate changes.

The returns for the stock, or equity, investment category are dependent on projected earnings for a specific firm or industry sector; therefore, stock price movements are more random.

The return-on-investments for the stock, or equity, investment category is a function of capital gains or losses and dividend income, neither of which is guaranteed.

Understanding the risk and return characteristics of different investment vehicles, asset classes, is, therefore, fundamental to the investment decision process if realistic assumptions are to be incorporated into the financial planning process.

In the development of a personal financial plan the impact of inflation on future purchasing power must also be an integral part of the planning process.

A review of historical performance statistics for the various asset classes is necessary, such that an investor may establish a reference benchmark of expected returns and risk.

Historical Investment Performance, 1926-1999

A review of historical investment performance will provide a basis as to the risk and return characteristics of various asset classes.

The primary reference source that will be references in the *Stock, Bonds, Bills & Inflation, SBBI Yearbook 2000*, published by Ibbotson Associates, Chicago, IL.

The SBBI Yearbook provides historical data for the following asset classes, starting in 1926.

Asset Class:
- Large company stocks
- Small company stocks
- Long term corporate bonds
- Long term government bonds
- Intermediate term government bonds
- US Treasury bills

The SBBI Yearbook also provides historical data, starting in 1926, on inflation, that is, the consumer price index, CPI.

Chart 3-1 provides a graphic presentation of the growth of $1.00, invested at the start of 1926, through 1999, for the respective asset classes and the consumer price index.

The projections of the growth of $1.00 are based on the assumption of the reinvestment of all dividends and interest and that the growth is before any income taxes.

Growth of $1.00 from 1925 - 1999

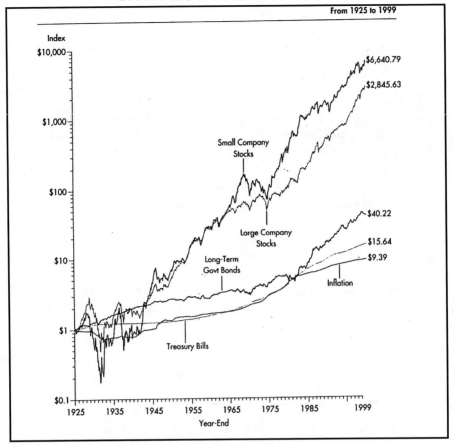

Source: Ibbotson Associates, SBBI Yearbook 2000

Chart 3-1

The interpretation of Chart 3-1 is as follows:

If $1.00 had been invested in the large company stock asset class at the start of 1926, it would have a market value of approximately $2846 at the end of 1999.

The increase in value of $1.00 to $2846 over the 74 year period for large company stocks represents an annualized compound rate of growth of 11.3%.

The average or arithmetic mean return for large company stocks, over the 74 year period was 13.3%.

At the lower end of the risk spectrum, the US Treasury bill asset class, $1.00 invested at the start of 1926 would have a market value of approximately $16 at the end of 1999.

The increase in value of $1.00 for US Treasury bills to $16 over the 74 year period represents an annualized compound rate of growth of 3.8%.

The average or arithmetic mean rate of growth for US Treasury bills over the 74 year period was also 3.8%.

The real growth of Treasury Bills (growth of T-Bills - growth of inflation) was very minimal over the 74 year period.

The compound annualized return represents the investment rate of return for an initial investment, present value, that has grown to a given market value, future value, after a designated period of time.

For example, if $1.00 is invested for a period of five years with the following annual returns, the market value at the end of five years is calculated as follows.

| Year | Annual Total Return, % | ------------Investment---------- | |
		Start Balance	End Balance
1	10%	$1.00	$1.10
2	8	1.10	1.19
3	15	1.19	1.37
4	-4	1.37	1.31
5	20	1.31	1.57
Arith Mean Return = 9.8%			

The present value, PV, of $1.00, which grows to a future value, FV, of $1.57, has a compound annualized rate of return of 9.44%. That is, if we were to substitute the 9.44% as the rate of return for each year in the above table, the ending market value will also be $1.57. (Note: see Chapter 9 on **Time Value of Money: "Simple and Compound Interest Concepts"**)

The arithmetic mean, or average, is calculated by adding up the annual returns and dividing by the number of years. The arithmetic mean, or average, for our example, is 9.8% (49/5).

Table 3-1 provides a summary of the performance statistics for the respective asset classes and inflation for the 1926 - 1999 period.

Table 3-1
Performance Statistics 1926-1999

Asset Class	Compound Rate of Return, %	Average Rate of Return, %	Future Value $1.00
Large company stocks	11.3%	13.3%	$2846
Small company stocks	12.6%	17.6%	$6641
Long term gov bonds	5.6%	5.9%	$4022
Intermediate term gov bonds	5.2%	5.4%	$43
US Treasury bills	3.8%	3.8%	$16
Inflation	3.1%	3.2%	$9.39

Source: Ibbotson Associates, SBBI Yearbook 2000

If we assume the data in Table 3-1 provides complete disclosure of the performance statistics for the respective asset classes, then an investor may ask "Why not invest 100% in stocks, in that the performance far exceeds the performance of bonds and Treasury bills?"

Risk and Volatility

As a famous radio commentator would say, "Now here is the rest of the story..."

Investment risk can be defined as the probability that the actual return for an investment will differ from the expected return. The greater the variation of returns above and below the arithmetic mean return for a given investment, the higher the probability that the actual return will differ from the expected return.

The statistical measurement of the variation in annual returns above and below the arithmetic mean, that is, risk, for a given investment, is called the standard deviation.

To get an insight into an investment's risk, we need to examine the variation of the period-to-period returns, that is, month-to-month, year-to-year, etc., returns above and below the average return.

The greater the range of variation above and below the average return, the higher the investment risk.

It should be noted that variations in an asset's returns are reflective of the asset's price variation.

Chart 3-2 is a graphic presentation of the variation in returns for large company stocks for the 1926-1999 period.

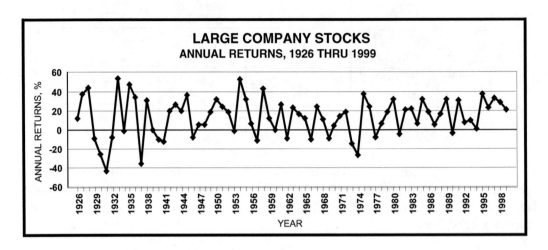

Source: Ibbotson Associates, SBBI Yearbook 2000

Chart 3-2

During the 1926-1999 period, large company stock returns ranged from a low of -43% in 1931 to a high of 54% in 1933, representing a range of variation in returns of 97 percentage points.

The arithmetic mean for large company stocks for the 1926-1999 period was 13.3%.

The statistical measurement of the variation of annual returns above and below the mean, the standard deviation, was 20.1%.

The interpretation of the risk measurement, standard deviation, implies that ⅔ of the annual returns will be within a range of the mean plus one standard deviation and the mean minus one standard deviation.

Therefore, for the large company stocks, with a mean return of 13.3% and a standard deviation of 20.1% for the 1926-1999 period, we would expect ⅔ of the annual returns to be in the mean return ± one standard deviation, as illustrated graphically in Chart 3 - 3.

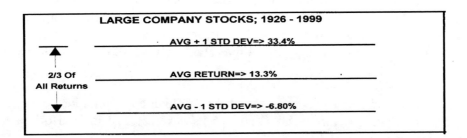

Chart 3-3

Chart 3-4 is a graphic presentation of the variation in returns for US Treasury bills for the 1926-1999 period.

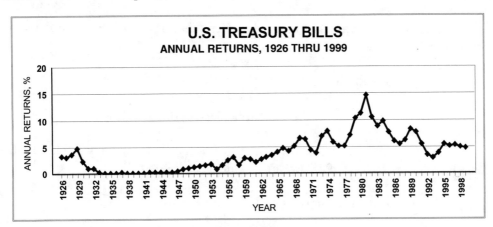

Source: Ibbotson Associates, SBBI Yearbook 2000

Chart 3-4

During the 1926-1999 period, US Treasury bill returns ranged from a low of 0.0% in 1940 to a high of 14.7% in 1981, representing a range of variation in returns of 14.7 percentage points.

The arithmetic mean for US Treasury bills for the 1926-1999 period was 3.8%.

The statistical measurement of the variation of annual returns above and below the mean, the standard deviation, was 3.2%.

Therefore, we would expect ⅔ of the returns during the 1926-1999 period for US Treasury bills to fall within the range of 0.6% (3.8 - 3.2) and 7.0% (3.8 + 3.2).

In that the standard deviation is a measurement of risk, when comparing the US Treasury bill standard deviation of 3.2% with the standard deviation of large company stocks, of 20.1%, it can easily be seen that the risk for US Treasury bills is significantly less than that of large company stocks, in that the actual returns will be nearer the expected return.

It should also be apparent that there is a high correlation between risk and return, in that the average return for US Treasury bills was 3.8%, as compared to the average return for large company stocks of 13.3%.

However, in looking at the risk and return relationship of two different investments or asset classes, where the means for the returns differ greatly, as for the large company stocks and Treasury bills, we do not get an accurate picture of the relative variation around the means by simply comparing the two standard deviations.

A measure of variation that overcomes this difficulty is the coefficient of variation, or risk/return ratio.

The formula for the coefficient of variation is as follows:

Coefficient of variation = (Standard deviation/Mean)

For example, the coefficients of variation for large company stocks and US Treasury bills for the 1926-1999 period are calculated as follows.

- Large company stocks–

  Coefficient of variation = Standard deviation/Mean return
  = 20.1/13.3
  = 1.51

- US Treasury bills–

  Coefficient of variation = Standard deviation/Mean return
  = 3.2/3.8
  = 0.84

The risk/return ratio for large company stocks of 1.51 implies that, for each unit of return, we incur 1.51 units of risk; whereas, the risk/return ratio for T-Bills implies that, for each unit of return, we incur only 0.84 units of risk.

The coefficient of variation, risk/return ratio, therefore, indicates how much the returns will vary around its mean, or average return.

For asset classes, it is obvious that the class with the highest potential return will most likely have the highest volatility and, thus, have the highest coefficient of variation, while the least risky class of investments will have the lowest probability of return and the lowest variation around its mean, or coefficient of variation. This is illustrated in Table 3-2.

Table 3-2 provides a summary of the risk and return statistics for various asset classes for the 1926-1999 period.

Table 3-2
Asset Classes, Performance Statistics, 1926-1999

Asset Class	Compound Return	Mean Rate of Return	Standard Deviation	Coefficient of Variation
Large company stock	12.6%	13.3%	20.1	1.5
Small company stocks	11.3%	17.6%	33.6	1.9
Long term gov bonds	5.6%	5.9%	9.3	1.6
Interm term gov bonds	5.2%	5.4%	5.8	1.1
US Treasury bills	3.8%	3.8%	3.2	0.84

Note: Numbers are rounded. Source: Ibbotson Associates, SBBI Yearbook 2000

The coefficient of variation for small company stocks, of 1.9, indicates that small company stocks are the highest risk asset class, whereas the US Treasury bills, with a coefficient of variation of 0.84, represents the lowest risk asset class.

The relationship of the mean rate of return of an investment and the standard deviation, based on historical data for various asset classes for the 1926-1999 period, is graphically illustrated in Chart 3-5.

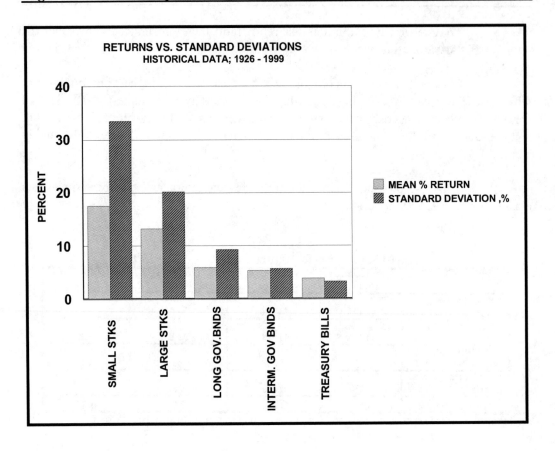

Chart 3 - 5

In the structure of an investment portfolio, investment dollars are allocated, called asset allocation, to different asset classes and within an asset class, such that return and risk conform to a stated investment policy.

In the structure of an investment portfolio the investment policy requires that one of the following two goals are met.

   <u>Goal 1:</u> The portfolio is structured such that, for a given level of expected return, the portfolio minimizes the risk.

   <u>Goal 2:</u> The portfolio is structured such that, for a given level of desired risk, the portfolio maximizes the return.

The following is a graphic representation of the stated investment policy goals.

In Chart 3-6, line 1-2 represents various investment portfolios for which the returns are maximized for a stated level of risk.

Portfolios A, B and C are optimal, whereas Portfolio D is not, in that it has the same level of risk as Portfolio C, but the return of Portfolio A.

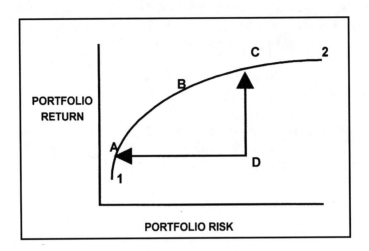

Chart 3-6

Historical Reference Period, 1970-1999

In the various analyses to follow, the following asset classes will be comprehended.

Asset Class	Investment Category
US Treasury bills	Cash
Interm term government bonds	Fixed income
Large company stocks	Stock (S&P 500 Index)

The historical reference period to be comprehended in our various analyses is the 30 year period starting in 1970 and continuing through the 1999 year.

This reference period is considered to be representative, in that the following market events occurred.

- The mean rate of return for stocks was 14.9%, with a low return of -26.5% and a high return of 37.4%, representing a range of 64 percentage points.

  The standard deviation for stocks during this period was 15.7%.

- The mean rate of return for intermediate term government bonds was 8.9%, with a low return of -5.1% and a high return of 29.1%, reflecting a range of 34 percentage points.

  The standard deviation for intermediate term government bonds during this period was 6.8%.

- The mean rate of return for US Treasury bills was 6.7%, with a low return of 2.9% and a high return of 14.7%, representing a range of 11.2 percentage points.

  The standard deviation for US Treasury bills during this period was 2.6%.

- The average inflation rate for the 1970-1999 period was 5.2%, with a low of 1.1% and a high of 13.3%.

The 1970-1999 year-by-year rates of return for the stocks, intermediate government bonds, US Treasury bills and inflation are tabulated in Table 3-3.

Table 3-3
Year-by-Year Returns, 1970-1999

YEAR	STOCKS	INTERM, GOV. BNDS	TREASURY BILLS	INFLATION
1970	4.01	16.86	6.52	5.49
1971	14.31	8.72	4.39	3.36
1972	18.98	5.16	3.84	3.41
1973	-14.66	4.61	6.93	8.80
1974	-26.47	5.69	8.00	12.20
1975	37.20	7.83	5.80	7.01
1976	23.84	12.87	5.08	4.81
1977	-7.18	1.41	5.12	6.77
1978	6.56	3.49	7.18	9.03
1979	18.44	4.09	10.38	13.31
1980	32.42	3.91	11.24	12.40
1981	-4.91	9.45	14.71	8.94
1982	21.41	29.10	10.54	3.87
1983	22.51	7.41	8.80	3.80
1984	6.27	14.02	9.85	3.95
1985	32.16	20.33	7.72	3.77
1986	18.47	15.14	6.16	1.13
1987	5.23	2.90	5.47	4.41
1988	16.81	6.10	6.35	4.42
1989	31.49	13.29	8.37	4.65
1990	-3.17	9.73	7.81	6.11
1991	30.55	15.46	5.60	3.06
1992	7.67	7.19	3.51	2.90
1993	9.99	11.24	2.90	2.75
1994	1.31	-5.14	3.90	2.67
1995	37.43	16.80	5.60	2.54
1996	23.07	2.10	5.21	3.32
1997	33.36	8.38	5.26	1.70
1998	28.58	10.21	4.86	1.61
1999	21.04	-1.77	4.68	2.68
AVG.RETURN, %	14.89	8.89	6.73	5.16
COMP RATE,%	13.72	8.68	6.69	5.11
MAXIMUM RATE,%	37.43	29.10	14.71	13.31
MINIMUM RATE,%	-26.47	-5.14	2.90	1.13
STANDARD DEV.%	15.70	6.83	2.60	3.22

Source: Ibbotson Associates, SBBI Yearbook 2000

Diversification: Overview

As historical data substantiates, stocks, over the long term, provide investors with the highest return as compared to bonds and US Treasury bills. Stocks, however, also represent higher risk.

The S&P 500 return for year 2000 was a -9.1%, the first down market since 1990 and the worst since 1974 when the stock market return was -26.5%.

Down markets are painful, but they do force investors to come to terms with stock market risk, as did the market drop in 2000.

Large lengthy drops can cause investors to act irrationally and make emotional decisions, possibly getting out of the market at inappropriate times.

An understanding of down markets can help an investor assess how much of a loss they can withstand.

Diversification addresses the issue of how to develop a portfolio in which the risk of loss from one investment can be mitigated, or offset, by gains, or at least smaller losses, from other investments. In other words, maximizing returns while minimizing losses.

Is this a guessing game? No, developing a portfolio through diversification uses many tools that help to make good selections of assets within asset classes, as well as which asset classes to use and what allocation to use in structuring a portfolio.

It is not a simple process, nor perfect. But knowledge and understanding of the tools will help the investor do a better job of investing money and achieving goals.

Significant losses can occur in a down market if an investment portfolio is not well diversified. The recovery of these losses may extend over several years; consequently, an investor in retirement requiring annual withdrawals will realize a reduction in retirement resources.

The combination of a major down market, and required withdrawals during the recovery period, is equivalent to a 'dollar-cost-averaging' in reverse; that is, the withdrawals will require the redemption of more shares to achieve a given withdrawal amount.

Table 3-4 is a tabulation of the bear markets since the second World War, as measured by the Standard & Poor 500 Index.

A bear market is defined as the loss of 20% or more in market value in the stock market.

For the purpose of this study, the duration of stock market declines start from the peak and end at the bottom.

The recovery period is the amount of time it takes for the market to go from the bottom back up to the same level as the previous peak.

Table 3-4
Bear Markets

Time Period	Length of Decline, Months	Percentage Loss	Recovery Period, Months
1946-49	37	-30%	16
1956-57	15	-22	11
1961-62	7	-28	16
1966	8	-22	10
1968-70	18	-36	23
1973-74	21	-48	70
1976-78	18	-20	18
1980-82	20	-27	5
1987	4	-34	19
1990	3	-20	6

Source: Leuthold Group

To avoid major losses in the stock market it is necessary to allocate dollars to other asset classes, such as bonds, cash, etc., whose returns are relatively uncorrelated.

The primary objective of diversification, that is, asset allocation, is to cut losses in down markets and still position the investment portfolio to participate in up markets.

Investment diversification comprehends diversification within a given asset class and among different asset classes, such that, the risk for a stated investment portfolio return is minimized.

When buying securities an investor is confronted with two important risks.

- Market risk
- Non-market risk

Market risk is the risk that is common to all securities in the same asset class, such as stocks and bonds.

Stocks' performances are directly impacted by the state of the economy, while bonds are impacted by changes in interest rates.

In that market risk is external to the specific industry sector or firm, you cannot diversify away market risk.

Approximately ⅓ of a stock's price movement is caused by the general movement of the market, that is, "all boats rise or fall with the tide."

Non-market risk is risk that is specific to a company or industry sector, that is, internal risk. For example, a report that a specific company did not meet forecasted earnings can have an adverse impact on the company's share price.

You can diversify against non-market risk by holding different securities from different industry sections in your investment portfolio.

The market risk and non-market risk represent the total risk inherent in equity investments, as illustrated in Chart 3-7.

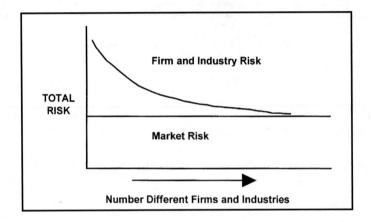

Chart 3-7

Diversification: Correlation

On review of the returns in Table 3-3, it becomes apparent that while stocks had the highest average return for the 30-year period, there were 11 different years in which bonds or Treasury bills, or both, outperformed the returns on stocks.

Table 3-5 provides the tabulation of the years in which stocks underperformed either bonds or Treasury bills or both.

Table 3-5

YEAR	STOCKS	INTERM. GOV. BNDS	TREASURY BILLS
1970	4.01	16.86	6.52
1973	-14.66	4.61	6.93
1974	-26.47	5.69	8.00
1977	-7.18	1.41	5.12
1978	6.56	3.49	7.18
1981	-4.91	9.45	14.71
1984	6.27	14.02	9.85
1987	5.23	2.90	5.47
1990	-3.17	9.73	7.81
1993	9.99	11.24	2.90
1994	1.31	-5.14	3.90

However, in 19 years out of 30, during the 1970-1999 period, stocks outperformed both bonds and Treasury bills.

It also should be noted that in year 2000 both bonds and Treasury bills outperformed stocks.

Correlation measures how closely two assets relate to one another, in terms of direction and magnitude of price movement.

Two assets with perfect negative correlation (-1) tend to move simultaneously in opposite direction and magnitude.

Two assets with perfect positive correlation (+1) tend to move in tandem in the same direction and magnitude.

A correlation of 0.00 indicates that there is no relationship at all between the price movement of two assets.

Chart 3-8 is a graphic illustration of the return profile, or price, for two asset classes, A and B, which are highly correlated.

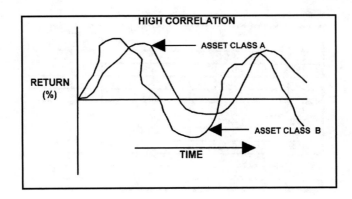

Chart 3-8

As illustrated in Chart 3-8, the return, or movements, for the respective asset classes, both upward and downward, tend to move in tandem.

Therefore, the addition of Asset Class B does not provide a significant improvement in the investment portfolio diversification; that is, lowering of the investment portfolio risk.

Chart 3-9 is a graphic illustration of two asset classes with low correlation. Two assets with low correlation tend to move simultaneously in opposite directions and magnitude.

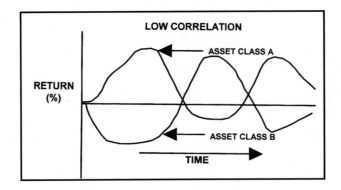

Chart 3-9

Table 3-6 is a tabulation of the correlation matrix for large company stocks, intermediate term government bonds, US Treasury bills and inflation for the return rates tabulated in Table 3-3 for the 1970-1999 period.

Table 3-6
Correlation Matrix

	1970 - 1999			
	STOCKS	BONDS	T-BILLS	INFLATION
STOCKS	1.00	0.32	-0.11	-0.39
BONDS	0.32	1.00	0.26	-0.26
T-BILLS	-0.11	0.26	1.00	0.59
INFL	-0.39	-0.26	0.59	1.00

There is a low positive correlation of 0.32 between stocks and bonds, that is, both asset classes move in the same direction; however, the movements for bonds is of a much lesser magnitude.

The correlation between stocks and Treasury bills is a negative 0.11, that is, an increase in stock price implies a decrease in Treasury bills.

A measure of the degree of correlation between two assets is as follows.

0.70	to	1.00	High Positive
0.11	to	0.69	Moderate Positive
0.10	to	-0.10	None
-0.11	to	-0.69	Moderate Negative
-0.70	to	-1.00	Highly Negative

The correlation factor for the *Vanguard 500 Index* fund and the *Vanguard Total Bond Market Index* fund was -0.07 for the 3-year period ending 6/30/01, representing no correlation.

The total returns for the *Vanguard 500 Index* and the *Vanguard Total Bond Index Market Index* fund, for the period of 12/31/99 through 8/9/01 are as follows.

Vanguard 500 Index fund .... -17.9%
Vanguard Total Bond Mkt Index ..... +19.1%

Therefore, an investment portfolio with 50% of the invested dollars allocated to the *Vanguard 500 Index* fund and 50% of the invested dollars allocated to the *Vanguard Total bond Market Index* fund has a return of +0.60% for the 12/31/99 - 8/9/01 period.

A well diversified investment portfolio must not only diversify between different asset classes, but diversify within a given asset class.

For example, investing in a single stock, as opposed to 8-10 different stocks may result in a potentially higher return. However, there is also a potential of losing the entire investment if the company falls on hard times and goes into bankruptcy.

When investing in 8-10 different stocks, the expected return for the investment portfolio will be the average return of the individual stocks in the investment portfolio.

The average return for the investment portfolio with 8-10 stocks may be lower than that of any single stock investment for any given time period, in that some of the stocks in the portfolio, which realized significant gains, are offset by other stocks with lower returns or losses.

However, the probability that all of the stocks in the investment portfolio will lose money over a given period is highly unlikely if the stocks are from different industry sectors with a low correlation of price movements.

Diversification: Hypothetical Stock Portfolio

To get further insight to diversification within a given asset class, stocks, we shall construct a hypothetical stock portfolio of eight different stocks from different industry sectors as follows

COMPANY NAME (TICKER)	SECTOR
ALCOA (AA)	INDUSTRIAL CYCLICALS
CITIGROUP (C)	FINANCIAL
ADOLPH COORS (RKY)	CONSUMER STAPLES
EXXON MOBILE (XOM)	ENERGY
IBM (IBM)	TECHNOLOGY
JOHNSTON&JOHNSTON (JNJ)	HEALTH
WAL-MART (WMT)	RETAIL
WORLDCOM (WCOM)	SERVICES

The reference period will be the 1998, 1999 and 2000 period, in that the total return for the S&P 500 Index was 28.6%, 21.0% and -9.1%, respectively, for the reference years.

The performance for common stocks in our hypothetical stock portfolio are illustrated in Table 3-7.

For the respective stocks in Table 3-7 the annual returns for 1998, 1999 and 2000, and the average return and standard deviation are provided.

Table 3-7
Hypothetical Portfolio

TICKER	ANNUAL RETURNS, %			AVG RETURN	COMP 3YR RETURN	3yr STD DEV
	1998	1999	2000			
AA	8.13	125.88	-18.02	38.66	26.04	65.9
C	-6.83	70.08	23.57	28.94	25.11	53.5
RKY	72.36	-5.83	54.91	40.48	35.98	37.7
XOM	22.40	12.56	10.24	15.07	14.95	21.6
IBM	77.48	17.57	-20.84	24.74	18.21	42.2
JNJ	28.99	12.47	14.24	18.57	18.34	34.6
WMT	107.55	70.44	-22.79	51.73	39.78	51.1
WCOM	137.19	10.93	-73.50	24.87	-11.32	47.9
MAXIMUM=>	137.19	125.88	54.91	51.73	39.78	65.9
MINIMUM=>	-6.83	-5.83	-73.5	15.07	-11.32	21.6
RANGE=>	144.02	131.71	128.41	36.67	51.1	44.3

Table 3-7 also provides a tabulation of the maximum returns, minimum returns and the differences between the maximum and minimum returns, that is, the range in any given year for the various stocks in the portfolio.

The years in which the respective stocks incurred a negative return are shaded.

The magnitude of the ranges for the respective years implies that the stocks in the hypothetical stock portfolio have a low correlation, as illustrated in the correlation matrix below, of 36 month returns for the period ending 12/31/00.

CORRELATION MATRIX								
		1	2	3	4	5	6	7	8
1	Adolph Coors B		0.06	-0.02	0.14	-0.01	0.27	0.31	-0.05
2	Alcoa	0.06		0.30	0.08	0.41	0.09	0.13	0.09
3	ExxonMobil	-0.02	0.30		0.12	0.39	0.21	0.03	-0.12
4	Gillette	0.14	0.08	0.12		0.01	0.27	0.28	0.32
5	IBM	-0.01	0.41	0.39	0.01		0.04	0.09	0.31
6	Johnson&Johnson	0.27	0.09	0.21	0.27	0.04		0.33	0.30
7	Wal-Mart	0.31	0.13	0.03	0.28	0.09	0.33		0.26
8	WorldCom	-0.05	0.09	-0.12	0.32	0.31	0.30	0.26	

The following assumptions are used in the construction of our hypothetical stock portfolio.

- Investment period 1998 through 2000
- Investment rates of return for the respective stocks are as tabulated in Table 3-7
- $1000 is allocated to each of the eight stocks at the start of 1998
- All dividends, interest income and capital gains are reinvested
- Investment assets are in a tax-deferred account; therefore no income taxes are generated

Diversification: Hypothetical Stock Portfolio Performance Statistics

Table 3-8 provides a tabulation of the annual earnings and total earnings for the respective stocks in our hypothetical portfolio over the 3-year period, based on a lump sum investment of $1000 in each stock at the start of 1998.

Table 3-8

ANNUAL EARNINGS PER STOCK, $			
INITIAL INVESTMENT ,$1000 PER STOCK			
YEAR=>	1998	1999	2000	TOTAL
AA	81	1361	-440	1002
C	-68	653	373	958
RKY	724	-101	891	1514
XOM	224	154	141	519
IBM	775	312	-435	652
JNJ	290	161	207	657
WMT	1076	1462	-806	1731
WCOM	1372	259	-1934	-303
TOTAL	4473	4261	-2003	6731
MAXIMUM	$1,372	$1,462	$891	$1,731
MINIMUM	($68)	($101)	($1,934)	($303)
RANGE	$1,440	$1,563	$2,825	$2,034

The calculation of earnings in Table 3-8 is as follows, using Alcoa (AA) as an example.

Lump sum investment, 1998	$1000
Times: 1998 rate of return, %	x 8.1%
Equals: Earnings, 1998, $	$81
Account balance, 1/1/99	$1081
Times: 1999 rate of return, %	x 125.9%
Equals: Earnings, 1999, $	$1361
Account balance, 1/1/00	$2442
Times: 2000 rate of return, %	x -18%
Equals, Earnings, 2000, $	$- 440
Account balance, 1/1/01	$2002 (= $1000 + $1002)

The total earnings for the lump sum investment of $8000 in the hypothetical portfolio was $6731 over the 3-year period, representing an annualized total return of 22.6%.

Wal-Mart had the highest earnings, of $1731, for an annualized return of 39.8%, whereas WorldCom lost $303, for an annualized return of -11.3%.

The range of differences in earnings in any given year among the eight stocks is a measure of the low correlation between the various stocks from different industrial sectors.

It should be noted that one or more stocks had a negative return in any given year, and the stocks with negative returns were different stocks each year.

Chart 3-10 is a graphic presentation of annual earnings over the 3-year period for the respective stocks in the hypothetical investment portfolio.

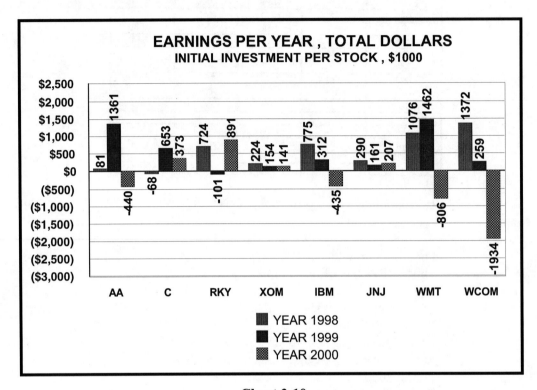

Chart 3-10

Table 3-9 presents the cumulative earnings for the respective stocks.

Table 3-9
Hypothetical Portfolio, Cumulative Dollars

STOCK	1998	1999	2000
AA	1081	2442	2002
C	932	1585	1958
RKY	1724	1623	2514
XOM	1224	1378	1519
IBM	1775	2087	1652
JNJ	1290	1451	1657
WMT	2076	3537	2731
WCOM	2372	2631	697
PORTFOLIO	$12,473	$16,734	$14,731

Table 3-10 is a tabulation of the annualized returns, average 3-year returns, 3-year standard deviations and the risk/return ratios for the respective stocks in the hypothetical stock portfolio.

Table 3-10

STOCK	ANNUALIZED RETURN	AVG RETURN	3 YEAR STD DEV	RISK / RETURN
AA	26.04	38.66	65.90	1.70
C	25.11	28.94	53.50	1.85
RKY	35.98	40.48	37.70	0.93
XOM	14.95	15.07	21.60	1.43
IBM	18.21	24.74	42.20	1.71
JNJ	18.34	18.57	34.60	1.86
WMT	39.78	51.73	51.10	0.99
WCOM	-11.32	24.87	47.90	1.93
PORT	22.59	26.03	23.85	0.92

The annualized hypothetical portfolio return is 22.6%. The annualized returns for the individual stocks ranged from a low of -11.3% for WorldCom to a high of 39.8% for Wal-Mart.

Over the 3-year period 50% of the individual stocks had annualized returns lower than that of the hypothetical portfolio.

In year 2000 the following stocks had negative returns: Alcoa, -18%; IBM, -20.8%; Wal-Mart, -27.8% and WorldCom, -73.5%, whereas the hypothetical investment portfolio return was -12%. In other words, the primary goal of diversification is to provide downside protection.

The risk/return ratio is calculated by dividing the 3-year standard deviation by the average return.

For example, the hypothetical investment portfolio's risk/return ratio is calculated as follows.

$$\text{Risk/Return ratio} \quad = \quad 23.85/26.03$$
$$= \quad 0.92$$

The individual stocks had risk/return ratios ranging from a low of 0.99 for Wal-Mart to a high of 1.93 for WorldCom.

It should be noted that all of the individual stock's risk/return ratios are greater than that of the hypothetical portfolio, which results from the low correlation between stocks in different industry sectors, reflecting the investment portfolio's diversification that results from the low correlation between stocks from different industry sectors.

Diversification: Hypothetical Portfolio Sector Weighting

The sector weighting for the eight stocks in the hypothetical portfolio are tabulated below in Table 3-11.

Table 3-11 provides the hypothetical portfolio sector weighting at the end of the three yeaar holding period, from 1998-2000.

Table 3-11

SECTOR WEIGHTING			
			PORTFOLIO/
% OF STOCKS=>	PORTFOLIO	S&P 500	S&P500
UTILITIES	0.00	3.00	0.00
ENERGY	10.31	7.30	1.41
FINANCIALS	13.29	17.50	0.76
INDUSTRIAL CYCL.	13.62	11.60	1.17
CONSUMER DURABLE	0.00	1.60	0.00
CONSUMER STABLES	17.06	6.70	2.55
SERVICES	4.73	11.10	0.43
RETAIL	18.53	6.00	3.09
HEALTH	11.25	13.90	0.81
TECHNOLOGY	11.21	21.20	0.53

It should be noted that the initial dollars invested in the eight stocks, respectively, was $1000 reflecting equal sector weighting at the beginning of the hypothetical holding period. Therefore, the difference in sector weighting in Table 3-11 reflects the change in market value for each of the stocks at the end of the three year holding period.

For example, the industry sector *retail*, which is the Wal-Mart stock, represents 18.5% of the investment portfolio at the end of the three year period, in that the annualized return for the Wal-Mart stock was 39.8% over the three year holding period, whereas the industry sector *services*, which is the WorldCom stock, represents 4.7% of the investment portfolio, in that the annualized return for WorldCom was -11.3% over the three year holding period.

Table 3-11 also provides the sector weighting for the S&P 500 as a benchmark for comparison.

The column 'Portfolio/S&P 500' provides the sector weighting ratio of the hypothetical investment portfolio relative to the sector weighting of the S&P 500 index.

The sector ratios for *consumer staples*, Adolph Coors, and *retail*, Wal-Mart, of 2.6 and 3.1, respectively, represent an investment portfolio bias in the *consumer staples* and *retail* industry sectors.

To maintain proper investment portfolio sector diversification, annual rebalancing is required for sectors that exceed that of the S&P 500 index by a ratio of 1.5 or greater.

Diversification: Risk/Reward Scatterplot

There is a direct correlation between the risk of an investment (standard deviation) and its annualized return. That is, an investment with higher risk should have a higher return than an investment with lower risk.

Therefore, plotting an investment's risk (standard deviation) and total annualized percent return, as compared to that of an appropriate benchmark such as the S&P 500 provides an insight as to the relative risk/reward for the investment vs the selected benchmark.

The plotting of the risk/reward for multiple investments vs an appropriate benchmark is called a 'scatterplot.'

The interpretation of a scatterplot relative to a selected benchmark is graphically illustrated below based on three years mean return and three year standard deviation..

I Low Risk High Reward	Benchmark Risk	II High Risk High Reward Benchmark Return
III Low Risk Low Reward		IV High Risk Low Reward

Annualized Return, Percent (vertical axis label)

Risk, Std Dev, %

The interpretation of the various quadrants are as follows:

I. Low Risk/High Reward
   This risk/reward relationship is highly desirable; however, due to the correlation of risk and return, very few investments will be in this *overachiever* quadrant.

II. High Risk/High Return
   This risk/reward relationship reflects the correlation of risk and return, in that, the higher the risk the higher the expected reward.

III. High Risk/Low Reward
   This risk reward relationship reflects the correlation of risk and return, in that the lower the risk the lower the expected reward.

IV. High Risk/Low Return
   This risk/reward relationship reflects investments that are *underachievers*, that is, the investor is not properly compensated for the level of risk taken.

Plotted below is the risk/reward scatterplot for the stocks in the hypothetical stock portfolio, based on the plotting of the 3-year standard deviation vs the 3-year mean return for the period ending 12/31/00.

The reference benchmark used in the scatterplot is the S&P 500 index three-year mean return of 12.3% and three-year standard deviation of 19.8% for the period ending 12/31/00.

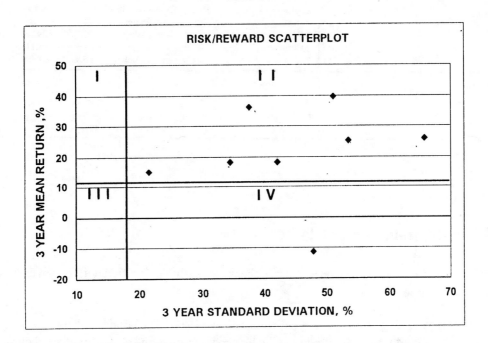

The dots in the above scatterplot represent the stocks in the hypothetical portfolio in the various risk/reward quadrants which are sorted on the three-year standard deviation from lowest to highest.

I	II				
				Std Dev	**Tot Ret.**
	Co Name	Ticker	Sector	3-Year	3-Year
	1 ExxonMobil	XOM	Energy	21.6	14.95
	2 Johnson & Johnson	JNJ	Health	34.6	18.34
	3 Adolph Coors B	RKY	Consumer Staple 37.7		35.98
	4 IBM	IBM	Technology	42.2	18.21
	5 Wal-Mart	WMT	Retail	51.1	39.78
	6 Citigroup	C	Financial	53.5	25.11
	7 Alcoa	AA	Indus Cyclical	65.9	26.04
III	IV				
				Std Dev	**Tot Ret.**
	Co Name	Ticker	Sector	3-Year	3-Year
	WorldCom	WCOM	Services	47.9	-11.32

Diversification: Asset Classes

The prior discussion addressed the issues of diversification within a given asset class, that is, stocks.

Diversification between asset classes, such as stocks, bonds, cash, etc., provides a greater opportunity to diversify due to the low correlation between different asset classes as was illustrated in Table 3-6.

Based on the historical data for the 1970-1999 period, Table 3-3, a hypothetical portfolio with an allocation of 50% in bonds and 50% in stocks was constructed.

Table 3-12 provides the tabulation of the year-by-year returns for stocks, bonds and the hypothetical stock/bond portfolio.

Table 3-12
Year-by-Year Returns, 1970-1999

YEAR	STOCKS	BNDS 50% STKS 50%	BONDS
1970	4.01	10.44	16.86
1971	14.31	11.52	8.72
1972	18.98	12.07	5.16
1973	-14.66	-5.03	4.61
1974	-26.47	-10.39	5.69
1975	37.20	22.52	7.83
1976	23.84	18.36	12.87
1977	-7.18	-2.89	1.41
1978	6.56	5.03	3.49
1979	18.44	11.27	4.09
1980	32.42	18.17	3.91
1981	-4.91	2.27	9.45
1982	21.41	25.26	29.10
1983	22.51	14.96	7.41
1984	6.27	10.15	14.02
1985	32.16	26.25	20.33
1986	18.47	16.81	15.14
1987	5.23	4.07	2.90
1988	16.81	11.46	6.10
1989	31.49	22.39	13.29
1990	-3.17	3.28	9.73
1991	30.55	23.01	15.46
1992	7.67	7.43	7.19
1993	9.99	10.62	11.24
1994	1.31	-1.92	-5.14
1995	37.43	27.12	16.80
1996	23.07	12.59	2.10
1997	33.36	20.87	8.38
1998	28.58	19.40	10.21
1999	21.04	9.64	-1.77
AVG.RET %	14.89	11.89	8.89
COMP RATE,%	13.72	11.47	8.68
MAX RATE,%	37.43	27.12	29.10
MIN RATE,%	-26.47	-10.39	-5.14
STD DEV.%	15.70	9.51	6.83
COEFF OF VAR	1.05	0.80	0.77

The 50/50 diversified portfolio average return over the 1970-1999 was 11.9%, as compared to stocks of 14.9% and bonds of 8.9%.

The worst year for the 50/50 portfolio was 1974, with a loss of -10.4%, whereas the best year was 1995, with a gain of 27.1%, representing a difference of 37.5 percentage points between the highest and the lowest annual portfolio returns.

The worst year for stocks was also 1974 with a loss of -26.5%, whereas the best year was also 1995, with a gain of 37.4%, representing a difference of 63.9 percentage points between the highest and the lowest.

It is significant to note that the average return for the 50/50 portfolio, of 11.9%, as compared to that of stocks, of 14.9%, represents a reduction of 20.1%, whereas the reduction in risk, that is, the standard deviation for the 50/50 portfolio, was 9.5%, as compared to the standard deviation for stocks, of 15.7%, representing a reduction in risk of 39.5%.

The average return for the hypothetical portfolio is calculated as follows.

$$
\begin{aligned}
\textbf{Avg Return} &= \textbf{0.5 x Avg Return Stks + 0.5 x Avg Return Bonds} \\
&= \textbf{0.5 x 14.89 + 0.5 x 8.89} \\
&= \textbf{11.89}
\end{aligned}
$$

However, it should be noted that the hypothetical portfolio's standard deviation, of 9.5%, is not equal to the weighted average of the standard deviation for the stocks and bonds, which is...

$$
\begin{aligned}
\textbf{Weighted Standard Deviation} &= \textbf{0.5 x Std Dev Stk + 0.5 x Std Dev Bonds} \\
&= \textbf{0.5 x 15.7 + 0.5 x 6.83} \\
&= \textbf{11.27}
\end{aligned}
$$

The standard deviation for the bond/stock investment portfolio, of 9.5%, as compared to the weighted portfolio standard deviation, of 11.3%, represents a reduction in volatility of 16%.

The reduction in the standard deviation of the investment portfolio vs the weighted portfolio standard deviation is the result of the low correlation, 0.32, between stocks and bonds.

The mathematical calculation of the standard deviation for two or more asset classes in an investment portfolio not only comprehends the allocation percentage of the respective asset classes, but also the correlation between the various asset classes.

The lower the correlation between asset classes in an investment portfolio, the greater the reduction of the investment portfolio's standard deviation, as compared to the weighted mean standard deviation.

The following three charts are graphic illustrations of the volatility of annual returns for stocks, for the 50% bond/50% stock hypothetical portfolio and for bonds for the 1970-1999 period.

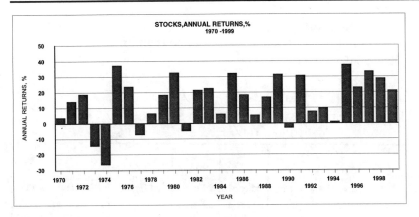

Avg Return = 14.9%

Std Dev = 15.7%

Maximum = 37.4%

Minimum = -26.5%

Chart 3-11

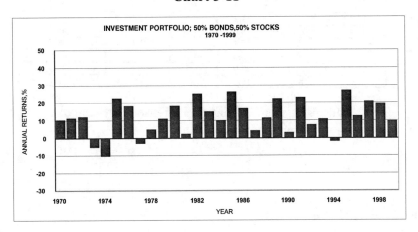

Avg Return = 11.9%

Std Dev = 9.5%

Maximum = 27.1%

Minimum = -10.4%

Chart 3-12

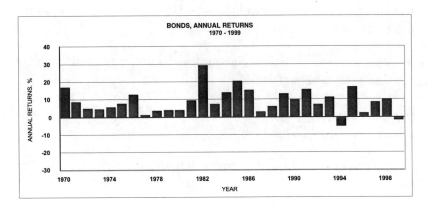

Avg Return = 8.9%

Std Dev = 6.9%

Maximum = 29.1%

Minimum = -5.1%

Chart 3-13

Table 3-13 provides the performance statistics for various hypothetical investment portfolios, combining the asset classes, stocks, bonds and T-Bills, based on the 1970-1999 historical data tabulated in Table 3-3.

Table 3-13
Hypothetical Investment Portfolio Statistics
1970 - 1999

Portfolio Asset Alloc			Average % Return	Compd % Return	Max % Return	Min % Return	Std Dev %	Risk/Return Ratio
Stocks	Bonds	T-Bills						
100%	0	0	14.9	13.7	37.4	-26.5	15.7	1.05
90	10	0	14.3	13.3	35.4	-23.2	14.1	1.0
80	20	0	13.7	12.9	33.3	-20.0	13.1	0.95
70	30	0	13.1	12.4	31.2	-16.8	11.8	0.90
60	35	5	12.4	11.9	28.6	-13.5	10.4	0.84
50	35	15	11.6	11.2	25.4	-10.0	8.9	0.77
40	40	20	10.9	10.6	22.8	-6.7	7.6	0.70
30	50	20	10.3	10.0	23.0	-3.5	6.7	0.65
15	25	60	8.5	8.4	16.8	1.3	3.8	0.44

As illustrated in Table 3-13, there is a direct relationship between investment return and risk, that is, average returns vs standard deviation.

Diversification: Asset Allocation

Establishing financial objectives such as funding college educations for children, retirement planning, etc., are long term objectives. However, most investors often pursue their long-term objectives with short-term strategies.

The asset allocation process balances investment risk and return and focuses on long-term goals rather than short-term performance.

As previously stated, the primary objective of portfolio structure, i.e. asset allocation, is to maximize expected return for any chosen level of risk.

In the construction of an investment portfolio, the portfolio asset allocation must comprehend the following constraints.

- Level of risk – safety of principal
- Income needs

- Liquidity
- Holding period
- Tax exposure

These constraints change with age as is illustrated in the following table.

	Early Career	Mid Career	Retirement
Risk	High	High	Low
Holding Period	Long	Long	Short
Income Needs	Low	Low	High
Taxes	Low	High	Low

The above constraints are general. For example, the following are issues that are to be comprehended, as a minimum, in structuring an asset allocation for retirement savings.

- Age
- Years prior to retirement
- Need to take distributions in the near future
- Future earnings potential
- Installment debt
- Dependents
- Emergency fund
- Retirement savings required to supplement other retirement income
- Investment knowledge and experience
- Risk tolerance

The objectives of asset allocation may be classified into the following generic groupings.

- Capital Preservation–

  An investment portfolio with a high level of bonds and cash, 70% - 80%.

  This investment portfolio will provide a lower return with correspondingly
   lower risk and high liquidity.

- Income and Growth–

    This portfolio provides a balance between bonds and cash vs stocks.

    The bonds and cash provide the required income, whereas the allocation to stocks allows for capital growth; consequently, a higher level of risk than the capital preservation investment portfolio.

- Long Term Growth–

    The objective of a growth portfolio is to achieve above average returns over the long term.

    In that a growth investment portfolio has 65% - 80% invested in stocks, representing an aggressive risk portfolio, this type portfolio should have a planning horizon of 10 - 20 years.

For individual investors, risk often is a more complex and subtle concept than the simple standard deviation of expected future returns. First, the risk/return trade-off must recognize that attempts to earn higher rates of return necessitate accepting higher risk levels. Secondly, diversification reduces risk. Rational investment management dictates that portfolios must be diversified among asset classes as well as among individual securities within asset classes.

Developing an appropriate asset allocation strategy requires that a person make a realistic assessment of the type and magnitude of the risk he/she is willing to accept that is commensurate with the rate of return he/she desires to earn.

For many investors, the use of index mutual funds should provide a good start. Index funds are designed to mimic the performance of the market they track, such as the S&P 500 stock index.

Because index funds don't actively buy and sell stocks like actively managed funds, index funds minimize capital gains taxes and offer low operating costs.

Index funds are designed to track the market, i.e. if the market goes down so will the index fund, as evidenced by funds tracking the S&P 500 stock index in year 2000, when the S&P 500 index fund was down an average of 9.2%.

In year 2000 actively managed funds outperformed index funds for the first time since 1993.

> ### Asset Allocation
> ### (Active vs Passive Management)
>
> As the numbers of investment style funds have increased, the number of stocks in a specific style fund decrease, resulting in loss of diversification, increased fees, and require an increase in management skills. Investment style funds which are actively managed to beat the market may, in reality, be counterproductive.
>
> Investment portfolio diversification is achieved through the use of passively managed *index funds*, not specific investment style funds.
>
> Therefore, the *core* of an investment portfolio should use index funds, which provides diversification and reduces costs, whereas specific style funds should be used to add value.

Summary

- With the ever increasing availability of investment products and the shifting of the investment decisions to the individual investor, understanding the risk and return characteristics of different investment products is fundamental to the investment decision process if realistic assumptions are to be incorporated in a personal financial plan.

- Historical performance statistics illustrate the basic relationship that increasing an investment portfolio's return requires a corresponding increase in risk.

- In the structuring of an investment portfolio, the investment policy requires that for a given level of expected return, the portfolio minimizes the risk.

- The structuring of an investment portfolio that minimizes risk requires diversification among investment classes and within investment classes.

- Investment portfolio diversification does not guarantee against potential losses. However, the objective of a properly diversified investment portfolio is to minimize losses in down markets and still position the portfolio to participate in up markets.

--INVESTMENT MANAGEMENT--
MEASUREMENT OF INVESTMENT PERFORMANCE

Investment Rates of Return: Overview

The purchase of common stock represents purchasing ownership in a corporation.

The decision to purchase common stock is complex, in that it requires the analysis of a company's 1) growth, 2) profitability, 3) financials and 4) valuation of the current share price.

The above factors will be reflected in the future share price of the stock.

Rate of return refers to how much an investment changed, on a percentage basis, from one period to another. A nominal rate of return is the rate of return stated for an investment that earns at a uniform, or fixed, rate over a given period of time. An example of a nominal rate of return is that of a certificate of deposit. Whether compounded annually, semi-annually, quarterly, etc., it always earns at the stated rate for a given period of time.

The measurement of return on stock investments is primarily the result of changes in share price and dividend payments. The share price varies constantly, depending on the market, whereas the dividend payments may be changed over time at the discretion of the company.

The measurement of the return on an investment, as reported in financial journals and newspapers, is based on various assumptions which may not be representative of an investor's return, when taking into consideration the timing of the investment, the frequency of contributions, withdrawals, reinvestment or distribution of capital gains and dividends, transaction costs, taxes, etc., over a designated holding period.

Investment Rates of Return, Equities: Computational Procedure

In the measurement of the rates of return for investment securities, such as stocks and stock mutual funds, where the share price is constantly changing, its investment rate of return is also constantly changing. Therefore, specific computational procedures are required for the evaluation of the rate of return over a designated holding period. This evaluation virtually transforms the widely varying actual rates of return into a nominal or uniform rate of return for the designated time period.

The common measurements of rates of return for such securities may be expressed as–

- Annual rate of return
- Annualized rate of return
- Total rate of return

The *annual rate of return* measures the equivalent constant rate of return that an investment earned over a one year period.

The *annualized rate of return* measures the equivalent constant rate of return that an investment earned per year over a multiple year period.

The *total rate of return* measures the cumulative return that the investment earned over the multiple year period, i.e. over 3 years, 5 years, etc.

The calculation of the rate of return for an investment security, such as a stock, requires the sequential compounding of the rates of return from one time period to the next time period within the holding period.

For example, the calculation of the annual rate of return, based on monthly rates of return, requires the compounding of the individual monthly returns as illustrated in Equation [1].

$$\text{Annual rate of return} = [(1.0 + M_1\%) \times (1.0 + M_2\%) .... \times (1.0 + M_{12}\%)] - 1.0 \qquad [1]$$

where M_1, M_2 ..... are the monthly percent returns for the respective months

The rates of return within the holding period also may be quarterly, semi-annually, etc. However, the same compounding concepts are applicable in the calculation of the annual rate of return, as illustrated using quarterly rates of return.

$$\text{Annual rate of return} = [(1.0 + Q_1\%) \times (1.0 + Q_2\%) \times (1.0 + Q_3\%) \times (1.0 + Q_4\%)] - 1.0$$

where Q_1, Q_2 ..... are the quarterly percent returns for the respective quarters

The average annual compounding rate for a holding period greater than one year is called the *annualized rate of return.*

The annualized rate of return is the geometric mean of the cumulative returns, calculated by taking the *root* of the cumulative returns, not simply by dividing the cumulative returns by the number of years in the holding period.

The mathematical expression for the calculation of the annualized return is as follows.

Annualized rate of return = [(1 + ROR₁) x (1 + ROR₂) ... x (1 + RORᵢ) ... x (1 + RORₙ)] ^1/N - 1.0   **[2]**

where ROR_i =   annual rate of return for the ith year
N   =   number of years in the holding period
1/N   =   root of the cumulative return

Equation [2] may be expressed mathematically as ...

$$\textbf{Annualized rate of return}\;=\;\left[\prod_{i=1}^{N}(1+ROR_i)\right]^{\wedge 1/N}-1.0 \qquad [3]$$

where $\displaystyle\prod_{i=1}^{N}$ is the mathematical symbol for multiplication of N different terms

The annualized rate of return is equivalent to a nominal rate of return over the holding period.

The annualized geometric mean may also be calculated using the concept of an index, where the starting index value is 1.00 and the index is compounded using the sequential period rates of return. The ending index value, therefore, represents the cumulative return over the holding period.

The mathematical expression for the annualized geometric mean, using the index concept, is as follows.

$$\textbf{Annualized return}=\left[\frac{\textbf{Cumulative Index}}{\textbf{Starting Index}}\right]^{\wedge 1/N}-1.0 \qquad [4]$$

The ending cumulative index also is a measure of the total return, TR, over the holding period.

The computational procedures used in the calculation of the *annual, annualized* and *total rates of return* are illustrated by the following example, using hypothetical monthly rates of return for a two year holding period, as tabulated in Table 4-1.

Table 4-1

(1) YEAR	(2) MONTH	(3) MO RETURN	(4) START INDEX	(5) CUM INDEX	(6) QRTLY RETURN	(7) ANNUAL RETURN	(8) ANNUALILIZED RETURN	(9) TOTAL RETURN
1	1	1.50%	1.000	1.015				
1	2	0.50%	1.015	1.020				
1	3	0.30%	1.020	1.023	2.31%			
1	4	2.50%	1.023	1.049				
1	5	3.00%	1.049	1.080				
1	6	0.30%	1.080	1.083	5.89%			
1	7	0.60%	1.083	1.090				
1	8	-0.70%	1.090	1.082				
1	9	2.00%	1.082	1.104	1.89%			
1	10	1.75%	1.104	1.123				
1	11	-0.30%	1.123	1.120				
1	12	1.65%	1.120	1.138	3.12%	13.84%		
2	1	0.50%	1.138	1.144				
2	2	0.25%	1.144	1.147				
2	3	5.00%	1.147	1.204	5.79%			
2	4	6.00%	1.204	1.277				
2	5	-5.00%	1.277	1.213				
2	6	-2.00%	1.213	1.188	-1.31%			
2	7	0.25%	1.188	1.191				
2	8	0.30%	1.191	1.195				
2	9	0.50%	1.195	1.201	1.05%			
2	10	0.60%	1.201	1.208				
2	11	0.80%	1.208	1.218				
2	12	2.00%	1.218	1.242	3.43%	9.12%	11.45%	24.22%

The interpretation of Table 4-1 is as follows:

Col (3):   The monthly rates of return during the two year holding period.

Col (4):   The cumulative index value at the start of each month.

Col (5):   The cumulative index value at the end of each month. The cumulative ending index value is calculated by compounding the cumulative start index with the respective monthly rates of return in Col (3).

For example, the cumulative index at the end of the <u>first quarter</u> in year 1, for months 1, 2 and 3, is calculated as follows:

Cum Index,Yr 1, 1st qtr $=$ $(1 + 1.5\%)$ x $(1 + 0.5\%)$ x $(1 + 0.3\%)$
$=$ **1.023**

Col (6): The entries in this column are the quarterly rates of return.

For example, the quarterly rate of return for year 1, for the *second quarter*, that is, compounding the rates of return for months 4, 5 and 6, Col (3), Table 4-1.

Second Qtr Return, Yr 1 $=$ $(1 + 2.5\%)$ x $(1 + 3.0\%)$ x $(1 + 0.3\%)$ - 1.0
$=$ **0.589 or 5.89%**

The second quarter return for year 1 may also be calculated using the change in the cumulative index during the second quarter in year 1, that is, dividing the cumulative index at the *end* of the 2nd quarter by the cumulative index at the *start* of the 2nd quarter, as follows:

$$\textbf{Second Qtr Return, Yr 1} \quad = \quad \left(\frac{1.083}{1.023}\right) - 1.0$$

$$= \quad \textbf{0.0589 or 5.89\%}$$

Col (7): The entries in this column are the annual geometric means for years 1 and 2.

The annual returns may be calculated using monthly or quarterly returns, using Equation [1].

For example, using quarterly rates for year 1, the annual returns is ...

Annual return $=$ $(1 + 2.31\%)$ x $(1 + 5.89\%)$ x $(1 + 1.89\%)$ x $(1 + 3.12\%)$ - 1.0
$=$ **0.1384 or 13.84%**

The annual return may also be calculated using the change in the cumulative index for year 1. For example, the annual rate of return for year 1 is calculated by dividing the cumulative index at the *end* of year 1 by the cumulative index at the *start* of year 1, as follows:

$$\text{Annual return} \quad = \quad \left(\frac{1.138}{1.00}\right) - 1.0$$

$$= \quad 0.1384 \quad \text{or} \quad 13.84\%$$

Col (8): The entry in this column is the annualized return for the two year holding period.

The annualized return for the two year holding period may be calculated using either Equation [3] or Equation [4].

Using Equation [3], the annualized return is calculated by taking the ½ root of the compounded return for the two year period, as follows...

$$\text{Annualized return} \quad = \quad [(1 + 13.84\%) \times (1 + 9.12)]^{\wedge\frac{1}{2}} - 1.0$$
$$= \quad 0.1145 \quad \text{or} \quad 11.45\%$$

Using Equation [4], the annualized return is calculated by dividing the cumulative index at the *end* of year 2 by the *starting* index in year 1 and taking the ½ root of the results, as follows...

$$\text{Annualized return} \quad = \quad \left(\frac{1.242}{1.00}\right)^{1/2} - 1.0$$

$$= \quad 0.1145 \quad \text{or} \quad 11.45\%$$

The annualized rate of return represents the equivalent nominal yearly rate of return over the two year holding period, as illustrated below.

$$\text{Annualized rate of return} \quad = \quad [(1 + 11.45\%) \times (1 + 11.45\%)]^{1/2} - 1.0$$
$$= \quad 0.1145 \quad \text{or} \quad 11.45\%$$

Col (9): The entry in this column is the total return, TR, over the two year holding period, which may be calculated using the annual returns, annualized returns or the cumulative index, as follows...

$$
\begin{aligned}
TR \; &= \; (1 + 13.84\%) \times (1 + 9.12\%) - 1.0 &&= \quad \text{annual return} \\
\text{or} \; &\quad (1 + 11.45\%) \times (1 + 11.45\%) - 1.0 &&= \quad \text{annualized return} \\
\text{or} \; &\quad (1.242/1.00) - 1.0 &&= \quad \text{cumulative index} \\
&= \; .242 \; \text{or} \; 24.2\%
\end{aligned}
$$

In summary, the total return, TR, over the two year holding period was 24.2%.

In Chapter 9, **Time Value of Money**, the various computational procedures are based on a constant rate of return over the holding period.

For example, in the calculation of the annual effective rate, AER, the mathematical Equation [1], in Chapter 9, is applicable if the nominal investment rate of return is constant over the holding period.

As was illustrated in Table 4-1, Col (3), the monthly rates of return in our hypothetical example are not constant, but vary from month-to-month from a low of -5.0% to a high of 6.0%.

The calculation of the effective annual or quarterly rates of return requires the use of Equations [3] or [4].

The effective monthly rate for year 1, using Equation [4], is calculated by dividing the cumulative index at the *end* of the 12th month by the index at the *start* of month 1, and taking the 1/12 root, as follows...

$$\textbf{Year 1, Effective monthly rate} \quad = \quad \left(\frac{1.138}{1.00}\right)^{1/12} - 1.0$$
$$= \quad \textbf{0.0109} \quad \textbf{or} \quad \textbf{1.09\%}$$

In other words, in our example, the annual effective rate, during year 1 was 1.09%.

The calculation of the effective monthly rates for year 2 is as follows...

$$\textbf{Year 2, Effective monthly rate} \quad = \quad \left(\frac{1.242}{1.138}\right)^{1/12} - 1.0$$
$$= \quad \textbf{0.0073} \quad \textbf{or} \quad \textbf{0.73\%}$$

Using the effective monthly rates of 1.09% and 0.73% for years 1 and 2, respectively, the cumulative index is calculated as illustrated in Table 4-2.

Table 4-2
Effective Monthly Returns

(1) MONTH	(2) MO RETURN	(3) EFF. MO. RETURN	(4) START INDEX	(5) END INDEX
1	1.50%	1.09%	1.000	1.011
2	0.50%	1.09%	1.011	1.022
3	0.30%	1.09%	1.022	1.033
4	2.50%	1.09%	1.033	1.044
5	3.00%	1.09%	1.044	1.055
6	0.30%	1.09%	1.055	1.067
7	0.60%	1.09%	1.067	1.079
8	-0.70%	1.09%	1.079	1.090
9	2.00%	1.09%	1.090	1.102
10	1.75%	1.09%	1.102	1.114
11	-0.30%	1.09%	1.114	1.126
12	1.65%	1.09%	1.126	1.138
13	0.50%	0.73%	1.138	1.147
14	0.25%	0.73%	1.147	1.155
15	5.00%	0.73%	1.155	1.163
16	6.00%	0.73%	1.163	1.172
17	-5.00%	0.73%	1.172	1.181
18	-2.00%	0.73%	1.181	1.189
19	0.25%	0.73%	1.189	1.198
20	0.30%	0.73%	1.198	1.207
21	0.50%	0.73%	1.207	1.215
22	0.60%	0.73%	1.215	1.224
23	0.80%	0.73%	1.224	1.233
24	2.00%	0.73%	1.233	1.242

It should be noted that the cumulative index, Table 4-2, Col (5), calculated using the effective annual rates at the *end* of 12 months and the *end* 24 months, are equal to the cumulative index in Table 4-1, Col (5), calculated using the actual monthly rates.

It should also be noted that the effective monthly rates are *not equal* to the respective annual rates divided by 12, as illustrated below.

Year 1:	**13.84%/12**	= 1.15%	≠	**Effective monthly rate of 1.09%**
Year 2:	**9.12%/12**	= 0.76%	≠	**Effective monthly rate of 0.73%**

The effective quarterly rates for year 1, using Equation [4] are calculated by dividing the *ending* cumulative index for each quarter, Table 4-1, by the *starting* index for each quarter, Table 4-1, and taking the ⅓ root, as follows...

$$\text{Qtr 1-1} \quad = \quad \left(\frac{1.023}{1.00}\right)^{1/3} - 1.0$$

$$= \quad 0.0077 \quad \text{or} \quad 0.77\%$$

$$\text{Qtr 1-2} \quad = \quad \left(\frac{1.083}{1.023}\right)^{1/3} - 1.0$$

$$= \quad 0.0193 \qquad \text{or} \quad 1.93\%$$

$$\text{Qtr 1-3} \quad = \quad \left(\frac{1.104}{1.083}\right)^{1/3} - 1.0$$

$$= \quad 0.0063 \qquad \text{or} \quad 0.63\%$$

$$\text{Qtr 1-4} \quad = \quad \left(\frac{1.138}{1.104}\right)^{1/3} - 1.0$$

$$= \quad 0.01303 \qquad \text{or} \quad 1.03\%$$

The effective quarterly rates for year 2 are calculated using the same concepts.

Using the effective quarterly rates for years 1 and 2, in Table 4-3, Col (3), in lieu of the actual monthly rates, Table 4-3, Col (2), the cumulative index in Col (5) of Table 4-3 is calculated.

Table 4-3
Effective Quarterly Rates

(1) MONTH	(2) MO RETURN	(3) EFF. QRTR RATE	(4) START INDEX	(5) END INDEX
1	1.50%	0.77%	1.000	1.008
2	0.50%	0.77%	1.008	1.015
3	0.30%	0.77%	1.015	1.023
4	2.50%	1.93%	1.023	1.043
5	3.00%	1.93%	1.043	1.063
6	0.30%	1.93%	1.063	1.083
7	0.60%	0.63%	1.083	1.090
8	-0.70%	0.63%	1.090	1.097
9	2.00%	0.63%	1.097	1.104
10	1.75%	1.03%	1.104	1.115
11	-0.30%	1.03%	1.115	1.127
12	1.65%	1.03%	1.127	1.138
13	0.50%	1.89%	1.138	1.160
14	0.25%	1.89%	1.160	1.182
15	5.00%	1.89%	1.182	1.204
16	6.00%	-0.44%	1.204	1.199
17	-5.00%	-0.44%	1.199	1.194
18	-2.00%	-0.44%	1.194	1.188
19	0.25%	0.35%	1.188	1.193
20	0.30%	0.35%	1.193	1.197
21	0.50%	0.35%	1.197	1.201
22	0.60%	1.13%	1.201	1.215
23	0.80%	1.13%	1.215	1.228
24	2.00%	1.13%	1.228	1.242

Again, it should be noted that the cumulative index at the end of 12 months and 24 months in Table 4-3, Col (5), calculated using the effective quarterly rates are equal to the cumulative index in Table 4-1, Col (5), calculated using the actual monthly rates.

In summary, the annual, annualized and total rates of return may be calculated by *compounding* the monthly, quarterly, annual, etc., rates of return.

Investment Rates of Return: Equities

As stated, the return on an investment in stocks (equities) and stock mutual funds is the result of appreciation or depreciation of share price and payments of dividends.

The basic components of the rate of return for equities comprehends the following:

- Change in share price over a designated holding period
- Distribution of income, that is, dividends and capital gains
- Reinvestment of income
- Additions or withdrawals of capital

In the calculation of an investment's rate of return, the timing of additions or withdrawals of capital over the holding period must be comprehended in the final determination of the investment's rate of return.

If the investment's rate of return is for a holding period greater than one year, the return represents a compounded return, or an annualized rate of return.

The returns that are published in financial journals and newspapers are reported as annualized rates of return for holding periods greater than one year, or as total returns.

The reported annualized investment rates of return are based on the following assumptions:

- The investment was a lump sum investment at the start of the holding period

- All dividends and capital gains are reinvested during the holding period

- No commissions, loads, taxes, etc. are comprehended

Therefore, an investor's rate of return over a designated holding period may significantly deviate from the published rate of return if the investor's activities do not conform to the above assumptions.

The following analysis will provide an insight into the impact that timing of investing has on the annualized return that an investor may realize.

In our analysis we shall use the Vanguard 500 Index fund which mimics the S&P 500 Index and is considered to be a measure of market performance for large corporate stocks.

Table 4-4 provides the quarterly rates of return for the Vanguard 500 Index fund, starting with the first quarter of 1996, and ending with the last quarter of 2000, for a holding period of five years.

Table 4-4

VANGUARD 500 INDEX FUND ; QUARTERLY RETURNS, %					
VANGUARD 500 INDEX FUND; 1996-2000					
YEAR	1996	1997	1998	1999	2000
Q1	5.36	2.63	13.91	4.98	2.25
Q2	4.44	17.41	3.29	7.00	-2.62
Q3	3.05	7.48	-9.95	-6.25	-0.93
Q4	8.36	2.84	21.39	14.96	-7.81

Chart 4-1 provides a graphic illustration of the quarterly returns as tabulated in Table 4-4.

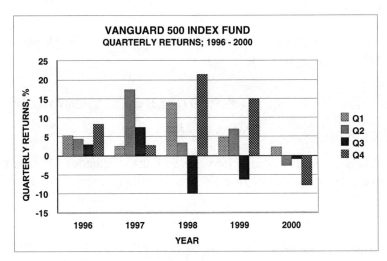

Chart 4-1

Table 4-5 provides the calculation of the cumulative index using the quarterly rates of return for the Vanguard 500 Index fund, as tabulated in Table 4-4 for the 1996-2000 holding period.

Table 4-5

(1)	(2)	(3)	(4)	(5)
	QTRLY	CUM	ANNUAL	ANNUALIZED
YEAR	RETURNS	INDEX	RETURNS	RETURNS
1996-Q1	5.36	1.054		
1996-Q2	4.44	1.100		
1996-Q3	3.05	1.134		
1996-Q4	8.36	1.229	22.87%	18.30%
1997-Q1	2.63	1.261		
1997-Q2	17.41	1.481		
1997-Q3	7.48	1.591		
1997-Q4	2.84	1.637	33.19%	17.19%
1998-Q1	13.91	1.864		
1998-Q2	3.29	1.926		
1998-Q3	-9.95	1.734		
1998-Q4	21.39	2.105	28.61%	12.29%
1999-Q1	4.98	2.210		
1999-Q2	7.00	2.364		
1999-Q3	-6.25	2.217		
1999-Q4	14.96	2.548	21.06%	4.93%
2000-Q1	2.25	2.605		
2000-Q2	-2.62	2.537		
2000-Q3	-0.93	2.514		
2000-Q4	-7.81	2.317	-9.06%	-9.06%

The annual rate of return shown in Table 4-5, Col (4), may be calculated using either Equation [3] or [4].

For example, the annual rate of return for year 1997, using Equation [3], and the quarterly 1997 rates are as follows.

$$\text{Annual rate return,1997} = \left[(1+2.63\%)\text{x}(1+17.41\%)\text{x}(1+7.48\%)\text{x}(1+2.84\%)\right]^{1/1} - 1.0$$

$$= 0.332 \quad \text{or} \quad 33.2\%$$

The annual rate of return for year 1997, using Equation [4], based on dividing the cumulative index at the *end* of year 1997 by the cumulative index at the *start* of 1997, is as follows.

$$\text{Annual rate return, 1997} = \left(\frac{1.637}{1.229}\right)^{1/1} - 1.0$$

$$= 0.332 \quad \text{or} \quad 33.2\%$$

The annualized rates in Table 4-5, Col (5), are...

Holding Period	Annualized Rate, %
5	18.3%
4	17.19
3	12.29
2	4.93
1	-9.06

The annualized rates of return shown in Table 4-5, Col (5), may be calculated using either Equation [3] or [4].

For example, the annualized rate of return for the five year holding period, using Equation [3] is as follows.

$$\text{Annualized return} = [(1 + 22.87\%)\text{x}(1 + 33.19\%)\text{x}(1 + 28.61\%)\text{x}(1 + 21.06\%)\text{x}(1 - 9.06\%)]^{1/5} - 1.0$$
$$= 0.183 \quad \text{or} \quad 18.3\%$$

The annualized rate of return for the five year holding period using Equation [4] is as follows.

$$\text{Annualized rate return} = \left(\frac{2.317}{1.00}\right)^{1/5} - 1.0$$
$$= 0.183 \quad \text{or} \quad 18.3\%$$

Tabulated below in Table 4-6 are the annualized rates of return for the Vanguard 500 Index fund, at the start of each quarter of each year for the five year holding period beginning 1/1/96 and through 12/31/00.

Table 4-6

ANNUALIZED RETURNS BASED ON STARTING QUARTER					
VANGUARD 500 INDEX FUND; 1996-2000					
YEAR	1996	1997	1998	1999	2000
Q1	18.30	17.18	12.30	4.92	-9.06
Q2	18.00	17.60	8.22	2.75	-11.10
Q3	17.90	13.60	7.68	-1.33	-8.67
Q4	18.31	12.24	13.74	3.62	-7.81

For example, the annualized 5-year return for a lump sum invested at the start of the first quarter in 1996 is 18.3%; for a lump sum invested at the start of the first quarter of 1998 the annualized 3-year return is 12.3%; and for a lump sum invested at the start of the first quarter of 2000 the annualized 1-year return is -9.06%.

The annualized returns shown in the first quarter of year 2000, 1998 and 1996 are the returns reported in the financial publications for the 1-, 3- and 5-year periods, respectively.

On review of the annualized returns tabulated in Table 4-6, an investor making a lump sum investment at the start of the 3rd quarter of 1998 realized an annualized return of 7.7% over the holding period from 7/1/98 through 12/31/00, whereas if the lump sum was invested at the start of the 4th quarter of 1998 the investor realized an annualized return of 13.7% over the holding period from 10/1/98 through 12/31/00.

The individual investing at the start of the 3rd quarter of 1998 lost 9.95% during that quarter, whereas the individual investing at the start of the 4th quarter of 1998 realized a gain of 21.4% in that quarter, as illustrated in Table 4-5, Col (2).

Assuming the lump sum investment was $1000 at the start of the 3rd and 4th quarters of 1998, the performance statistics over the holding period ending 12/31/00 are as follows.

1998	Initial Invest,$	Total Return, TR,%	Annualized Return, %	Ending Mkt Value
3Q	$1000	20.3%	7.68%	$1203
4Q	$1000	33.1%	13.74%	$1336

Note: Reinvestment of all dividends and capital gains is assumed.

In summary, the individual investing at the start of the 4th quarter realized an increase in ending market value, on 12/31/00, of 11%.

The difference in annualized returns of 6.0% (13.7% - 7.7%) reflects the difference in the timing of investing by one quarter.

In the above analysis the basic assumption is that an investor makes a lump sum investment at the start of the holding period, and no additional contributions are made during the holding period, whereas, in reality, an investor is contributing to a savings plan, such as a 401-k, and, as a minimum, is making monthly contributions.

The computation of the annualized rate of return over a holding period, where multiple contributions are made, must comprehend the respective contributions.

For example, Table 4-7 illustrates contributing $1000 at the *start* of each year into the Vanguard 500 Index fund for the holding period of 1996 - 2000.

Table 4-7

YEAR=>	1996	1997	1998	1999	2000	ANNUALIZED RETURN
ANNUAL RET	22.87%	33.19%	28.61%	21.06%	-9.06%	
	$1,229	$1,637	$2,105	$2,548	$2,317	18.30%
		1,332	1,713	2,074	1,886	17.18%
			1,286	1,557	1,416	12.30%
				1,211	1,101	4.92%
					909	-9.06%
				TOTAL=>	$7,630	

The interpretation of Table 4-7 is as follows...

The annual contributions of $1000 are compounding over their respective holding periods.

For example, $1000 invested at the start of 1996 has an ending market value of $1229 at the end of 1996, based on the 1996 annual rate of return of 22.87%, whereas the market value at the end of year 1997 is the compounding of the $1229, at the end of 1996, with the rate of return for year 1997 of 33.19%, resulting in a market value of $1637 at the end of 1997.

The ending market value for the $1000 invested in 1996 is $2317 at the end of year 2000, representing an annualized rate of return of 18.3%.

The same compounding procedure is followed for each of the annual contributions and the total market value of the investment at the end of 2000 is $7630.

In summary, the annual contributions of $1000 over the five year period resulted in a total savings of $7630, representing an annualized return of 14.4%.

The above analysis again illustrates that timing of an investment in any given calendar year and frequency of contributions over the holding period makes a significant difference in the annualized returns as opposed to a lump sum contribution at the start of a holding period.

Evaluating The Investment Rate of Return

As previously stated, the investment performance, as reported in financial journals, may not be representative of the rate of return that an investor realizes, as a consequence of the assumptions used in the calculation of the returns published in financial journals and newspapers.

The following is a simple approach that will provide an *approximation* of the investment rate of return which will be precise enough to make an informed decision.

The information used in the calculation of the rate of return is available in typical account statements.

The calculation of the return consists of the changes in value of the investment during the investment period.

If the income from the investment is reinvested, such as in mutual funds, the income is reflected in the change in market value.

For a common stock, if the dividend paid is invested into a cash account, the ending investment balance must comprehend the market value of both the stock and the cash account.

The change in market value also needs to be adjusted to comprehend any cash additions or withdrawals from the account during the investment period.

The calculation of the investment return compares the ending market value with the starting market value and adjusts for the net additions or withdrawals from the portfolio during the investment period.

This adjustment is made by *decreasing* the ending value by 50% of the net additions or withdrawals and *increasing* the beginning value by 50% of the net additions or withdrawals.

The following example illustrates the adjustment to the ending and starting values.

If the starting value is $10,000 and the ending value is $10,750, and during the investment period $1000 was added to the account and $500 was withdrawn, the net addition was $500 ($1000 - $500).

The adjustment to the ending value is -0.50 x $500, or $250, resulting in an adjusted ending value of $10,500 ($10,750 - $250).

The adjustment to the starting value is +0.50 x $500, or $250, resulting in an adjusted starting value of $10,250 ($10,000 + $250).

The return for the holding period is then calculated by dividing the adjusted ending value by the adjusted starting value and subtracting 1.0, as follows:

$$\frac{\textbf{Adjusted End Value}}{\textbf{Adjusted Start Value}} \quad -1.0 \quad = \quad \frac{10,500}{10,250} \quad -1.0$$

$$= \quad 0.0244 \quad \text{or } 2.44\%$$

The approximate rate of return equation may be expressed mathematically as follows.

$$\textbf{Rate of Return} \quad = \quad \left(\frac{\textbf{Ending value} - \textbf{0.5x(Net additions / withdrawals)}}{\textbf{Starting value} + \textbf{0.5x(Net additions / withdrawals)}} \right) - 1.0 \quad [5]$$

Substituting in the values from our example, the rate of return is calculated as follows:

$$\textbf{Rate of Return} \quad = \quad \left(\frac{10,750 - 0.5 \text{x} \$500}{10,000 + 0.5 \text{x} \$500} \right) - 1.0$$

$$= \quad 0.244 \quad \text{or} \quad 2.44\%$$

Table 4-8 is a tabulation of quarterly investment transactions for a hypothetical portfolio over a one year holding period.

Table 4-8

(1) QUARTER-MO	(2) STARTING BALANCE	(3) ADDITIONS/ WITHDRAWALS	(4) ENDING VALUE	(5) QTR RETURN
QTR1-1	$10,000			
QTR1-2		($500)		
QTR1-3			$10,000	
NET ADD./WITHDRAWALS=>		($500)		5.13%
QTR2-1	$10,000	($500)		
QTR2-2		$1,000		
QTR2-3			$10,750	
NET ADD./WITHDRAWALS=>		$500		2.44%
QTR3-1	$10,750			
QTR3-2		($750)		
QTR3-3			$9,750	
NET ADD./WITHDRAWALS=>		($750)		-2.41%
QTR4-1	$9,750			
QTR4-2		($1,200)		
QTR4-3			$9,500	
NET ADD./WITHDRAWALS=>		($1,200)		10.38%
			ANNUAL % RETURN=>	16.01%

The quarterly rates of return in Table 4-8, Col (5),are calculated using Equation [5]. The example given before Table 4-8 illustrated the calculation of the rate of return for the second quarter in Table 4-8.

The annual rate of return is calculated by compounding the quarterly rates of return.

For an investment holding period greater than one quarter, Equation [5] does not recognize the specific month in which additions or withdrawals are made. Consequently, the longer the holding period, the higher the potential for error.

Therefore, it is recommended that Equation [5] not be used for investment period greater than one quarter.

The annual rate of return may be computed by compounding the return for the respective monthly or quarterly investment periods, using Equation [3].

The calculation of an investment's or an investment portfolio's rate of return, for a designated holding period, is complex and requires the use of portfolio management software programs, such as *Quicken 2000* from *Intuit*, or *Money 2000* from *Microsoft*.

These types of programs utilize the *value weighted internal rate of return* calculation methodology.

In the past 15 years, from 1984 - 1999, a very favorable stock market period, the average mutual stock fund gained 15% annually, but the average mutual stock fund investor realized only 10% return annually.

In other words, one-third of the investors' available return was lost by switching from one fund to another – all to often selling low and buying high.

To reiterate once again, the annualized statistics listed in financial publications may not be representative of what an individual investor may have realized.

Inflation: Overview

The development of a personal financial plan must comprehend the impact of inflation on future purchasing power.

The average inflation rate for the 1926-1999 period was 3.2%, ranging from a low of -10.3% in 1932 to a high of 18.2% in 1946.

In the calculation of financial goals that may be many years in the future, and require an income over many years, such as retirement, the required savings will be significantly impacted by inflation rate assumptions, as illustrated in Table 4-9.

Table 4-9

Years to Retirement	Inflation Rate	BFT Infl Adjusted Retirement Inc, $/Yr(1)	Savings Required at Start of Retirement(2)
10	3%	$25,000	$525,168
15	3%	25,000	608,814
20	3%	25,000	705,782
10	4%	25,000	652,036
15	4%	25,000	793,301
20	4%	25,000	965,172

(1) In current dollars
(2) Based on 8% before-tax rate of return and a 30 year retirement period.

As illustrated in Table 4-9, a 1.0% difference in future inflation rates may result in underestimating the savings required at the start of retirement by 25% to 40%.

The majority of defined benefit pension plans and tax-deferred retirement plans have no inflation protection, resulting in a significant loss of purchasing power over the retirement period.

With the increase in life expectancy, the projected retirement period may exceed the working years, resulting in the possibility of "running out of money before time."

A recent trend reflecting this phenomenon is that individuals are delaying retirement or working part-time after retirement.

The real rate of return is defined as the actual rate minus the inflation rate. For example, if the actual rate of return is 14.0% and inflation is 4.0%, the real rate of return is 10.0% (14.0 - 4.0).

Inflation: Loss of Purchasing Power

The loss of purchasing power over time is illustrated in Table 4-10, based on a purchasing power of $10,000 in today's dollars.

Table 4-10

Year	Inflation Rate	Purchasing Power	% Loss of Purchasing Power
1		$10,000	
10	3%	7,374	26.3%
20	3%	5,438	45.6%
30	3%	4,010	59.9%
10	4%	6,648	33.5%
20	4%	4,420	55.8%
30	4%	2,939	70.6%

As illustrated in Table 4 - 10, in 30 years at a 4.0% inflation rate, $10,000 in today's dollars will purchase goods and services worth approximately $3000 in today's dollars, representing a 71% loss in purchasing power.

Historical Real Rates of Return and Purchasing Power

Using the historical data for large corporate stocks, intermediate government bonds and Treasury bills for the 1970-1999 period, the real rates of return were calculated for the respective securities.

The real rates of return are tabulated in Table 4 - 11. Years with negative real rates of return are highlighted. A negative real rate of return indicates loss of purchasing power for the investor in that year.

Table 4 - 11
Real vs Actual Returns, 1970-1999

YEAR	STOCKS ACTUAL RETURNS	STOCKS REAL RETURNS	BONDS ACTUAL RETURNS	BONDS REAL RETURNS	T-BILLS ACTUAL RETURNS	T-BILLS REAL RETURNS	INFL
1970	4.01	-1.48	16.86	11.37	6.52	1.03	5.49
1971	14.31	10.95	8.72	5.36	4.39	1.03	3.36
1972	18.98	15.57	5.16	1.75	3.84	0.43	3.41
1973	-14.66	-23.46	4.61	-4.19	6.93	-1.87	8.80
1974	-26.47	-38.67	5.69	-6.51	8.00	-4.20	12.20
1975	37.20	30.19	7.83	0.82	5.80	-1.21	7.01
1976	23.84	19.03	12.87	8.06	5.08	0.27	4.81
1977	-7.18	-13.95	1.41	-5.36	5.12	-1.65	6.77
1978	6.56	-2.47	3.49	-5.54	7.18	-1.85	9.03
1979	18.44	5.13	4.09	-9.22	10.38	-2.93	13.31
1980	32.42	20.02	3.91	-8.49	11.24	-1.16	12.40
1981	-4.91	-13.85	9.45	0.51	14.71	5.77	8.94
1982	21.41	17.54	29.10	25.23	10.54	6.67	3.87
1983	22.51	18.71	7.41	3.61	8.80	5.00	3.80
1984	6.27	2.32	14.02	10.07	9.85	5.90	3.95
1985	32.16	28.39	20.33	16.56	7.72	3.95	3.77
1986	18.47	17.34	15.14	14.01	6.16	5.03	1.13
1987	5.23	0.82	2.90	-1.51	5.47	1.06	4.41
1988	16.81	12.39	6.10	1.68	6.35	1.93	4.42
1989	31.49	26.84	13.29	8.64	8.37	3.72	4.65
1990	-3.17	-9.28	9.73	3.62	7.81	1.70	6.11
1991	30.55	27.49	15.46	12.40	5.60	2.54	3.06
1992	7.67	4.77	7.19	4.29	3.51	0.61	2.90
1993	9.99	7.24	11.24	8.49	2.90	0.15	2.75
1994	1.31	-1.36	-5.14	-7.81	3.90	1.23	2.67
1995	37.43	34.89	16.80	14.26	5.60	3.06	2.54
1996	23.07	19.75	2.10	-1.22	5.21	1.89	3.32
1997	33.36	31.66	8.38	6.68	5.26	3.56	1.70
1998	28.58	26.97	10.21	8.60	4.86	3.25	1.61
1999	21.04	18.36	-1.77	-4.45	4.68	2.00	2.68
AVERAGE	14.89	9.73	8.89	3.72	6.73	1.56	5.16

Source: Ibbotson Associates, SBBI Yearbook 2000

The real rate of return for *stocks* was negative for eight different years over the 1970-1999 period, as illustrated in Table 4-11.

The average real rate of return for stocks was 9.7%, as compared to the average actual rate of return of 14.9% over the 1970-1999 period.

The average inflation rate over the 30 year period, 1970-1999, was 5.2%.

The real rate of return for *bonds* was negative for ten different years over the 1970-1999 period, as illustrated in Table 4-11.

The average real rate of return for bonds was 3.7%, as compared to the actual average rate of return of 8.9% over the 1970-1999 period.

The real rate of return for *Treasury bills* was negative for seven different years over the 1970-1999 period, as illustrated in Table 4-11.

The average real rate of return for Treasury bills was 1.6%, as compared to the average actual rate of return of 6.7% over the 1970-1999 period.

Table 4-12 provides the indexes, that is, the growth of $1.00 is illustrated for stocks, bonds and Treasury bills for the 1970 - 1999 period, based on the annual returns for the respective securities in Table 4-11 (stocks, bonds, and T-Bills).

Table 4-12 also provides the inflation index based on the assumption of a hypothetical portfolio earning at the inflation rate.

Table 4-12

YEAR	STOCK INDEX	BOND INDEX	T BILLS	INFL INDEX
======	======	======	======	======
1970	1.04	1.17	1.07	1.05
1971	1.19	1.27	1.11	1.09
1972	1.41	1.34	1.15	1.13
1973	1.21	1.40	1.23	1.23
1974	0.89	1.48	1.33	1.38
1975	1.22	1.59	1.41	1.47
1976	1.51	1.80	1.48	1.54
1977	1.40	1.82	1.56	1.65
1978	1.49	1.89	1.67	1.80
1979	1.77	1.96	1.84	2.04
1980	2.34	2.04	2.05	2.29
1981	2.22	2.23	2.35	2.49
1982	2.70	2.88	2.60	2.59
1983	3.31	3.10	2.83	2.69
1984	3.52	3.53	3.11	2.79
1985	4.65	4.25	3.35	2.90
1986	5.51	4.89	3.55	2.93
1987	5.79	5.03	3.75	3.06
1988	6.77	5.34	3.99	3.20
1989	8.90	6.05	4.32	3.35
1990	8.62	6.64	4.66	3.55
1991	11.25	7.67	4.92	3.66
1992	12.11	8.22	5.09	3.77
1993	13.32	9.14	5.24	3.87
1994	13.50	8.67	5.44	3.97
1995	18.55	10.13	5.75	4.07
1996	22.83	10.34	6.05	4.21
1997	30.44	11.21	6.37	4.28
1998	39.14	12.35	6.67	4.35
1999	47.38	12.13	6.99	4.47

The interpretation of Table 4-12 is as follows.

● $1.00 invested at the start of 1970 in stocks, has a market value of $47.38 at the end of 1999.

The $47.38 has a before-tax purchasing power, after being adjusted for inflation, of $10.60 ($47.38/$4.47).

The *real compounded* rate of return over the 30-year period for stocks is 8.2%, as compared to the actual compounded rate of 13.7% (see Chapter 3, **Investment Management–Risk and Diversification**, Table 3-3).

● $1.00 invested in T-bills at the start of 1970 has an index value of $6.99 at the end of 1999.

The $6.99 has a before-tax purchasing power, after being adjusted for inflation, of $1.56 ($6.99/$4.47).

The *real compounded* rate of return over the 30-year period is 1.50%, as compared to the actual rate of 6.7% (see Chapter 3, **Investment Management–Risk and Diversification**, Table 3-3).

Chart 4-2 is a graphic illustration of the indexes as tabulated in Table 4-12.

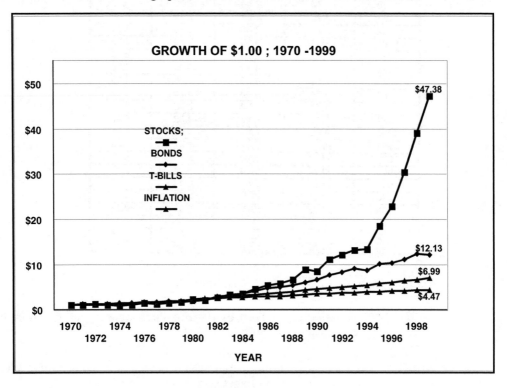

Chart 4-2

As illustrated in Table 4-11, T-bills had positive returns in all years from 1970 through 1999. Therefore, the loss of principal is not a consideration.

The risk incurred by investing in T-bills was that of loss of purchasing power on an after-tax basis.

If we assume a 39.6% marginal tax rate, the *after-tax real purchasing power* for the $1.00 invested in T-Bills, over the 30-year period, is calculated as follows.

$$\textbf{After-tax real purchasing power} \ = \ \textbf{\$1.56 x (1 - 0.396)}$$
$$= \ \textbf{\$0.94}$$

Therefore, the investor has incurred a loss of purchasing power in that the $1.00 invested in T-bills in 1970 has a purchasing power of only $0.94 in year 1999 on an after-tax basis.

Summary

- The measurement of the return, as reported in financial journals and newspapers, is based on various assumptions which may not be representative of an investor's return when taking into consideration the timing of the investment, the frequency of contributions, withdrawals, reinvestment or distribution of capital gains and dividends, transaction costs, taxes, etc.

- The common measurements of rates of return for stocks may be expressed as ...

  → Annual rate of return
  → Annualized rate of return
  → Total rate of return

- The calculation of annual rates of return requires the compounding of the rates of return for the respective investment periods, such as months, quarters, etc.

  The annual rate of return, calculated by the compounding of the returns for each time period within the holding period, is called the *geometric mean*.

- The real rate of return is defined as the actual rate of return minus the inflation rate.

- The development of a personal financial plan must comprehend the impact of inflation on future purchasing power.

Bonds: Overview

A bond is a debt security. When a person purchases a bond you are lending money to a government, a municipality, a corporation, etc.

In return for the loan, the issuer promises to pay the bond owner a fixed rate of interest during the term of the bond, and to repay the face value of the bond, the principal, when it matures. An individual bond has a stated finite life, or date of maturity, whereas, a bond mutual fund portfolio is made up of many different bonds; therefore, the fund has no finite date of maturity or termination.

The array of bonds available to an investor include: US Government securities, municipal bonds, corporate bonds, federal agency bonds, etc.

Because stock prices are correlated with projected earnings for a specific firm or industry sector, stocks tend to move independently of one another.

In contrast, bonds tend to move up or down in tandem, but in a direction opposite to the movement of interest rates.

The market price of a bond tends to rise when interest rates fall, and the bond market price falls when interest rates rise.

The volatility of a bond price, that is, the variation of the bond's market price above or below its par value, called interest rate risk, is a risk an investor is subject to if the bond is sold prior to its maturity.

If the bond is held to maturity, the interim price volatility is of no concern to an investor, in that, at maturity, the investor receives the par value, face value, of the bond.

The primary variables that impact bond prices are: 1) bond coupon rate, 2) time to maturity and 3) credit rating of the issuer.

The magnitude of a bond's market price change is correlated with time-to-maturity. The prices of bonds with longer maturities will rise or fall more than bonds with shorter maturities for a given interest rate change.

Bond maturities can range from one to 30 years.

The financial strength of the issuer of the bond establishes the bond's credit rating.

Bond credit ratings range from the highest credit rating, such as US Treasury securities, to bonds that are considered to be below investment grade, such as high yield or junk bonds.

Investment grade bonds with the highest quality are assigned an AAA credit rating. Investment grade bonds with the lowest credit rating are assigned a BBB credit rating.

Ratings below BBB are considered not to be investment grade bonds.

The most important measurement used in the valuation of a bond is yield-to-maturity, YTM. The yield-to-maturity bond measurement evaluates both interest income and price appreciation/depreciation and comprehends the total cash flow over the term of the bond.

Bond Pricing

The buying and selling of bonds requires an understanding of how bonds are priced. The bond price, as published in newspapers, is different than the pricing of stocks, in that, for a specific stock you can find its latest closing price, high price and low price.

There are a limited number of stocks listed on the major exchanges, approximately 9000, whereas there are millions of bonds. Therefore, it is not feasible to list the prices for individual issues.

In that only a small fraction of bonds are traded on any given day, the listing of representative bond prices will provide an investor with sufficient information such that an informed buy/sell decision may be made.

The bond price tables for various bond securities, such as Treasury, municipal, corporate and agency bonds will vary in format.

Treasury Bonds--

The format for Treasury bond price tables is as follows:

Table 5-1
Treasury Bond Price Table

Rate	Maturity	Bid	Ask	Chg	Yield,%
6¾	July 05	103:12	103:14		6.00
5⅜	Aug 07	99:14	99:16		5.46

Note: Purchase date 1/1/2000

The interpretation of Table 5-1 is as follows.

Rate/Maturity: The coupon rate of the bond; that is, the annual interest paid on the par value.

The Treasury bonds are identified by the coupon rate and date of maturity. In our example, the 6¾ bond has a maturity date of July 2005, whereas the 5⅜ bond has a maturity date of August 2007.

Bid/Ask: The price table includes the bid price and the ask price. The bid price is the current price that buyers will pay, whereas the ask price is the price at which the current sellers are offering the bond.

The prices are stated as a percentage of the bond's face value of $1000. The price fractions after the colon represent 32^{nds}.

For example, the bid price, 103:12, for the 6¾% bond is 103 12/32%, or 103.375% of $1000, which is a bid price of $1033.75.

Similarly, the ask price for the 6¾% July 2005 bond is 103:14, or 103.438% of $1000, or an ask price of $1034.38.

Yield: The yield to maturity, YTM, is based on the ask price. The YTM is what an investor would realize if the bond is purchased at the ask price and held until maturity.

The YTM is the most important and widely used bond valuation measure.

The 6¾% bond, maturity July 2005, with a current ask price of $1034.38, exceeds the bond par value of $1000. The ask price <u>premium</u> is the result of the coupon rate, 6¾%, being higher than current issues of Treasury bonds with the same time to maturity.

But, because the investor paid a premium of $34.38 ($1034.38 - $1000), the yield to maturity is 6.00% which is below the coupon rate of 6.75%.

The 5⅜% bond, maturity August 2007, with a current ask price of $995.00, is <u>discounted</u> from the par value of $1000 because rates on new issues with the same time to maturity have coupon rates higher than the 5⅜% bond.

Because the investor is buying the bond below par value, the bond's yield to maturity, YTM, of 5.46%, exceeds the bond coupon rate of 5.37%.

Tax-Exempt Bonds–

The format for the tax-exempt bond price table is as follows.

Table 5-2
Tax-Exempt Bond Price Table

Issuer	Coupon	Maturity	Price	Yld to Maturity
ABC	3.95%	3/01/05	100⅛	3.92%
XYZ	4.47%	1/01/10	98¼	4.69%

Note: Purchase date 1/1/2000

The interpretation of Table 5-2 is as follows:

Issuer: The issuing municipality or agency.

Coupon: The bond coupon rate.

Price: The most recent price, expressed as a percent of the par value.

Yld/Maturity: The yield to maturity based on the current price.

The ABC tax-exempt bond price of 100⅛%, or $1001.25, priced at a premium to its par value of $1000, is a result of the bond's coupon rate of 3.95% which is higher than current issues of tax-free bonds with the same time to maturity.

In that the investor is purchasing this bond at a *premium*, the yield to maturity of 3.92% is less than the coupon rate of 3.95%.

The XYZ tax-free bond, priced at 98.25% of par, is selling at a *discount* to par value.

Here, because the investor is purchasing the bond at a discount, the yield to maturity of 4.69%, is greater than the coupon rate of 4.47%.

Corporate Bonds–

The format for the corporate bond price table is as follows.

Table 5-3
Corporate Bond Price Table

Bonds	Cur Yld	Vol	Close	Net Change
IBM5⅜ 09	5.6%	–	95⅞	–
CocaCola8½ 22	7.2%	–	117¾	–

The interpretation of Table 5-3 is as follows:

Bonds: The name of the company issuing the bond; immediately following the name is the interest rate paid by the bond as a percentage of its par value, and the year the bond matures.

Current Yield: The IBM current yield of 5.6% is

based on its closing price of 95⅞%, or $958.75, and the 5⅜% coupon rate. The current yield, 5.6%, for the IBM bond is the annual interest payment, $53.75 (5⅜% x $1000), divided by the closing price, $958.75.

Bond Risk

Interest Rate Risk–

The market price of a bond is a function of its coupon rate, the time to maturity and the movement of market interest rates.

The coupon rate of a bond, relative to market interest rates, establishes the current bond market price.

If market interest rates are below the bond's coupon rate, the market price of the bond is above its par value, that is, the bond is selling at a *premium*.

If market interest rates are higher than the bond coupon rate, the market price of the bond is below its par value, that is, the bond is selling at a *discount*.

Changes in the inflation rate have a direct impact on interest rates, in that, as inflation increases, corresponding market interest rates will increase, resulting in lower bond prices. If inflation rates decrease, corresponding market interest rates will decrease, resulting in higher bond prices.

The magnitude of movement in bond market price is also correlated with time to maturity, in that the longer the time to maturity, the greater the movement in bond prices.

Table 5-4 provides a tabulation of the change in bond prices for various interest rates, above and below the coupon rate.

The bond coupon rate in Table 5-4 is 10.0%.

In that the change in bond price is also a function of time to maturity, three different bonds are evaluated, with times to maturity of 5-, 10- and 20-years.

Table 5-4
Bond Price, Percent of Par

MARKET	YEARS TO MATURITY		
INTR RATES	5 YRS	10 YRS	20YRS
============	============	============	============
6	116.85	129.44	145.88
7	112.30	121.07	131.78
8	107.98	113.42	119.64
9	103.89	106.42	109.13
10	100.00	100.00	100.00
11	96.30	94.11	92.04
12	92.79	88.70	85.06
13	89.44	83.72	78.93
14	86.27	79.14	73.51

The interpretation of Table 5-4 is as follows:

If the market interest rates are the same as the coupon rate, 10.0%, the bond's market price is as 100% of par value, or $1000.

If market interest rates decrease to 6.0%, the bond will sell at a premium rate; for example, the 5-year bond price is $1168.50 (116.85% x $1000), the 10-year bond price is $1294.40 and the 20-year bond price is $1458.80.

The difference in the bond prices reflects the difference in times to maturity of 5, 10 and 20 years.

If the market interest rate increases to 14.0%, the bond will sell at a discount; for example, the 5-year bond price would be $862.70, the 10-year bond price would be $791.40 and the 20-year bond price would be $735.10.

Chart 5-1 provides a graphic illustration of the change in bond price resulting from changes in market interest rates.

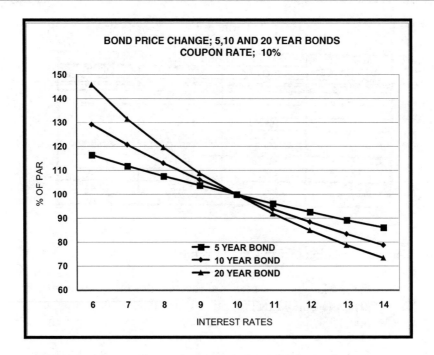

Chart 5-1

Chart 5-1 graphically illustrates the inverse relationship between bond prices and interest rates; that is, as interest rates go down below the coupon rate, the bond price will go up, and when interest rates go above the coupon rate the bond price will decrease.

Purchasing Power Risk–

Purchasing power risk occurs during periods when inflation exceeds the returns on bonds. For example, during the 70's, there were 5 years in which inflation rates exceeded the return on bonds.

In that a bond is a fixed income security, even if market interest rates are increasing as the result of inflation, the return on a bond is locked in until the bond's maturity date.

Table 5-5 is a tabulation of intermediate government bond returns and inflation rates for the 1970-1999 period. The shaded returns represent years in which the inflation rates exceeded returns on bonds.

Also provided in Table 5-5 is the cumulative bond index, the growth of $1.00 invested in bonds and the cumulative inflation index. It should be noted that the cumulative bond index in 1981 is 2.23, whereas the cumulative inflation index is 2.49. For the period of 1970 through 1981, the cumulative inflation index exceeded the return on bonds, representing a loss of purchasing power during this period.

Table 5-5
Bond Returns vs Inflation Rates

YEAR	INTERM GOV BOND RETURNS	CUM BOND INDEX	RATE OF INFL	CUM INFL INDEX
1970	16.86	1.17	5.49	1.05
1971	8.72	1.27	3.36	1.09
1972	5.16	1.34	3.41	1.13
1973	4.61	1.40	8.80	1.23
1974	5.69	1.48	12.20	1.38
1975	7.83	1.59	7.01	1.47
1976	12.87	1.80	4.81	1.54
1977	1.41	1.82	6.77	1.65
1978	3.49	1.89	9.03	1.80
1979	4.09	1.96	13.31	2.04
1980	3.91	2.04	12.40	2.29
1981	9.45	2.23	8.94	2.49
1982	29.10	2.88	3.87	2.59
1983	7.41	3.10	3.80	2.69
1984	14.02	3.53	3.95	2.79
1985	20.33	4.25	3.77	2.90
1986	15.14	4.89	1.13	2.93
1987	2.90	5.03	4.41	3.06
1988	6.10	5.34	4.42	3.20
1989	13.29	6.05	4.65	3.35
1990	9.73	6.64	6.11	3.55
1991	15.46	7.67	3.06	3.66
1992	7.19	8.22	2.90	3.77
1993	11.24	9.14	2.75	3.87
1994	-5.14	8.67	2.67	3.97
1995	16.80	10.13	2.54	4.07
1996	2.10	10.34	3.32	4.21
1997	8.38	11.21	1.70	4.28
1998	10.21	12.35	1.61	4.35
1999	-1.77	12.13	2.68	4.47

Source: Ibbotson Associates, SBBI Yearbook 2000

Business/Financial Risk, Credit Risk

The credit risk is the risk to the investor that the issuer of a bond will default on interest payments and/or principal payments.

Therefore, there are rating agencies, such as *Moody's* and *Standard & Poor*, who evaluate the financial strength and stability of a firm or governing body, and assign a credit rating.

Table 5-6 lists the various ratings assigned to bonds by Moody's and Standard & Poor.

Table 5-6
Bond Ratings

Moody's	S&P	Definition
Investment Grade--	Investment Grade--	
Aaa	AAA	High-grade investment bonds. The highest rating assigned, denoting extremely strong capacity to pay principal and interest. Often called "gilt edge" securities.
Aa	AA	High-grade investment bonds. High quality by all standards, but rated lower primarily because the margins of protection are not quite as strong.
A	A	Medium-grade investment bonds. Many favorable investment attributes, but elements may be present that suggest susceptibility to adverse economic changes.
Baa	BBB	Medium-grade investment bonds. Adequate capacity to pay principal and interest but possibly lacking certain protective elements against adverse economic times.
Non Investment Grade--	Non Investment Grade--	
Ba	BB	Speculative issues. Only moderate protection of principal and interest in varied economic times. (This is one of the ratings carried by junk bonds.)
B	B	Speculative issues. Generally lacking desirable characteristics of investment bonds. Assurance of principal and interest may be small; this is another junk bond rating.
Caa	CCC	Default. Poor-quality issues that may be in default or in danger of default.
Ca	CC	Default. Highly speculative issues, often in default or possessing other market shortcomings.
C		Default. These issues may be regarded as extremely poor in investment quality.
	C	Default. Rating given to income bonds on which no interest is paid.
	D	Default. Issues actually in default, with principal or interest in arrears.

Source: Moody's Bond Record and Standard & Poor's Bond Guide.

Note that the top four ratings designate investment grade bonds. All other ratings are classified as non investment grade.

The Ba/B or BB/B ratings are reserved for high yield bonds or junk bonds.

From the time the bond is issued until maturity, it is not uncommon for the rating of the bond to be revised up or down. Correspondingly, revision of bond ratings will impact the bond's yield.

Bonds with the highest rating have the lower yields, while bonds with low rating, representing a greater risk to the investor, have higher yields.

Bond Funds: Morningstar Style Box

The Morningstar Inc. bond fund data base defines an investment style box for fixed income investments, i.e. bonds, which focuses on interest rate sensitivity and credit quality.

The interest rate sensitivity, that is, years to maturity, is divided into three maturity groups.

Short:	1 to 4 years
Intermediate:	4 to 10 years
Long:	10 years or more

The style box also divides the credit quality into three groups: high, medium and low.

The Morningstar fixed income style box and the relative risks are graphically displayed in Chart 5-2.

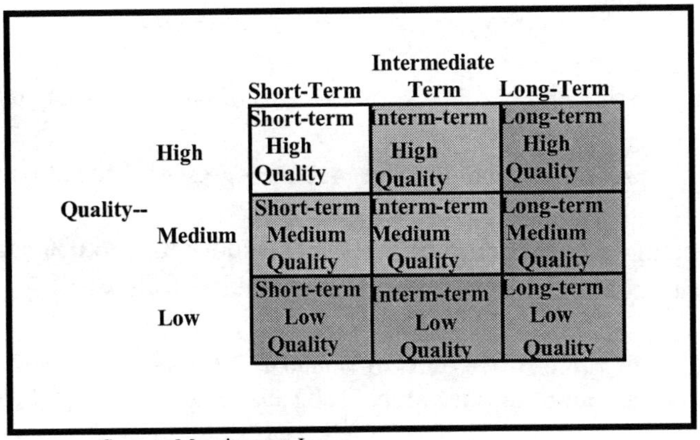

		Intermediate	
	Short-Term	Term	Long-Term
High	Short-term High Quality	Interm-term High Quality	Long-term High Quality
Quality-- Medium	Short-term Medium Quality	Interm-term Medium Quality	Long-term Medium Quality
Low	Short-term Low Quality	Interm-term Low Quality	Long-term Low Quality

Source: Morningstar, Inc.

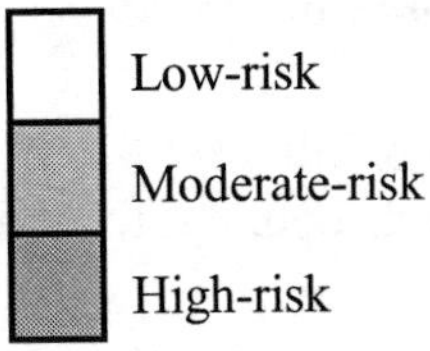

☐ Low-risk

▨ Moderate-risk

▨ High-risk

Chart 5-2

Measurement of Fixed Income Performance

Yield to Maturity–

All bonds, taxable or tax-free, have a standard methodology for the way the bonds are priced. Bond prices are established based on market yields.

The cash flow components of a bond are 1) the annual interest income over the life of the bond and 2) the recovery of the bond's principal, par value, at the time of maturity.

The valuation of a bond comprehends the valuation of the annuity of coupon payments plus a lump sum cash flow at the time of maturity.

Using the concepts of *time value of money*, the present value of the coupon payments plus the present value of the lump sum payment represent the current bond price.

The calculation of the present values are based on current market yields.

To summarize, the bond price is expressed mathematically as ...

Bond Price = present value of interest income + present value of bond par value

For example, the pricing of a 10-year bond with a 6.0% coupon rate, being priced with current market yields of 7.0%, is calculated as follows.

Present value* of 10 pmts of $60.00 @ 7.0%	**=**	**$421.42**
Present value* of par value, $1000 @ 7.0%	**=**	**$508.35**
Current Bond price =		**$929.77**

* See *Chapter 9, Time Value of Money* **for computational procedures**

In that the current market interest rate, of 7.0%, is greater than the coupon rate, 6.0%, the bond price of $929.77 is discounted from its par value of $1000.00.

For an investor, however, the measurement of return is based on the ask price, that is, the yield to maturity. The yield to maturity represents the compounded rate of return earned by an investor, assuming that the bond is held to maturity.

This procedure is the reverse of the above procedure used to calculate the bond price, in that the bond price, ask price, is known while the yield to maturity is *unknown*.

Therefore, it is necessary to estimate a yield rate, yield to maturity, for which the sum of the present values of interest payments plus the present value of the bond's par value is equal to the ask price.

The calculation of the yield to maturity is a matter of trial and error. Therefore, the use of a *financial calculator* or *computer software* is required.

Current Yield–

Current yield is the annual return on the dollar amount paid for the bond, and is derived by dividing the bond interest payments by its purchase price. If an investor bought a $1000 bond (at par) and the interest rate is 6.0% ($60/year), the current yield is 6.0% ($60/$1000).

However, if the 6.0% bond was bought at $950, i.e. discounted, the current yield is 6.3% ($60/$950).

As previously discussed, the more meaningful measure of return is the yield to maturity.

Taxable Equivalent Yield vs Tax-Exempt Yield–

The decision to purchase tax-free bonds vs taxable bonds must take into consideration the investor's taxable income.

The higher the individual's tax bracket, the more attractive tax-free bonds become. Generally speaking, an investor has to be in one of the higher tax brackets, such as 28% or higher, before tax-free bonds offer yields that are competitive with taxable bonds. This is because tax-free bond yields are lower than those of taxable bonds.

The basic equation to calculate the taxable equivalent return for tax-free bonds is as follows.

$$\text{Taxable equiv yield} = \frac{\text{Tax-free bond yield}}{1.0 - [\text{Federal tax rate} + \text{State tax rate} \times (1.0 - \text{Federal tax rate})]}$$

For example, for an investor whose taxable income is in the 31% marginal tax bracket and the state tax rate is 2.0%, the taxable equivalent of a tax-free bond with a 6.0% coupon rate is calculated as follows.

$$
\begin{aligned}
\text{Taxable equivalent yield} &= \frac{0.06}{1.0 - [0.31 + 0.02 \times (1.0 - 0.31)]} \\[2mm]
&= \frac{0.06}{1.0 - [0.31 + 0.014]} \\[2mm]
&= \frac{0.06}{1.0 - 0.324} \\[2mm]
&= 8.88\%
\end{aligned}
$$

Based on the above assumptions, a taxable bond would have to have a yield of 8.88% to be equivalent to the 6.0% tax-free bond.

The above computational procedure is based on the assumption that the investor itemized his deductions and the bond was taxed by the state in which the investor lives.

If the investor is using the standard deduction, then the calculation of the taxable equivalent yield is as follows.

$$\text{Taxable equivalent yield} \quad = \quad \frac{\textbf{Tax-free bond yield}}{\textbf{1.0 - (Federal tax rate + State tax rate)}}$$

Table 5-7 is a tabulation of taxable equivalent yield for the year 2001 federal tax brackets when purchasing tax-exempt bonds at yields of 4%, 5%, 6% and 7%.

Table 5-7
Tax Equivalent Yields

Taxable Income		Federal	Tax-Exempt Returns & Equivalents			
Single Return	**Joint Return**	**Tax Brackets**	**4%**	**5%**	**6%**	**7%**
$0 - $27,050	$0 - $45,200	15%	4.71%	5.88%	7.06%	8.24%
$27,050-65,550	$45,200-109,250	28%	5.56%	6.94%	8.33%	9.72%
$65,550-$136,750	$109,250-166,450	31%	5.80%	7.25%	8.70%	10.14%
$136,750-297,300	$166,450-297,300	36%	6.25%	7.81%	9.38%	10.94%
$297,300 and over	$297,300 and over	39.6%	6.62%	8.28%	9.93%	11.59%

For example, if you are married and have taxable income of $80,000, you would fall into the 28% federal tax bracket. You would need to earn 9.72% on a taxable security in order to match a 7.0% yield from a tax-exempt security.

Bond Investment Strategy

The buy-and-hold strategy will provide a bond investor with a fixed income and return of principal at the time of maturity. The buy-and-hold strategy avoids the loss of principal and minimizes the transaction costs.

The down side of the buy-and-hold strategy is that it restricts the potential of earning above average returns.

An investment strategy that is more active than the buy-and-hold strategy is the so called *bond laddering* strategy, wherein equal dollar amounts are invested in a series of bonds with staggered maturities.

For example, if an investor confined his investing to fixed income securities with maturities of 10 years or less, equal dollar amounts could be allocated to three-, five-, seven- and ten-year issues.

At such time as the 3-year issue matures, the principal received from the 3-year issue is invested in a new 10-year issue. When the 5-year issue matures, the money received from this issue is rolled into a new 10-year issue. This process would continue until the investor has a series of 10-year bonds with staggering maturities.

The *bond laddering* strategy is, in essence, dollar cost averaging, and thereby reduces the impact of changes in market rates.

A bond investment portfolio should be diversified: investing in high yield corporate bonds will generate higher returns, whereas investment grade bonds will generate somewhat lower yields. However, the investment grade bonds will offset potential credit-quality concerns that could affect high yield securities in an economic downturn.

The issue of whether to invest in individuals bonds vs bond mutual funds are as follows.

- An individual bond has a stated finite life, or date of maturity, whereas a bond mutual fund has no finite date of maturity.

- If an investor holds an individual bond to maturity, there is no loss of principal; however, when investing in a bond fund there is no assurance of not losing principal when the investor sells his interest in the bond mutual fund.

- The purchase of individual bonds requires a greater outlay of cash, in that individual bonds, such as municipal bonds, are issued in $5000 denominations, whereas the initial purchase in an bond mutual fund may range from $500 to several thousand dollars.

- An investment of several thousand dollars in a bond fund purchases hundreds of bonds, thereby providing diversification, as compared to the purchase of one or more individual bonds.

- Individual bonds may incur a liquidity risk, that is, the risk that a bond will be difficult to sell at a particular point in time, in that there just isn't much trading done in the secondary market, particularly with corporate and municipal bonds.

Summary

- A bond is a debt security where the issuer promises to pay the bond owner a fixed rate of interest during the term of the bond and to repay the face value of the bond, the principal, when it matures.

- The volatility of a bond price, that is, the variation of the bond's market price above or below its par value is a function of 1) the bond coupon rate, 2) the time to maturity and 3) the credit rating of the issuer.

- The bond market price varies inversely with market interest rates, that is, when market interest rates are greater than the bond coupon rate, the bond market price is less than its par value, and when market interest rates are lower than the bond coupon rate, the bond market price is greater than its par value.

- The true measure of the return on a bond investment is the *yield to maturity*.

- An investment strategy to be considered when purchasing individual bonds is *bond laddering*, wherein equal dollar amounts are invested in a series of bonds with staggered maturities.

—RETIREMENT PLANNING—

Overview:

Retirement Planning is a continuing process in that the planning comprehends both the *pre-retirement* period and the *post-retirement* period.

1. Pre-retirement period–
    The primary objective of pre-retirement planning is to determine the *annual savings required*, such that a desired retirement standard of living will be achieved.

2. Post-retirement period–
    Based on available retirement resources, that is, savings, pensions, Social Security, etc., the primary objective of the post-retirement planning is to determine a withdrawal rate such that the retirement resources are not depleted over the life expectancy of the individual and his/her spouse.

The various interacting variables which must be comprehended in establishing the retirement withdrawal rate are investment rates of return, inflation and life expectancy. In reality, the only variable really controlled by the individual is the *withdrawal rate*.

During the pre-retirement period the employee makes contributions to various retirement savings plans to provide capital accumulation for retirement years. The retirement savings plans provide various tax advantages, in that the earnings from these plans are tax-deferred until withdrawals are made and, normally, the contributions are made with dollars which are pre-tax.

In addition to the retirement savings plans for employees, some employers provide options to participate in various types of pension plans. The contributions to these plans are primarily made by the employer; however, a majority of the plans also provide for additional contributions by the employee.

At retirement the distribution of the pension is usually as an annuity payment over the life of the employee or over the joint lives of the employee and his/her spouse. When provisions are made for payment over joint lives, the annuity payments are reduced based on the option selected.

Defined benefit types of pension plans are normally distributed as annuity payments over the retiree's life or joint life expectancies. However, some employers have provisions which allow the pension to be distributed as an equivalent lump sum at the date of retirement.

Social Security benefits also provide a source of income during the retirement years. For individuals whose year of birth is year 1937 or earlier, full Social Security benefits start at age 65; whereas, for individuals with a year of birth as of 1960 or later, full Social Security benefits start at age 67. For birth years between 1937 and 1960, full benefits are phased in between age 65 and age 67 under current regulations. Reduced benefits, however, may be started at age 62 for all retirees.

Age 62 is the youngest eligible age at which a retiree can begin to receive Social Security benefits. If an individual starts to receive Social Security benefits prior to the age at which full benefits are available, the monthly benefits are permanently reduced. The reduction is a function of the number of months prior to eligibility for full benefits that the individual starts receiving benefits. The reduction in benefits for selected years of birth are summarized as follows:

	Age 62--	
Yr of Birth	**% Reduction**	**Full Benefit Age**
1937	20%	65
1943-1954	25%	66
1960 and later	30%	67

The issue of starting at the youngest age eligible, 62, which results in a permanent reduction, or starting at the age at which full benefits are available, is a decision for which various factors must be taken into consideration.

The decision to elect reduced retirement benefits at age 62, as opposed to waiting until the age needed for full benefits, should be based on the comparison of the *present value*, economic value, of the Social Security benefits to be received over a normal life expectancy for the respective scenarios.

If an individual attains age 62 after year 2000, the economic value of electing Social Security benefits at age 62 will be greater than waiting until the age needed for *full* benefits. The economic value of electing benefits at age 62 increases as the age needed for full benefits increases.

Over the last decade the number of employers offering pension plan benefits has been on the decrease.

The solvency of Social Security in the year 2035 and beyond has been a major political issue for some time.

Therefore, based on the trend relative to retirement resource options, the primary burden of saving for retirement is shifting to the employee.

Chart 6-1 depicts the retirement resources and the interacting variables which must be comprehended in evaluating pre-retirement savings contributions and post-retirement spending rates.

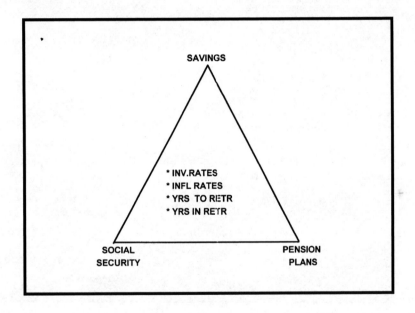

Chart 6-1

The 'baby boom' generation, those born between 1946 and 1964, has transformed every stage of life as it has passed through it. Now this generation is headed for perhaps the greatest transformation of all —— retirement.

Surveys of this generation show that–

- Their savings rate continues at a historical low.

- They do not know how much they will need at retirement, or how to plan to meet these needs.

- They do not fully understand their employer retirement benefits, Social Security, etc.

Consumer debt, outstanding balances on credit cards, auto loans and other consumer loans, has been on the rise over the last decade. The consumer debt for the year 2000 was approximately twice that of the year 1990.

For the year 2000, Americans were spending 14.3% of their take-home pay on debts–the highest percentage since 1986, based on *Federal Reserve Board* data.

Credit card delinquencies, that is, accounts at least 30 days past due are approximately 5.0% of total credit card debt.

Mortgage delinquencies rose to 4.5% of outstanding loans in the last quarter of 2000, the highest since 1992.

One of the best indicators of American debt is the rise of bankruptcies. In the first quarter of 2001, the number of bankruptcy cases files was 17.5% more than a year earlier. The majority of the debtors filing for bankruptcy were consumers.

Retirement: Investment Portfolio and Withdrawal Rate Limits

Retirement is a longer, more active period than ever before. Therefore, how retirement investment assets are to be invested is significantly different than 15-20 years ago, in that, individuals retiring at age 65 then had a pension and a shorter life expectancy.

At that time, upon retirement, investment savings were invested in bonds to generate required supplemental income. Today, retirees are living longer and the money needs to last longer; therefore, the investment portfolio requires 35% or more to be invested in stocks to provide growth.

Today's retirees must discard the idea that they shouldn't spend principal; in other words, an individual's investment portfolio asset allocation should not be dictated by income needs alone.

The investment portfolio asset allocation should be dictated by *total return*, that is, income *plus* growth.

The old rule that the percent of stock in the investment portfolio should be 100 minus the individual's age is no longer valid.

Therefore, if a higher percentage of the investment portfolio is to be invested in stocks, during retirement and to protect against bear markets the investment allocation should provide for two year's worth of supplemental living expenses to be held as cash reserves, while the balance of the investment portfolio is invested for total return.

Income from both the cash reserves and the investment portfolio are used under normal market conditions; however, in a bear market, drawing only on the cash reserves gives the investment portfolio equities time to recover.

There is a significant difference between pre-retirement investing and post-retirement investing.

In the pre-retirement years, earning a good average return over an extended number of years is the primary objective.

However, during the retirement years the *rate of withdrawal* dictates whether an individual's savings will last 20 or 30 years.

The assumption that if the investment portfolio is earning ten percent, as an average, and the annual withdrawal rate is six percent, the individual will not only have sufficient savings to support his/her life style, but also leave a significant estate for heirs, is not true.

In the real world no one earns an average rate of return year after year, in that, actual returns vary from year to year. The variability of returns has a significant impact on the chance that an individual will outlive his/her money.

Not only the variability of returns is significant. If one retires at the start of a *bull market*, there is a high probability that he will live well and also leave an estate for his heirs.

On the other hand, if one retires at the start of a *bear market*, there is a high probability that he will outlive his money, i.e. deplete his savings during retirement.

Some well publicized studies have indicated that if starting with a retirement withdrawal rate equal to 4.0% to 5.0% of the investment portfolio value, and adjusted for inflation each year, there is a high probability that the individual will not deplete his savings even if there is a repeat of the 1973-1974 bear market.

The following scenarios put into perspective the above concepts, using the returns for stocks over the 1970 through 1999 period.

Table 6-1 provides a tabulation of the actual total returns for stocks and inflation for the 1970-1999 period.

Table 6-1
Actual Returns, %: Stocks and Inflation
1970-1999

YEAR	STOCKS %	INFL %
1970	4.01	5.49
1971	14.31	3.36
1972	18.98	3.41
1973	-14.66	8.80
1974	-26.47	12.20
1975	37.20	7.01
1976	23.84	4.81
1977	-7.18	6.77
1978	6.56	9.03
1979	18.44	13.31
1980	32.42	12.40
1981	-4.91	8.94
1982	21.41	3.87
1983	22.51	3.80
1984	6.27	3.95
1985	32.16	3.77
1986	18.47	1.13
1987	5.23	4.41
1988	16.81	4.42
1989	31.49	4.65
1990	-3.17	6.11
1991	30.55	3.06
1992	7.67	2.90
1993	9.99	2.75
1994	1.31	2.67
1995	37.43	2.54
1996	23.07	3.32
1997	33.36	1.70
1998	28.58	1.61
1999	21.04	2.68
AVERAGE	14.89	5.16

Source: Ibbotson Associates, SBBI Yearbook 2000

The average return for stocks for the 1970-1999 period was 14.9%, whereas the average inflation rate was 5.2%.

Using the returns for stocks for the 1970-1999 period, the following three scenarios were evaluated to determine the impact of the sequence of investment rates of return on a retirement investment portfolio. The respective scenarios are:

Scenario	**Investment Rate of Return**
A	Using actual stock investment rates of return for the 30-year period, starting with 1970, that is, a rate of return of 4.01% in the 1st year of retirement, etc.

B   Using the average stock investment rate of return, of 14.9%, for each year over the 30-year retirement period.

C   In this scenario the stock investment rates of return are *reversed*, that is, the 1st year of retirement starts with the 1999 rate of return of 21.04%, etc.

For the respective scenarios the following assumptions are comprehended:

- Starting retirement savings of $100,000

- Annual withdrawal rate is 5% of the starting investment portfolio value, that is, $5000.

- The annual withdrawals are increased each year by the assumed inflation rate of 5.0%, resulting in a withdrawal of $20,580 in the 30th year of retirement.

- All withdrawals are taken at the start of each year.

Table 6-2 provides the cash flow profiles for the respective scenarios.

Table 6-2
Impact of Returns on the Retirement Investment Portfolio

	SCENARIO A				SCENARIO B				SCENARIO C		
YEAR	PERCENT RETURN	WITH-DRAWAL	ENDING BALANCE	YEAR	PERCENT RETURN	WITH-DRAWAL	ENDING BALANCE	YEAR	PERCENT RETURN	WITH-DRAWAL	ENDING BALANCE
1970	4.01	$5,000	$98,810	1970	14.89	$5,000	$109,146	1999	21.04	$5,000	$114,988
1971	14.31	5,250	106,948	1971	14.89	5,250	119,367	1998	28.58	5,250	141,101
1972	18.98	5,513	120,688	1972	14.89	5,513	130,808	1997	33.36	5,513	180,821
1973	-14.66	5,788	98,055	1973	14.89	5,788	143,636	1996	23.07	5,788	215,413
1974	-26.47	6,078	67,631	1974	14.89	6,078	158,042	1995	37.43	6,078	287,690
1975	37.20	6,381	84,035	1975	14.89	6,381	174,244	1994	1.31	6,381	284,993
1976	23.84	6,700	95,771	1976	14.89	6,700	192,492	1993	9.99	6,700	306,094
1977	-7.18	7,036	82,364	1977	14.89	7,036	213,072	1992	7.67	7,036	321,997
1978	6.56	7,387	79,895	1978	14.89	7,387	236,313	1991	30.55	7,387	410,723
1979	18.44	7,757	85,441	1979	14.89	7,757	262,590	1990	-3.17	7,757	390,192
1980	32.42	8,144	102,356	1980	14.89	8,144	292,334	1989	31.49	8,144	502,354
1981	-4.91	8,552	89,199	1981	14.89	8,552	326,039	1988	16.81	8,552	576,811
1982	21.41	8,979	97,394	1982	14.89	8,979	364,272	1987	5.23	8,979	597,529
1983	22.51	9,428	107,767	1983	14.89	9,428	407,683	1986	18.47	9,428	696,723
1984	6.27	9,900	104,004	1984	14.89	9,900	457,015	1985	32.16	9,900	907,706
1985	32.16	10,395	123,714	1985	14.89	10,395	513,126	1984	6.27	10,395	953,572
1986	18.47	10,914	133,634	1986	14.89	10,914	576,994	1983	22.51	10,914	1,154,850
1987	5.23	11,460	128,564	1987	14.89	11,460	649,746	1982	21.41	11,460	1,388,190
1988	16.81	12,033	136,119	1988	14.89	12,033	732,672	1981	-4.91	12,033	1,308,588
1989	31.49	12,635	162,370	1989	14.89	12,635	827,256	1980	32.42	12,635	1,716,101
1990	-3.17	13,266	144,377	1990	14.89	13,266	935,198	1979	18.44	13,266	2,016,837
1991	30.55	13,930	170,299	1991	14.89	13,930	1,058,451	1978	6.56	13,930	2,134,298
1992	7.67	14,626	167,612	1992	14.89	14,626	1,199,257	1977	-7.18	14,626	1,967,479
1993	9.99	15,358	167,465	1993	14.89	15,358	1,360,190	1976	23.84	15,358	2,417,507
1994	1.31	16,125	153,322	1994	14.89	16,125	1,544,204	1975	37.2	16,125	3,294,696
1995	37.43	16,932	187,441	1995	14.89	16,932	1,754,694	1974	-26.47	16,932	2,410,140
1996	23.07	17,778	208,804	1996	14.89	17,778	1,995,554	1973	-14.66	17,778	2,041,641
1997	33.36	18,667	253,566	1997	14.89	18,667	2,271,258	1972	18.98	18,667	2,406,935
1998	28.58	19,601	300,833	1998	14.89	19,601	2,586,944	1971	14.31	19,601	2,728,962
1999	21.04	20,581	339,217	1999	14.89	20,581	2,948,512	1970	4.01	20,581	2,816,987

The interpretation of Table 6-2 is as follows:

Scenario A:

Under this scenario the actual sequence of investment rates of return for stocks are used, starting with the 1970 rate of return.

Under this scenario the retirement investment portfolio has an ending balance of $339,217.

The 1973 and 1974 *bear market*, near the start of the retirement period, had a significant impact on the ending value of the retirement investment portfolio.

If a 6.0% inflation adjusted withdrawal rate had been used in lieu of the 5.0% rate, the retirement investment portfolio was *depleted* at the end of the 21st year of retirement.

Scenario B:

Using the average rate of return of 14.9% for stocks for all years of the 1970-1999 period and a 5.0% inflation adjusted withdrawal rate, the retirement investment portfolio at the end of 30 years has a balance of $2,948,512.

Scenario C:

Under this scenario the sequence of investment rates of return are reversed, that is, in year one of retirement the 1999 rate of return of 21% is used, for year 2 the 1998 rate of return of 28.6% is used, etc.

Under this scenario the retirement investment portfolio has an ending balance of $2,816,987.

The reversing of the stock rates of return simulated the start of retirement in a *bull market*.

It should be noted that the average investment rate of return, of 14.9%, is the same for all three scenarios.

Chart 6-2 provides a graphic illustration of the investment portfolio balances for the respective scenarios.

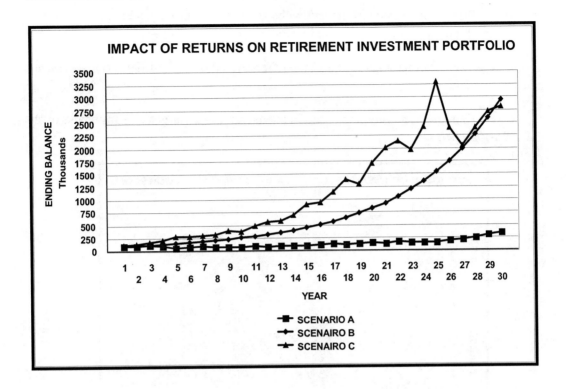

Chart 6-2

Simulation Analysis (Monte Carlo)

As illustrated in Scenario A and Scenario C, the *reversing* of the sequence of occurrences of the investment rates of return resulted in ending investment portfolio balances of $339,217 and $2,816,987, respectively, representing a significant difference.

If one were to randomly select an investment rate of return from Table 6-1 for each year and develop a new sequence of returns over the 30-year period, and using the withdrawal rates in Table 6-2, the ending investment portfolio balances would be different than Scenario A or Scenario C.

If this procedure were repeated a few hundred times, that is, developing random sequences of investment rates of return for each 30-year period, we would generate hundreds of different ending investment portfolio balances.

Statistical analysis of the ending balances would provide an insight as to the probability of not depleting an individual's money.

The stock investment annual rates of return over the 1926-1999 period represent a random variable.

Chart 6-3 is a histogram of the 74 annual returns for large company stocks over the 1926-1999 period.

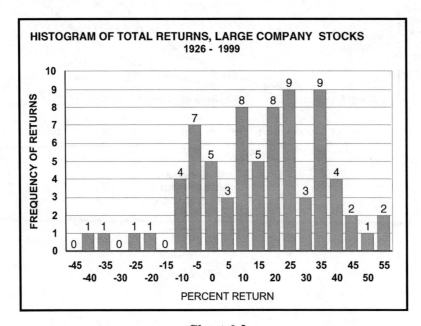

Chart 6-3

The returns are grouped into 15 different cells with a cell width of 5%. For example, in the cell labeled '5', there are 3 different annual returns out of 74, with annual returns ranging from 0% to 5%.

The following observations are provided pertaining to Chart 6-3 histogram of large company stocks.

- Over the 74 year period, there are two annual returns greater than 50%, that is, year 1933 of 54% and year 1954 of 52.6%.

- Over the 74 year period there is one annual return of less than -40%, that is, year 1931 of -43.3%.

- The majority of the annual returns, 57%, are in the 10% to 40% range of returns.

The statistical parameters for large company stocks for the 1926-1999 period are as follows.

Arithmetic mean, average 13.3%
Maximum return 54.0%
Minimum return .... -43.4%
Standard deviation 20.1%

The interpretation of the above statistical parameters is as follows.

The average annual return for large company stocks, over the 1926-1999 period was 13.3%, with a maximum return of 54% and a minimum return of -43.4%.

Using the above statistical parameters, a frequency distribution for the large company stocks may be developed, as illustrated in Chart 6-4.

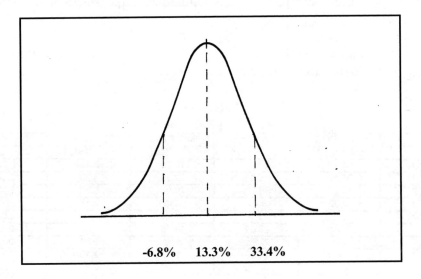

-6.8%   13.3%   33.4%

Chart 6-4

The area under the frequency curve in Chart 6-4, between the average minus one standard deviation, -6.8% (13.3% -20.1%), and the average plus one standard deviation,

33.4% (13.3% + 20.1%), represents 68% of the total area. This implies that 68% of all returns will be between -6.8% and +33.4%.

Each tail of the distribution (left and right) represents 16% of the area under the curve.

Therefore, if we randomly selected annual returns from the frequency distribution seen in Chart 6-4, 68 out of 100 returns will be in the range from -6.8% to 33.4%, 16 out of 100 will be above 33.4% and 16 out of 100 will be below -6.8%.

Simulation modeling (Monte Carlo) is a method for analyzing problems involving random variables, such as investment rates of return. In the development of a simulation model, the random variables are defined by frequency distributions.

The frequency distribution for the specific variable is a function of the mean value, or average, and the measure of variation around the mean, that is, the standard deviation.

The mean value and standard deviation for a random variable are based on a reference period of historical data. Table 6-3 provides the historical data for years 1950-2001 for various investment portfolio asset mixes of large stocks and intermediate government bonds.

The average and standard deviation statistics for the returns for the respective investment portfolios are also tabulated in Table 6-3.

Table 6-3
Statistical Parameters

Year	100% STKS 0% BNDS	75% STKS 25% BNDS	50% STKS 50% BNDS	25% STKS 75% BNDS	0% STKS 100% BNDS
1950	31.71	23.96	16.21	8.45	0.70
1951	24.02	18.11	12.19	6.28	0.36
1952	18.37	14.19	10.00	5.82	1.63
1953	-0.99	0.07	1.12	2.18	3.23
1954	52.62	40.14	27.65	15.17	2.68
1955	31.56	23.51	15.46	7.40	-0.65
1956	6.56	4.82	3.07	1.33	-0.42
1957	-10.78	-6.13	-1.47	3.19	7.84
1958	43.36	32.20	21.04	9.87	-1.29
1959	11.96	8.87	5.79	2.70	-0.39
1960	0.47	3.29	6.12	8.94	11.76
1961	26.89	20.63	14.37	8.11	1.85
1962	-8.73	-5.16	-1.59	1.99	5.56
1963	22.80	17.51	12.22	6.93	1.64
1964	16.48	13.37	10.26	7.15	4.04
1965	12.45	9.59	6.74	3.88	1.02
1966	-10.06	-6.37	-2.69	1.00	4.69
1967	23.98	18.24	12.50	6.75	1.01

Year	100% STKS 0% BNDS	75% STKS 25% BNDS	50% STKS 50% BNDS	25% STKS 75% BNDS	0% STKS 100% BNDS
1968	11.06	9.43	7.80	6.17	4.54
1969	-8.50	-6.56	-4.62	-2.68	-0.74
1970	4.01	7.22	10.44	13.65	16.86
1971	14.31	12.91	11.52	10.12	8.72
1972	18.98	15.53	12.07	8.62	5.16
1973	-14.66	-9.84	-5.03	-0.21	4.61
1974	-26.47	-18.43	-10.39	-2.35	5.69
1975	37.20	29.86	22.52	15.17	7.83
1976	23.84	21.10	18.36	15.61	12.87
1977	-7.18	-5.03	-2.89	-0.74	1.41
1978	6.56	5.79	5.03	4.26	3.49
1979	18.44	14.85	11.27	7.68	4.09
1980	32.42	25.29	18.17	11.04	3.91
1981	-4.91	-1.32	2.27	5.86	9.45
1982	21.41	23.33	25.26	27.18	29.10
1983	22.51	18.74	14.96	11.19	7.41
1984	6.27	8.21	10.15	12.08	14.02
1985	32.16	29.20	26.25	23.29	20.33
1986	18.47	17.64	16.81	15.97	15.14
1987	5.23	4.65	4.07	3.48	2.90
1988	16.81	14.13	11.46	8.78	6.10
1989	31.49	26.94	22.39	17.84	13.29
1990	-3.17	0.06	3.28	6.51	9.73
1991	30.55	26.78	23.01	19.23	15.46
1992	7.67	7.55	7.43	7.31	7.19
1993	9.99	10.30	10.62	10.93	11.24
1994	1.31	-0.30	-1.92	-3.53	-5.14
1995	37.43	32.27	27.12	21.96	16.80
1996	23.07	17.83	12.59	7.34	2.10
1997	33.36	27.12	20.87	14.63	8.38
1998	28.58	23.99	19.40	14.80	10.21
1999	21.04	15.34	9.64	3.93	-1.77
2000	-9.11	-3.69	1.74	7.17	12.59
2001	-11.81	-6.95	-2.10	2.76	7.62
=============	=============	=============	=============	=============	=============
AVG=>	13.87	12.01	10.16	8.31	6.46
STD DEV=>	16.85	12.83	9.18	6.57	6.41
MAX=>	52.62	40.14	27.65	27.18	29.10
MIN=>	-26.47	-18.43	-10.39	-3.53	-5.14

A cash flow simulation model was used to determine the probability of not depleting an individual's retirement savings.

The cash flow simulation model's structure is as follows:

- Starting retirement savings of $100,000

- Inflation adjusted withdrawal rate: three different withdrawal rates, 4%, 5% and 6%, were analyzed. The withdrawal rate represents the percent of the starting retirement savings.

For example, if the starting retirement savings are $100,000 and the withdrawal rate is 4.0%, the withdrawal rate, in dollars, in year one is $4000 ($100,000 x .04). The withdrawal rate is increased annually by an inflation rate of 4.0%. Therefore, the withdrawal rate for year two is $4160 [$4000 x (1 + .04)], for year three it is $4326 [$4160 x (1 + .04)], etc.

- The savings at the end of any given year during the retirement period is calculated as follows:

Ending Savings = [(Start savings - Withdrawal $) x (1 + Random Inv Rate of Return)]

where the random rate of return is a function of the investment portfolio's frequency distribution.

Monte Carlo simulations of cash flow analyses, based on the above assumptions, were conducted to develop the probability of not depleting the retirement savings over the retirement period.

The probability percents of not depleting the retirement savings are tabulated in Table 6-4. Each cell entry in Table 6-4 represents the results of 1000 30-year cash flow analyses.

Table 6-4
Probability of <u>Not</u> Depleting Savings

	Investment Portfolio Asset Mix				
Stocks =>	100%	75%	50%	25%	0%
Bonds =>	0%	25%	50%	75%	100%
Withdrawal Rates:					
4%	97%	98%	98%	97%	73%
5%	92	92	88	71	27
6%	83	79	65	27	4

The interpretation of Table 6-4 is, for example: using an inflation adjusted withdrawal rate of 4.0%, there is a 97%-98% probability that the retirement savings will <u>not</u> be depleted, or less than 3 chances in 100 that the savings will be depleted if the investment portfolio includes stocks.

The shaded areas in Table 6-4 represent retirement scenarios with a confidence level for non-depletion of savings of 90% or higher.

The results shown in Table 6-4 support other studies. That is, when using a 4.0%-5.0% inflation adjusted withdrawal rate during retirement, i.e., there is a high level of confidence that an individual will not deplete his/her retirement savings with an investment portfolio allocation of 50% or more in stocks.

Lump Sum Retirement Savings Calculations:

The retirement savings required at the start of retirement to supplement various retirement incomes, such as pensions, Social Security, etc., must comprehend the following.

- Annual income required from retirement savings
- Years in retirement
- Investment rates of return
- Inflation rates

The required lump sum of retirement savings is very sensitive to the number of years in retirement, investment rates and inflation rates, as illustrated in Table 6-5.

The required retirement lump sum savings shown in Table 6-5 are based on the assumption that the required annual supplemental income to be generated by the savings is $10,000 per year in year one, and is inflation adjusted for each following year. The required lump sums in Table 6-5 are based on annual withdrawals at the *start* of each year.

Table 6-5
Required Retirement Savings

Yrs in Retr	Infl Rates	Investment Rates of Return				
		6%	7%	8%	9%	10%
15	3%	$126,637	$116,448	$109,915	$103,964	$98,534
	4%	131,720	123,854	116,712	110,215	104,293
	5%	140,488	131,878	124,069	116,972	110,511
20	3%	154,352	142,649	132,300	123,122	114,955
	4%	167,903	154,712	143,074	132,771	123,523
	5%	183,052	168,172	155,067	143,491	133,234
25	3%	180,961	164,305	149,963	137,556	126,776
	4%	200,799	181,481	164,901	150,606	138,225
	5%	223,644	201,197	181,992	165,488	151,240
30	3%	204,012	182,205	163,898	148,432	135,284
	4%	230,705	204,700	182,974	164,708	149,257
	5%	262,357	231,428	205,379	183,734	165,510

As illustrated in Table 6-5, with a 30-year retirement period, an investment rate of return of 8.0% and an inflation rate of 4.0%, the required retirement lump sum would be $182,974.

Table 6-6 illustrates the retirement cash flow generated by the $182,974 over the 30-year retirement period, based on an investment rate of return of 8.0% and annual distributions being increased at the assumed inflation rate of 4.0%.

Using Table 6-5, the required retirement lump sum may be calculated for any other required supplemental income. For example, if the required supplemental income is $15,000 per year, using the 30-year retirement period, an 8.0% investment rate of return and a 4.0% inflation rate, the required lump sum would be $274,461 ($182,974 x 1.5).

Table 6-6
Retirement Cash Flow

RETR YEAR	START BAL	ANNUAL WITHDRAWAL	END BAL
1	$182,974	$10,000	$186,812
2	186,812	10,400	190,524
3	190,524	10,816	194,085
4	194,085	11,249	197,463
5	197,463	11,699	200,626
6	200,626	12,167	203,536
7	203,536	12,653	206,154
8	206,154	13,159	208,434
9	208,434	13,686	210,328
10	210,328	14,233	211,783
11	211,783	14,802	212,739
12	212,739	15,395	213,132
13	213,132	16,010	212,891
14	212,891	16,651	211,939
15	211,939	17,317	210,192
16	210,192	18,009	207,558
17	207,558	18,730	203,934
18	203,934	19,479	199,211
19	199,211	20,258	193,270
20	193,270	21,068	185,977
21	185,977	21,911	177,191
22	177,191	22,788	166,756
23	166,756	23,699	154,501
24	154,501	24,647	140,242
25	140,242	25,633	123,778
26	123,778	26,658	104,889
27	104,889	27,725	83,338
28	83,338	28,834	58,864
29	58,864	29,987	31,187
30	31,187	31,187	

As illustrated in Table 6-6 the $182,974, earning 8%, will support an annual withdrawal of $10,000 per year, being inflation adjusted at 4.0% each year, for 30 years.

The *real rate of return* is the difference between the investment rate of return and inflation (see Chapter 4, **Investment Management, Measurement of Investment Performance**).

An important concept to understand is that the required lump sum is virtually the same with higher or lower investment returns, as long as the *real rate of return* remains the same.

This concept is illustrated in Table 6-7 using a real rate of return of 4.0%.

Table 6-7
Real Rate of Return

Inv Rate Return,%	6%	7%	8%	9%	10%
Inflation Rate	2%	3%	4%	5%	6%
Real Rate Return	4%	4%	4%	4%	4%
Req. Lump Sum	$181,425	$182,205	$182,974	$183,734	$184,484

As you can see from Table 6-7, if the real rate of return does not change, the lump sum required to provide an annual inflation adjusted withdrawal over a 30-year period remains essentially the same, regardless of investment returns or inflation rates.

As a point of reference, the real rates of return for large company stocks, intermediate government bonds and various investment portfolio allocations for the 1970-1999 period are tabulated in Table 6-8.

Table 6-8
Real Rates of Return, 1970-1999

Type of Investment	Real Rates of Return,%
100% Large Company Stock, 0% Bonds	9.7%
75% Large Company Stock, 25% Bonds	8.2%
50% Large Company Stock, 50% Bonds	6.7%
25% Large Company Stock, 75% Bonds	5.2%
0% Large Company Stock, 100% Bonds	3.7%

In conclusion, for the achievement of major financial goals, an investor must focus on the *real rate of return*, not the absolute values of investment and inflation rates.

Sample Family Retirement Cash Flow Analysis

Retirement Budgeting--

The budgeting changes, as an individual goes into retirement, generally comprehend reductions in food, transportation and clothing; however, offsetting these reductions are increases in travel and health and medical expenditures.

The early years on retirement are active years, in that retirees are often involved in taking extended vacations, entertaining, etc.

In later years retirees gradually become less active as health declines, as does interest in travel.

On the assumption that the home mortgage and college funding are completed at the start of retirement, it has been our experience that there is not a significant decrease in expenditures when entering retirement.

In fact, expenditures in retirement may increase immediately if the retiree does not have health insurance coverage in the pre-Medicare period. The current trend with employers is to reduce or eliminate pre-Medicare health insurance coverage.

In the development of the Sample family retirement budget the following changes were implemented at the start of retirement.

- Decrease food and household expenditures by 20%.
- Decrease transportation expenditures by 20%.
- Decrease clothing expenses by 20%.
- In that the Sample's employers did not provide retirement health insurance coverage, the following additional expenditures are comprehended.
  - Health insurance, pre-Medicare of $6000/year, in today's dollars
  - Age 65 plus Supplemental health insurance of $3000/year, in today's dollars
- Increase doctor and medical expenditures by 20%.
- Travel expenses are increased from $1500 per year, in today's dollars, to $5000 per year for ages 60-70. After age 70, the expense is reduced to $2500 per year, in today's dollars.

In that health insurance and medical expenditures will probably continue to increase at a greater rate than inflation, and other expenditures will increase at or below the inflation rate, a 4.0% annual inflation rate is used over the retirement period.

Table 6-8, the living expense worksheet, is a tabulation of the Sample family's living expenses as of 1/1/2027 at the start of retirement, expressed in today's dollars.

Table 6-8
Living Expense Worksheet

1. Food and Household:			**7. Insurance:**		
At home (groc store)	$ 4160		Life–		
Meals out	2080		Term insurance	$_____	
Total		$ 6240	Fixed term	_____	
			Health--		
2. Housing:			Fixed cost	_____	
Mortgage/Rent Pmts	$_____		Variable cost	6000	
Property taxes	2685		Disability	_____	
Property Insurance	434		Total		$ 6000
Repair & Maint/Yard	700				
Furnishings & Equip	200		**8. Doctor & Medical:**		$ 672
Total		$ 4019	(Not covered by insurance)		
3. Utilities:		$ 3029	**9. Education:**		
			Reading materials	$ 285	
4. Transportation:			School supplies	_____	
Car Payments	$_____		Tuition	_____	
Gas & oil	1200		Other	_____	
Car upkeep	300		Total		$ 285
Car Insr/Lic/Etc.	1212				
Total		$ 2712	**10. Recreation/Vacation:**		
			Travel	$ 5000	
5. Other Debt:			Entertaining	200	
Home equity loans	$_____		Club fees	70	
Installment debt	_____		Sports, etc	500	
Personal loans	_____		Total		$ 5770
Credit card pmts	_____				
Other	_____		**11. Other/Miscellaneous:**		
Total		$_____	Charity	$ 500	
			Gifts	750	
6. Clothing/Personal Care:			Child support	_____	
Clothing	$ 1600		Alimony	_____	
Personal care	1104		Household help	_____	
Other	150		Prof & business exp	500	
Total		$ 2854	Tax preparation	_____	
			Other	_____	
			Total		$ 1750
			12. Total Living Expenses:		$ 33,331
			(Sum of items 1-11).		

The Sample's base living expenses in year 2027, in today's dollars, is $33,331.

Table 6-9 provides a summary of the retirement living expenses for the first ten years of retirement, as adjusted for inflation, that is, for years 2027 through 2036.

Table 6-9
Inflation Adjusted Budget, Years 2027-2036

Year =>	2027	2028	2029	2030	2031	2032	2033	2034	2035	2036
Food	$17,300	$17,992	$18,712	$19,460	$20,239	$21,048	$21,890	$22,766	$23,677	$24,624
Housing	11,143	11,588	12,052	12,534	13,035	13,557	14,099	14,663	15,249	15,859
Utilities	8,398	8,734	9,083	9,446	9,824	10,217	10,626	11,051	11,493	11,953
Transportation	7,519	7,820	8,132	8,458	8,796	9,148	9,514	9,894	10,290	10,702
Other Debt	0	0	0	0	0	0	0	0	0	0
Clothing/Pers.	7,913	8,229	8,558	8,901	9,257	9,627	10,012	10,412	10,829	11,262
Insurance	16,635	17,300	17,992	18,712	9,730	10,119	10,524	10,945	11,383	11,838
Doctor/Medical	1,863	1,938	2,015	2,096	2,180	2,267	2,357	2,452	2,550	2,652
Education	790	822	855	889	924	961	1,000	1,040	1,081	1,125
Rec/Vacation	15,997	16,637	17,303	17,995	18,714	19,463	20,241	21,051	21,893	22,769
Other	3,966	4,104	4,248	4,398	4,554	4,716	4,885	5,060	5,243	5,433
Infl Adj Budget	$91,523	$95,164	$98,950	$102,888	$97,254	$101,124	$105,149	$109,335	$113,688	$118,216

It should be noted that the inflation adjusted budget for the Sample's is $91,523 in the first year of retirement, 2027, as compared to $72,500 in year 2026.

This increase in living expenses reflects the increases in health insurance and travel.

Retirement Investment Portfolio Asset Allocation and Rates --

The retirement investment portfolio asset allocation is as follows:

> Cash/Bonds 40%
> Stocks 60%

The investment rates of return used in the retirement cash flow analysis are as follows:

Investment Group	Rate Return,%
Cash/Bonds	5.5%
Stocks–	
Dividends	1.5%
Growth	8.0%

The 5.5% rate of return for the cash/bonds reflects the holding of two years of cash reserves in combination with intermediate term government and corporate bonds.

The combined investment portfolio total rate of return, based on the investment asset allocation and assumed rates of return, is approximately 8.0%.

Therefore, with a 4.0% inflation rate, the projected real rate of return is 4.0% (8.0% - 4.0%), which is considered to be a conservative strategy.

Retirement Planning–Investment Asset Allocation

Having established retirement goals, that is, the age of retirement and retirement savings required to supplement other income resources, such as pension income, social security, etc., a realistic evaluation of the income to be generated from the retirement savings is required.

The retirement decision requires the development of a cash flow over the joint life expectancies of a couple, based on an assumed *investment rate of return*. The assumed investment rate of return will dictate the retirement investment portfolio asset allocation. Increasing the retirement portfolio's rate of return correspondingly increases the investment portfolio's volatility, that is, its risk.

If the investment portfolio volatility exceeds the individual's risk tolerance, then the following actions, or combination of actions, are required.

- Delay retirement
- Reduce retirement withdrawal rates

The steps used in the development of the retirement investment portfolio asset allocation are as follows.

Step 1:   Identify the annual cash needs for a minimum of two years in retirement and invest this portion of the retirement savings in *cash equivalents*.

Step 2:   Identify the required lump sum withdrawals, such as major home repairs, purchase of a new car, etc., anticipated in the first five years of retirement, and invest this portion of the retirement savings in *cash equivalents*.

Step 3:   The residual savings are to be invested into an investment portfolio containing assets suitable for long term retirement investing.

Based on historical returns, develop a hypothetical asset allocation of stocks and bonds, such that the required investment rate of return is realized.

The following expected returns and risk are provided as benchmarks:

Investment Portfolio Expected Return, %	Risk
6.0% - 7.0%	Low
7.0% - 8.0%	Moderate
Above 8.0%	High

Retirement Resources:

The projected Sample family retirement savings, for the end of year 2026, are as follows:

Taxable Savings:		
Cash/Bonds	$456,183	
Stock/Stock funds	684,275	
Total Taxable Savings		$1,140,458
Tax-Deferred Savings:		
John Sample–		
Employer plan	$1,513,722	
Roth IRA	100,486	
Total, John		$1,614,208
Mary Sample–		
Employer plan	$ 215,606	
Roth IRA	100,486	
Total, Mary		$ 316,092
Total Savings		$3,070,758

The Sample's do not have employer pension plans.

In as much as the Sample's are planning to retire when John reaches age 60, in year 2026, there was considerable discussion relating to the inclusion of Social Security benefits as a retirement resource. The issue of ignoring Social Security would overstate the amount of savings required.

The various proposed solutions for maintaining the Social Security solvency, such as increasing payroll taxes, eliminating the wage-base cap, privatizing, etc., were discussed.

In that the Sample's were maximizing their pre-tax contributions to their respective retirement plans (see Chapter 2, **Financial Position: Goal Setting and Cash Flow**), they decided not to include Social Security as a retirement resource.

Therefore, it was mutually agreed that Social Security would not be included as a retirement resource in the retirement cash flow analysis.

Retirement Cash Flow Analysis:

Table 6-10 is a tabulation of the Sample's cash flow profile for the 30-year retirement period, starting in year 2027 and continuing through year 2056.

Table 6-10
Retirement Cash Flow

(1) YEAR	(2) AGE CLIENT	(3) INTR & DIV.INC	(4) USE SAVINGS	(5) MIN REQ DISTR	(6) TOTAL TAXES	(7) LIVING EXPENSE	(8) TAXABLE SAVINGS	(9) REG IRA	(10) ROTH IRA	(11) TOTAL ASSETS
2027	61	$35,370	$57,131		$978	$91,523	$1,138,597	$1,867,676	$217,827	$3,224,100
2028	62	35,297	60,699		832	95,164	1,132,550	2,017,091	235,253	3,384,894
2029	63	35,109	64,510		669	98,950	1,122,403	2,178,458	254,073	3,554,934
2030	64	34,794	68,573		479	102,888	1,107,705	2,352,734	274,399	3,734,839
2031	65	34,339	62,915			97,254	1,097,960	2,540,953	296,351	3,935,265
2032	66	34,037	67,087			101,124	1,083,575	2,744,229	320,059	4,147,864
2033	67	33,591	71,558			105,149	1,064,028	2,963,768	345,664	4,373,460
2034	68	32,985	76,350			109,335	1,038,752	3,200,869	373,317	4,612,938
2035	69	32,201	81,487			113,688	1,007,125	3,456,939	403,183	4,867,246
2036	70	31,221	113,444	$115,494	26,447	118,218	1,057,517	3,618,000	435,437	5,110,954
2037	71	32,783	109,586	124,605	29,704	112,665	1,123,297	3,782,835	470,272	5,376,404
2038	72	34,822	115,891	134,431	33,562	117,151	1,195,755	3,951,030	507,894	5,654,680
2039	73	37,068	129,220	165,748	44,471	121,817	1,289,680	4,101,365	548,525	5,939,570
2040	74	39,980	136,431	178,116	49,741	126,670	1,393,270	4,251,358	592,407	6,237,035
2041	75	43,191	144,298	192,140	55,772	131,717	1,507,989	4,399,327	639,800	6,547,116
2042	76	46,748	152,523	207,257	62,306	136,965	1,635,106	4,544,016	690,984	6,870,106
2043	77	50,688	160,736	222,455	69,000	142,424	1,775,311	4,685,082	746,263	7,206,655
2044	78	55,035	169,696	239,932	76,630	148,101	1,930,762	4,819,956	805,964	7,556,682
2045	79	59,854	178,619	257,536	84,468	154,005	2,102,355	4,948,017	870,441	7,920,812
2046	80	65,173	187,025	276,180	92,053	160,145	2,292,422	5,067,678	940,076	8,300,177
2047	81	71,065	194,801	296,270	99,315	166,551	2,503,928	5,176,822	1,015,282	8,696,033
2048	82	77,622	202,668	317,495	107,077	173,213	2,738,944	5,273,473	1,096,505	9,108,922
2049	83	84,907	210,118	338,163	114,884	180,141	2,998,459	5,357,187	1,184,225	9,539,871
2050	84	92,952	218,208	362,100	123,813	187,347	3,286,277	5,423,662	1,278,963	9,988,902
2051	85	101,875	225,685	385,092	132,719	194,841	3,603,425	5,472,463	1,381,280	10,457,169
2052	86	111,706	233,018	408,860	142,090	202,635	3,952,231	5,501,400	1,491,783	10,945,414
2053	87	122,519	240,354	434,068	152,133	210,740	4,335,653	5,507,444	1,611,125	11,454,222
2054	88	134,405	246,464	456,533	161,700	219,169	4,753,833	5,491,506	1,740,015	11,985,355
2055	89	147,369	253,311	483,223	172,744	227,936	5,211,929	5,447,604	1,879,217	12,538,749
2056	90	161,570	258,671	506,565	183,187	237,054	5,709,996	5,376,847	2,029,554	13,116,396

The interpretation of Table 6-10 is as follows:

Col (3):   The entries in this column are the interest and dividend income, as generated from the taxable savings shown in Col (8).

The interest and dividend income is based on the asset allocation and investment rates of returns, as detailed in the prior section, *"Retirement Investment Portfolio Assets and Rates."*

Col (4): Use of savings represents the annual savings required to supplement the retirement income to offset any shortfalls, as required to meet taxes, Col (6) and living expenses, Col (7).

The general planning strategy is the use of taxable savings prior to the use of tax-deferred savings, such as IRA's, etc., to supplement income sources in pre-70½ years.

This planning strategy provides for continued deferral of taxation for the tax-deferred savings.

However, as it will be discussed later, depending on the effective tax rates during the pre-70½ period, tax planning opportunities are to be considered, such as taking distributions from tax-deferred savings or conversion to Roth IRA's.

After the start of minimum required distributions, the distributions from the tax-deferred savings are used to supplement other income. For example, in year 2036, the required minimum distribution is $115,494 and the required use of savings is $113,444, leaving a balance of $2050 to be invested in taxable savings.

The issue of using savings needs to be put into proper perspective. Using savings must be viewed from the point of view of investment portfolio *total return*, in that interest and dividend return represents income only, portfolio yield, whereas total return comprehends both investment portfolio income and growth.

As previously discussed, there is a high probability that retirement savings will not be depleted if the inflation adjusted withdrawal rates are 5.0% or less.

The Sample's withdrawal rate is tabulated in Table 6-11, where the withdrawal rate is defined as follows.

Withdrawal rate, % = **(Taxes + Living expenses)/(Total Savings) * 100**

= **(Total Withdrawals)/(Total Savings) * 100**

Table 6-11
Sample's Withdrawal Rate

YEAR	TOTAL TAXES	LIVING EXPENSES	TOTAL WITHDRAWAL	TOTAL SAVINGS	% WITHDRAWAL
2027	$978	$91,523	$92,501	$3,224,100	2.87%
2028	832	95,164	95,996	3,384,894	2.84
2029	669	98,950	99,619	3,554,934	2.80
2030	479	102,888	103,367	3,734,839	2.77
2031		97,254	97,254	3,935,265	2.47
2032		101,124	101,124	4,147,864	2.44
2033		105,149	105,149	4,373,460	2.40
2034		109,335	109,335	4,612,938	2.37
2035		113,688	113,688	4,867,246	2.34
2036	26,447	118,218	144,665	5,110,954	2.83
2037	29,704	112,665	142,369	5,376,404	2.65
2038	33,562	117,151	150,713	5,654,680	2.67
2039	44,471	121,817	166,288	5,939,570	2.80
2040	49,741	126,670	176,411	6,237,035	2.83
2041	55,772	131,717	187,489	6,547,116	2.86
2042	62,306	136,965	199,271	6,870,106	2.90
2043	69,000	142,424	211,424	7,206,655	2.93
2044	76,630	148,101	224,731	7,556,682	2.97
2045	84,468	154,005	238,473	7,920,812	3.01
2046	92,053	160,145	252,198	8,300,177	3.04
2047	99,315	166,551	265,866	8,696,033	3.06
2048	107,077	173,213	280,290	9,108,922	3.08
2049	114,884	180,141	295,025	9,539,871	3.09
2050	123,813	187,347	311,160	9,988,902	3.12
2051	132,719	194,841	327,560	10,457,169	3.13
2052	142,090	202,635	344,725	10,945,414	3.15
2053	152,133	210,740	362,873	11,454,222	3.17
2054	161,700	219,169	380,869	11,985,355	3.18
2055	172,744	227,936	400,680	12,538,749	3.20
2056	183,187	237,054	420,241	13,116,396	3.20

Col (5) of Table 6-10, Retirement Cash Flow: The entries in this column represent the required minimum distributions from tax-deferred savings, that is, employer's savings plans and regular IRA's, starting at age 70½.

In January, 2000, the IRA unveiled new regulations as they relate to minimum required distributions. These can be summarized as follows:

    ✓   Providing a simple, uniform table that all employees can use to determine the minimum required distribution during their lifetime. This makes it far easier to calculate the required minimum distribution because employees would

➜ no longer need to determine their beneficiary by their required beginning date,

➜ no longer need to decide whether or not to recalculate their life expectancy each year in determining required minimum distributions, and

✓ Permit the required minimum distribution during the employee's lifetime to be calculated without regard to the beneficiary's age (except when required distributions can be reduced by taking into account the age of a beneficiary who is a spouse more than 10 years younger).

The uniform table provides the required distribution factors for all retirees, starting in year 2002, according to the age of the participant.

Uniform Table for Determining Applicable Factors											
Age	Divisor	Age	Divisor	Age	Divisor	Age	Divisor	Age	Divisor	Age	Divisor
70	27.4	78	20.3	86	14.1	94	9.1	102	5.5	110	3.1
71	26.5	79	19.5	87	13.4	95	8.6	103	5.2	111	2.9
72	25.6	80	18.7	88	12.7	96	8.1	104	4.9	112	2.6
73	24.7	81	17.9	89	12.0	97	7.6	105	4.5	113	2.4
74	23.8	82	17.1	90	11.4	98	7.1	106	4.2	114	2.1
75	22.9	83	16.3	91	10.8	99	6.7	107	3.9	115	1.9
76	22.0	84	15.5	92	10.2	100	6.2	108	3.7		
77	21.2	85	14.8	93	9.6	101	5.9	109	3.4		

The calculation of the minimum required distribution, MRD, is as follows.

$$\text{MRD} = \frac{\text{Retirement sav acct bal, end of prior year}}{\text{Applicable factor from the Uniform table}}$$

Table 6-12 provides the Sample family minimum required distribution detail for their respective tax-deferred retirement savings. It should be noted that the required minimum distribution factors are based on the distribution factors applicable in 2001.

Table 6-12
Sample's Minimum Required Distributions

YEAR	CLIENT	SPOUSE	STARTING BALANCE	DISTR. FACTOR	MINIMUM DISTR.	START BALANCE	DISTR FACTOR	MRD	TOTAL MRD
2027	61	58	$1,513,722			$215,608			
2028	62	59	1,634,820			232,857			
2029	63	60	1,765,605			251,485			
2030	64	61	1,906,854			271,604			
2031	65	62	2,059,402			293,332			
2032	66	63	2,224,154			316,799			
2033	67	64	2,402,087			342,143			
2034	68	65	2,594,253			369,514			
2035	69	66	2,801,794			399,075			
2036	70	67	3,025,937	26.20	$115,494	431,001			$115,494
2037	71	68	3,152,518	25.30	124,605	465,482			124,605
2038	72	69	3,280,114	24.40	134,431	502,720			134,431
2039	73	70	3,408,093	23.50	145,025	542,938	26.20	$20,723	165,748
2040	74	71	3,535,715	22.70	155,758	565,650	25.30	22,358	178,116
2041	75	72	3,662,814	21.80	168,019	588,544	24.40	24,121	192,140
2042	76	73	3,787,820	20.90	181,235	611,507	23.50	26,022	207,257
2043	77	74	3,909,610	20.10	194,508	634,406	22.70	27,947	222,455
2044	78	75	4,027,871	19.20	209,785	657,211	21.80	30,147	239,932
2045	79	76	4,140,316	18.40	225,017	679,641	20.90	32,519	257,536
2046	80	77	4,246,524	17.60	241,280	701,493	20.10	34,900	276,180
2047	81	78	4,344,966	16.80	258,629	722,712	19.20	37,641	296,270
2048	82	79	4,433,934	16.00	277,121	742,888	18.40	40,374	317,495
2049	83	80	4,511,528	15.30	294,871	761,945	17.60	43,292	338,163
2050	84	81	4,577,579	14.50	315,695	779,608	16.80	46,405	362,100
2051	85	82	4,628,090	13.80	335,369	795,572	16.00	49,723	385,092
2052	86	83	4,662,969	13.10	355,952	809,494	15.30	52,908	408,860
2053	87	84	4,680,054	12.40	377,424	821,345	14.50	56,645	434,068
2054	88	85	4,677,035	11.80	396,359	830,409	13.80	60,175	456,533
2055	89	86	4,654,839	11.10	419,355	836,667	13.10	63,868	483,223
2056	90	87	4,607,871	10.50	438,845	839,732	12.40	67,720	506,565

Col (6) of Table 10, Retirement Cash Flow: The entries in this column represent the federal taxes, based on current IRS regulations, as of year 2000.

It should be noted that the taxes for the Sample's incurred significant changes in the pre-70½ period. The effective tax rate is defined as *total taxes divided by taxable income.*

Table 6-13 illustrates the Sample's annual effective tax rates over the 30-year retirement period. The effective tax rate profile in Table 6-13 illustrates the need to calculate taxes based on IRS regulations, as opposed to using an 'average' tax rate.

The need for use of savings in the pre-70½ age period is usually taken from taxable savings, thereby maximizing the continued deferral of taxation of tax-deferred savings.

In that the effective tax rates for the Sample's in the pre-70½ age period is zero or minimal, a tax planning strategy would be to convert some of the regular IRA savings to a Roth IRA during this time.

Table 6-13

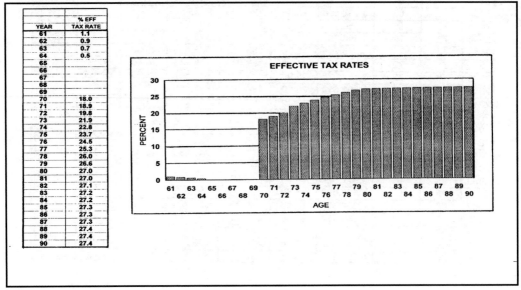

YEAR	% EFF TAX RATE
61	1.1
62	0.9
63	0.7
64	0.5
65	
66	
67	
68	
69	
70	18.0
71	18.9
72	19.8
73	21.9
74	22.8
75	23.7
76	24.5
77	25.3
78	26.0
79	26.6
80	27.0
81	27.0
82	27.1
83	27.2
84	27.2
85	27.3
86	27.3
87	27.3
88	27.4
89	27.4
90	27.4

The determination of the dollars of regular IRA to be converted annually must comprehend the following, based on IRS regulations as of year 2000.

- The "taxpayer's adjusted gross income, AGI, in the year of conversion cannot exceed $100,000." In the determination of the AGI cap, the dollars converted to a Roth IRA are not included. Also, a married taxpayer filing a separate return cannot do a rollover to a Roth IRA.

The minimum required distributions, MRD, from tax-deferred savings are currently included in the AGI; however, starting in year 2005 the MRD are not included in the AGI for the purposes of establishing the Roth IRA adjusted gross income (AGI) cap.

- The assets to be "converted" must be in a "regular" IRA. Savings in a 401-k plan or any qualified plan must first be rolled over to a regular IRA before conversion to a Roth IRA.

- Converting to a Roth IRA is treated as a distribution from the regular IRA; therefore, income taxes must be paid.

In addition to the above IRS regulations, the dollars of regular IRA to be converted to a Roth IRA must take into consideration the marginal tax brackets and AMT taxes (Alternative Minimum Tax).

Comprehending the above constraints, a scenario based on converting $50,000 of regular IRA funds for the pre-70½ period, from years 2027 through 2035, was developed for the Sample's.

Table 6-14 is a summary of the ending investment assets, year 2056, without and with the Roth conversion. The numbers shown are based on before and after taxation of the regular IRA savings at 39.6% tax rate.

Table 6-14
Investment Assets, Year 2056

	Roth Conversion	
Before Taxes:	**No**	**Yes**
Taxable Savings	$ 5,709,996	$ 3,835,890
Regular IRA	5,376,847	4,440,538
Roth IRA	2,029,544 (1)	4,706,705 (2)
Total:	$13,116,396	$12,983,132
After Taxes:		
Taxable Savings	$ 5,709,996	$ 3,835,890
Regular IRA (3)	3,247,615	2,682,085
Roth IRA	2,029,544	4,706,705
Total:	$10,987,155	$11,224,680

(1) Roth account based on pre-retirement years, contributions only
(2) Roth account includes pre-retirement contributions and post-retirement
    conversion. Converted IRA dollars are taxed at 39.6%.
(3) The after-tax IRA accounts are based on a 39.6% tax rate.

The after-tax total investment assets for the Roth scenario, of $11,224,680, as compared to without the Roth conversion, of

$10,987,155, represents an increase of $237,525, or approximately 2.0%.

It is important to note that Roth IRA's are not subject to minimum required distribution rules and future earnings and distributions are *tax free*.

Col (8), (9), & (10) of Table 6-10, Retirement Cash Flow: These entries represent the allocation of investment assets among taxable savings, regular IRA's and Roth IRA's, assuming no Roth IRA conversion.

The Sample family's projected retirement savings, Col (10), are based on a real rate of return of 4.0% and a withdrawal rate of approximately 3.0% over the retirement period.

The real rate of return of 4.0% and a withdrawal rate of 3.0% are conservative; therefore the probability of the Sample's *not depleting* their savings in retirement is very high.

Chart 6-5 provides a graphic profile of the investment asset allocation over the 30-year retirement period before taxes.

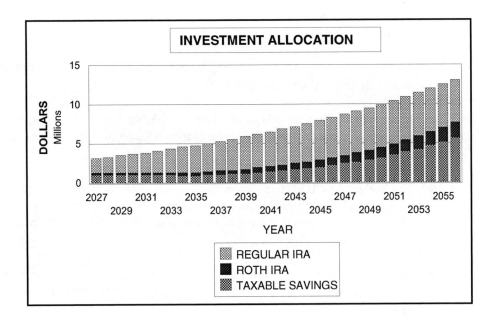

Chart 6-5

Summary:

- Retirement planning is a continuing process, in that the planning comprehends both the pre-retirement period and the post-retirement period.

- The various interacting variables which must be comprehended in establishing the retirement withdrawal rate are investment rates of return, inflation and life expectancy. In reality, the only variable really controlled by the individual is the *withdrawal rate*.

- Today's retirees must discard the idea that they shouldn't spend principal; in other words, an individual's investment portfolio asset allocation should not be dictated by income needs alone. The investment portfolio asset allocation is to be dictated by *total return*, that is, income *plus* growth.

- The assumption that, if the investment portfolio is earning ten percent, as an average, and the annual withdrawal rate is six percent, that the individual will not only have sufficient savings to support his/her life style, but also leave a significant estate for heirs, is not true. In the real world no one earns an average rate of return year after year, in that, actual returns vary from year to year. The variability of returns has a significant impact on the chance that an individual will deplete his/her money.

- In retirement there is a high level of confidence that a retiree will not outlive his retirement savings if the inflation adjusted withdrawal rate does not exceed 5.0%.

- The budgeting changes, as an individual goes into retirement, generally comprehend reductions in food, transportation and clothing; however, offsetting these reductions are increases in travel and health and medical expenditures.

- In the development of retirement cash flow projections, the use of an average income tax rate over the retirement period will result in unrealistic results.

- If cash flow retirement projections are based on 4.0% real rates of return and 3% to 5% withdrawal rates, there is a high probability that the retirement savings will not be depleted.

RETIREMENT CAPITAL NEEDS WORKSHEET

This worksheet calculates the savings required at the *start* of retirement to supplement other retirement income resources, such that a *desired inflation adjusted income* is provided over the retirement years. The worksheet is based on the assumption that, if both spouses are working, both retire in the same year. Referenced tables are on pages 168 and 169.

Worksheet Description–

Line #	Description	Example	Your Numbers
1	Enter your current age.	40	
2	Enter your spouse's age.	38	
3	Enter your age at retirement.	55	
4	Enter assumed investment rate of return, %..	8.0%	
5	Enter assumed inflation rate, %.	4.0%	
6	Real rate of return (Inv rate, Line 4 - Infl rate, Line 5) (Recommended real rate of return = 3.0% to 5.0%)	4.0%	
7	Enter expected number of years in retirement.	30	
8	Enter desired after-tax spending rate for retirement, in today's dollars, $/yr	$60,000	
9	Enter tax filing status, Joint = J; Single = S.	J	
10	Select a tax factor from *Table A*, corresponding to the spending rate, Line 8, and tax filing status, Line 9. Enter as a decimal.	0.109	
11	Subtract from 1.00 the tax factor, Line 10.	0.891	
12	Divide the after-tax retirement spending, Line 8, by Line 11. This entry = your *before-tax* spending rate in today's dollars.	$67,340	
13	Enter years prior to your retirement, Line 3 - Line 1.	15	
14	Select a future value factor from *Table B*, corresponding to your years prior to retirement, Line 13, and the inflation rate, Line 5.	1.801	

15	Multiply Line 12 x Line 14. This entry represents the _inflation adjusted_ budget at the _start_ of retirement.	$121,276	
16	Select a capital need factor from _Table C_, corresponding to the years in retirement, Line 7, and the real rate of return, Line 6.	17.984	
17	Miltiply Line 15 x Line 16. This entry represents the present value, lump sum, of equivalent savings required at the start of retirement to support the inflation adjusted budget, Line 15.	$2,180,987	
18	Enter an estimate of your annual social security benefits at _age 62_, in _today's dollars_, or at attained age if retirement is after age 62.	$14,700	
19	Enter an estimate of your spouse's annual SS benefits at age 62 based on _spouse's earning base_, in today's dollars; if spouse is older than 62 at your retirement, enter spouse's SS benefits at attained age.	$12,240	
20	Enter an estimate of Cost-of-Living, COLA, the adjustment for social security (recommend 2% - 3%).	3.0%	
21	Select a future value factor from _Table B_, corresponding to years before your retirement, Line 13, and the COLA rate, Line 20.	1.558	
22	Multiply Line 18 x Line 21. This entry represents your COLA adjusted soc sec at the _start of your retirement_.	$22,902	
23	Multiply Line 19 x Line 21. This entry represents your spouse's COLA adjusted soc sec at start of your retirement.	$19,070	
24	Multiply Line 22 x Line 16. This entry represents the present value, lump sum, of equivalent savings required _if your SS was paid_ from date of retirement over the entire retirement period, Line 7.	$411,865	
25	If SS starts at age 62 or later, go to Line 28, else enter the number of years prior to age 62 (62 - Line 3).	7	
26	Select a capital needs factor from _Table D_, corresponding to the real rate of return, Line 6, and Line 25.	6.242	
27	Multiply Line 22 x Line 26. This entry represents the present value, lump sum of the _shortfall_ of SS for your pre-age 62 period.	$142,958	

| 28 | If SS starts at 62 or later enter Line 24 data, else subtract Line 27 from Line 24. This entry represents the *adjusted* present value, PV, of your SS benefits. | $268,907 | |

| 29 | Multiply Line 23 x Line 16. Same interpretation as Line 24, except applies to spouse. | $342,941 | |

| 30 | If spouse is 62 or older at your retirement, go to Line 33, else enter years prior to age 62, [(62 - Line 3 + (Line 1 - Line 2)]. | 9 | |

| 31 | Select a capital needs factor, *Table D,* corresponding to the real rate of return, Line 6, and Line 30. | 7.333 | |

| 32 | Multiply Line 23 x Line 31. This entry represents the PV, lump sum, of the *shortfall* of SS for your spouse's pre-age 62 period. | $147,960 | |

| 33 | If spouse's SS starts at 62 or later, enter Line 29 data, else subtract Line 32 from Line 29. This entry represents the adjusted PV of your spouse's SS benefits. | $195,481 | |

| 34 | Enter annual pension, if any, $/year. | $38,400 | |

| 35 | Select annuity factor, *Table E*, corresponding to inv rate of return, Line 4, and retirement years, Line 7. | 9.604 | |

| 36 | Multiply Line 34 x Line 35. This entry represents the PV, lump sum, of the pension over the retirement years. | $432,299 | |

| 37 | Enter the sum of Line 17 - Line 28 - Line 33 - Line 36. This entry represents the savings required at the start of retirement to supplement incomes, that is, SS plus pensions. | $1,284,300 | |

TRACKING RETIREMENT SAVINGS WORKSHEET

Having established the required retirement savings at the start of retirement, it is necessary during the *pre-retirement* years to monitor the progress toward the achievement of the retirement savings goal.

The following worksheet calculates whether the annual savings required to supplement your current cumulative savings to meet the stated goal is to be realized.

The annual savings required is expressed as a percent of your wages, which is then compared to the *actual* percent of annual savings being saved.

Worksheet Description--

Line #	Description	Example	Your Numbers
1	Enter the years to retirement.	12	
2	Enter the total of current gross wages.	$60,000	
3	Enter the tax filing status, that is, joint = J, or single = S	J	
4	Enter the expected investment rate of return for retirement savings during the pre-retirement period.	8.0 %	
5	Choose a tax factor from Table A, corresponding to the wages in Line 2. Enter as a decimal.	0.109	
6	Subtract the tax factor in Line 5 from 1.00.	0.891	
7	Choose a future value factor from Table B, corresponding to Line 1, the years to retirement, and Line 4, the investment rate of return.	2.518	
8	Enter the current <u>taxable savings</u> available for retirement, if applicable.	$30,000	
9	Multiply the taxable savings, Line 8, times the future value factor, Line 7, times the (1.0 - tax factor), Line 6. This entry is an estimate of the future value of taxable savings at the start of retirement.	$67,311	
10	Enter the total of the current tax-deferred savings, that is, the 401-k's, IRA's, etc.	$425,000	
11	Multiply the current tax-deferred savings, Line 10, times the future value factor, Line 7. This entry is an estimate of the tax-deferred savings at the start of retirement.	$1,070,222	

12	Enter the required retirement savings, as calculated in the *"Retirement Capital Needs"* worksheet, Line 37.	$1,284,300	
13	From Line 12, retirement capital needs, subtract Line 11, the tax-deferred savings, and Line 9, the taxable savings available at the start of retirement. This entry represent additional savings required at the start of retirement.	$146,767	
14	Choose from Table E the annual savings factor corresponding to the years to retirement, Line 1, and the investment rate of return, Line 4.	18.977	
15	Divide the additional savings required, Line 13, by the savings factor in Line 14. This entry represents the annual savings required if the additional savings necessary, Line 13, is to be realized by the start of retirement.	$7,734	
16	Divide Line 15, the annual required savings, by the total wages in Line 2. This entry represents the current percent of your wages that must be saved to meet your retirement savings goal.	12.89%	

WORKSHEET TABLES A, B AND C

TABLE A   **TAX FACTORS**

RETR SPENDING	JOINT	SINGLE
20000	3.1%	8.2%
25000	4.7%	9.5%
30000	6.3%	10.4%
35000	7.6%	11.3%
40000	8.5%	13.1%
45000	9.2%	14.5%
50000	9.8%	15.6%
55000	10.3%	16.5%
60000	10.9%	17.3%
70000	12.9%	18.5%
80000	14.5%	19.7%
90000	15.8%	20.7%
100000	16.9%	21.5%
120000	18.5%	22.7%
140000	20.2%	23.8%
160000	21.6%	25.0%
180000	22.8%	26.1%
200000	24.0%	27.0%

TABLE C   **CAPITAL NEED FACTORS**

REAL RATES OF RETURN	YEARS IN RETIREMENT			
	20	25	30	35
2%	16.678	19.914	22.844	25.499
3%	15.324	17.936	20.188	22.132
4%	14.134	16.247	17.984	19.411
5%	13.085	14.799	16.141	17.193
6%	12.158	13.550	14.591	15.368
7%	11.336	12.469	13.278	13.854
8%	10.604	11.529	12.158	12.587
9%	9.950	10.707	11.198	11.518

TABLE B   **FUTURE VALUE FACTORS**

YEARS TO RETR	RATES							
	2%	3%	4%	5%	6%	7%	8%	9%
1	1.000	1.030	1.040	1.050	1.060	1.070	1.080	1.090
2	1.040	1.061	1.082	1.103	1.124	1.145	1.166	1.188
3	1.061	1.093	1.125	1.158	1.191	1.225	1.260	1.295
4	1.082	1.126	1.170	1.216	1.262	1.311	1.360	1.412
5	1.104	1.159	1.217	1.276	1.338	1.403	1.469	1.539
6	1.126	1.194	1.265	1.340	1.419	1.501	1.587	1.677
7	1.149	1.230	1.316	1.407	1.504	1.606	1.714	1.828
8	1.172	1.267	1.369	1.477	1.594	1.718	1.851	1.993
9	1.195	1.305	1.423	1.551	1.689	1.838	1.999	2.172
10	1.219	1.344	1.480	1.629	1.791	1.967	2.159	2.367
11	1.243	1.384	1.539	1.710	1.898	2.105	2.332	2.580
12	1.268	1.426	1.601	1.796	2.012	2.252	2.518	2.813
13	1.294	1.469	1.665	1.886	2.133	2.410	2.720	3.066
14	1.319	1.513	1.732	1.980	2.261	2.579	2.937	3.342
15	1.346	1.558	1.801	2.079	2.397	2.759	3.172	3.642
16	1.373	1.605	1.873	2.183	2.540	2.952	3.426	3.970
17	1.400	1.653	1.948	2.292	2.693	3.159	3.700	4.328
18	1.428	1.702	2.026	2.407	2.854	3.380	3.996	4.717
19	1.457	1.754	2.107	2.527	3.026	3.617	4.316	5.142
20	1.486	1.806	2.191	2.653	3.207	3.870	4.661	5.604
21	1.516	1.860	2.279	2.786	3.400	4.141	5.034	6.109
22	1.546	1.916	2.370	2.925	3.604	4.430	5.437	6.659
23	1.577	1.974	2.465	3.072	3.820	4.741	5.871	7.258
24	1.608	2.033	2.563	3.225	4.049	5.072	6.341	7.911
25	1.641	2.094	2.666	3.386	4.292	5.427	6.848	8.623
26	1.673	2.157	2.772	3.556	4.549	5.807	7.396	9.399
27	1.707	2.221	2.883	3.733	4.822	6.214	7.988	10.245
28	1.741	2.288	2.999	3.920	5.112	6.649	8.627	11.167
29	1.776	2.357	3.119	4.116	5.418	7.114	9.317	12.172
30	1.811	2.427	3.243	4.322	5.743	7.612	10.063	13.268

WORKSHEET TABLES D, E AND F

TABLE D   CAPITAL NEED FACTORS

REAL RATES OF RETURN	YEARS FROM START RETIREMENT TO AGE 62											
	1	2	3	4	5	6	7	8	9	10	11	12
2%	1.000	1.980	2.942	3.884	4.808	5.713	6.601	7.472	8.325	9.162	9.983	10.787
3%	1.000	1.971	2.913	3.829	4.717	5.580	6.417	7.230	8.020	8.786	9.530	10.253
4%	1.000	1.962	2.886	3.775	4.630	5.452	6.242	7.002	7.733	8.435	9.111	9.760
5%	1.000	1.952	2.859	3.723	4.546	5.329	6.076	6.786	7.463	8.108	8.722	9.306
6%	1.000	1.943	2.833	3.673	4.465	5.212	5.917	6.582	7.210	7.802	8.360	8.887
7%	1.000	1.935	2.808	3.624	4.387	5.100	5.767	6.389	6.971	7.515	8.024	8.499
8%	1.000	1.926	2.783	3.577	4.312	4.993	5.623	6.206	6.747	7.247	7.710	8.139
9%	1.000	1.917	2.759	3.531	4.240	4.890	5.486	6.033	6.535	6.995	7.418	7.805

TABLE E   PRESENT VALUE ORDINARY ANNUITY FACTOR

YRS IN RETR.	INVESTMENT RATE OF RETURN					
	5%	6%	7%	8%	9%	10%
15	10.380	9.712	9.108	8.559	8.061	7.606
20	12.462	11.470	10.594	9.818	9.129	8.514
25	14.094	12.783	11.654	10.675	9.823	9.077
30	15.372	13.765	12.409	11.258	10.274	9.427
35	16.374	14.498	12.948	11.655	10.567	9.644

TABLE F   ANNUAL SAVINGS FACTOR

YRS TO GOAL	4.5%	5.0%	5.5%	6.0%	6.5%	7.0%	7.5%	8.0%	8.5%	9.0%
1	1.000	1.000	1.000	1.000	1.000	1.000	1.000	1.000	1.000	1.000
2	2.045	2.050	2.055	2.060	2.065	2.070	2.075	2.080	2.085	2.090
3	3.137	3.153	3.168	3.184	3.199	3.215	3.231	3.246	3.262	3.278
4	4.278	4.310	4.342	4.375	4.407	4.440	4.473	4.506	4.540	4.573
5	5.471	5.526	5.581	5.637	5.694	5.751	5.808	5.867	5.925	5.985
6	6.717	6.802	6.888	6.975	7.064	7.153	7.244	7.336	7.429	7.523
7	8.019	8.142	8.267	8.394	8.523	8.654	8.787	8.923	9.060	9.200
8	9.380	9.549	9.722	9.897	10.077	10.260	10.446	10.637	10.831	11.028
9	10.802	11.027	11.256	11.491	11.732	11.978	12.230	12.488	12.751	13.021
10	12.288	12.578	12.875	13.181	13.494	13.816	14.147	14.487	14.835	15.193
11	13.841	14.207	14.583	14.972	15.372	15.784	16.208	16.645	17.096	17.560
12	15.464	15.917	16.386	16.870	17.371	17.888	18.424	18.977	19.549	20.141
13	17.160	17.713	18.287	18.882	19.500	20.141	20.806	21.495	22.211	22.953
14	18.932	19.599	20.293	21.015	21.767	22.550	23.366	24.215	25.099	26.019
15	20.784	21.579	22.409	23.276	24.182	25.129	26.118	27.152	28.232	29.361
16	22.719	23.657	24.641	25.673	26.754	27.888	29.077	30.324	31.632	33.003
17	24.742	25.840	26.996	28.213	29.493	30.840	32.258	33.750	35.321	36.974
18	26.855	28.132	29.481	30.906	32.410	33.999	35.677	37.450	39.323	41.301
19	29.064	30.539	32.103	33.760	35.517	37.379	39.353	41.446	43.665	46.018
20	31.371	33.066	34.868	36.786	38.825	40.995	43.305	45.762	48.377	51.160
21	33.783	35.719	37.786	39.993	42.349	44.865	47.553	50.423	53.489	56.765
22	36.303	38.505	40.864	43.392	46.102	49.006	52.119	55.457	59.036	62.873
23	38.937	41.430	44.112	46.996	50.098	53.436	57.028	60.893	65.054	69.532
24	41.689	44.502	47.538	50.816	54.355	58.177	62.305	66.765	71.583	76.790
25	44.565	47.727	51.153	54.865	58.888	63.249	67.978	73.106	78.668	84.701
26	47.571	51.113	54.966	59.156	63.715	68.676	74.076	79.954	86.355	93.324
27	50.711	54.669	58.989	63.706	68.857	74.484	80.632	87.351	94.695	102.723
28	53.993	58.403	63.234	68.528	74.333	80.698	87.679	95.339	103.744	112.968
29	57.423	62.323	67.711	73.640	80.164	87.347	95.255	103.966	113.562	124.135
30	61.007	66.439	72.435	79.058	86.375	94.461	103.399	113.283	124.215	136.308

–RISK MANAGEMENT–

Overview

Risk management is the financial planning process of protecting your family and assets against financial problems arising from catastrophes or unexpected events, such as...

- Death
- Disability
- Medical expenses
- Property loss
- Liability claims

The basic risk management techniques include the following.

- Risk avoidance
- Risk reduction (loss prevention)
- Risk assumption
- Risk transfer

Risk avoidance requires an individual to completely avoid the exposure to the specific risk element, such as avoiding air transportation.

Risk reduction does not avoid the risk exposure. However, it comprehends the use of various loss prevention strategies, such as proper diet, use of smoke detectors in the home, etc.

Risk assumption implies that an individual will be financially accountable for any losses incurred. In accepting the decision to assume risk, a person must evaluate the potential loss relative to one's wealth. As the potential loss increases relative to an individual's wealth, the risk assumption strategy becomes less desirable and less practical.

The major vehicle for risk management is the use of *insurance*, which is a means of transferring the risk. In the transferring of risk to an insurance company there is a financial cost, that is, a premium which must be paid to the insurance carrier. Therefore, an individual must evaluate how much of the risk they are willing to retain and how much should be transferred.

Life Insurance

Life insurance is unique in that there is no other financial instrument which can create an immediate "estate" so readily when it is needed most – at the death of a provider. It can supply both liquidity for estate costs and income for survivors.

Insurance can provide:

- cash for immediate needs: final illness, burial, taxes, payment of debts
- readjustment income for a period of time, i.e. until a spouse can become employed or until children complete their education
- a trust fund for another
- an estate for heirs
- charitable gifts
- payment of business debt or money to buy out a business partner

Once a person has decided on the purpose of life insurance for his/her needs, then the primary considerations in the purchase of insurance are...

1. What type of insurance should be bought?
2. How much insurance should be purchased?

Most families don't have enough insurance protection because they buy the wrong kind of life insurance. One of the most important expenditures the average family makes in its lifetime is the purchase of life insurance. It is also one of the most misunderstood. It is absolutely critical that a person make the right decision about the kind and amount of life insurance to buy.

There are various "rules of thumb" used to determine how much life insurance is needed; such as, 'multiply your annual salary by seven or eight,' or 'cover your debts,' etc. However, these "rules of thumb" overlook so many other factors which must be considered.

The most common misconception about life insurance is that it is a permanent need that each family has. Life insurance is a way to *buy time* until a person or family gets their personal financial estate in order. A family needs more coverage when it is young, and less when it is older. This is referred to as *"the theory of decreasing responsibility."*

The need for insurance is greatest when responsibilities are greatest, i.e. when children are young, there is a mortgage payment, etc. As a person or family grows older, responsibilities decrease: children are grown and on their own, routine payments are reduced, the home is paid for, etc. This is the time when a family or person needs very little "death protection" in the form of insurance, and should rely instead on the wealth they have accumulated.

Chart 7-1 illustrates the concepts of "Theory of Decreasing Responsibility."

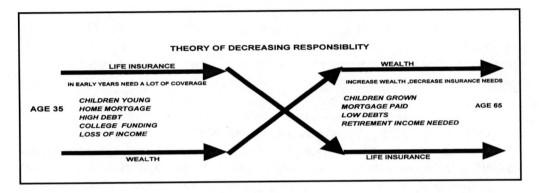

THEORY OF DECREASING RESPONSIBLITY

LIFE INSURANCE   WEALTH

IN EARLY YEARS NEED A LOT OF COVERAGE   INCREASE WEALTH ,DECREASE INSURANCE NEEDS

AGE 35   CHILDREN YOUNG   CHILDREN GROWN
          HOME MORTGAGE   MORTGAGE PAID   AGE 65
          HIGH DEBT   LOW DEBTS
          COLLEGE FUNDING   RETIREMENT INCOME NEEDED
          LOSS OF INCOME

WEALTH   LIFE INSURANCE

Chart 7-1

Type of Life Insurance

All Policies Fall into Two Catagories:

1 - Term insurance
2 - Cash value insurance

Term Insurance:

As the name indicates, term insurance covers a person for a specific term, such as one-year, five-years, ten-years, etc. When the term is over, so is the life insurance coverage–unless the person has purchased *renewable* term. Renewable term guarantees the right to renew the coverage, regardless of any changes in the person's health. The premium for renewable term insurance rises at the beginning of each new term. The increased premium reflects the increasing probability of death. The use of term insurance provides the lowest cost per $1,000 of protection.

Cash Value Insurance:

Cash value insurance combines insurance with savings. As the name indicates it includes a cash value account within the life insurance policy. With most cash value policies, the annual premium stays level throughout the life of the policy. In effect, the buyer pays more than is needed to cover the low statistical risk of death in the early years, and less than the amount needed to cover the higher statistical risk of death in later years.

A person is not entitled to withdraw money from the savings component of a cash value policy before its maturity date. But the policy holder can borrow against it at whatever interest rate that is guaranteed in the policy. If the policy holder dies, the beneficiary receives no more than the face amount of the policy, regardless of how much or how little money has accumulated in the savings component. If the policy holder dies with a loan outstanding, the beneficiary receives the face amount minus the loan and interest amount.

In recent years the insurance industry has introduced various new policies, such as Universal, Variable Life, etc., which combine some of the components of term and cash value insurance. These policies provide a more competitive savings component and greater flexibility as it pertains to changes in coverage and premium payments. However, even with these enhancements, insurance policies are <u>not</u> a substitute for the standard investment vehicles or retirement planning options that are available.

The criteria for making the decision to buy term or cash value insurance should be based on the need for a defined time period, such as 10-20 years or permanent.

In that term policy premiums are lower than cash value premiums for the same face amount, a rule of thumb is to 'buy term insurance and then invest the difference between the term and cash value premiums.' Depending on various factors, a cash value policy may require 15 years or more to accumulate enough after-tax surrender value to outperform the 'buy term and invest the difference' strategy.

If the insurance needs will exceed 20 years, purchase of some form of cash value insurance will provide the greatest economies, in that, term premiums continue to increase with age, whereas with a cash value policy, the individual can select a policy with level premiums for the life of the coverage.

Who Requires Coverage?

There is a need for financial protection when one or more persons must depend on another person for money to live on. Emphasis is on the word 'must.' A family with two working adults and no dependents has a lesser need for financial protection than a family with one working adult and a dependent spouse with young children.

When both parents contribute vital portions of the family income, both should be insured. If both are working, but one is the family's economic mainstay, the urgent priority is adequate insurance on that person.

The need for insurance for the homemaker depends on the following.

- Insurance premiums should not be diverted to the homemaker until the breadwinner is adequately insured.

- In the event of the homemaker's death, there must be adequate savings to help the family over the immediate cash drain required to cover baby sitters, daycare facilities, etc. If there are not funds for these needs, then life insurance on the homemaker may be needed.

- Consideration should be given to the ability of the family to afford the premiums for insurance on the homemaker. A family that is hard pressed to pay for food and shelter would not be wise to allocate resources for life insurance on a homemaker.

Although one or both parents may have good reason to be insured, their children seldom need life insurance unless they have debts.

Unless a single person contributes to the support of one or more people, a single person does not usually need life insurance.

Insurance Needs

The determination of life insurance coverage depends upon many factors; however, the starting point is the acceptance of a person's own mortality, that is, literally to assume that he/she might die tomorrow.

The immediate or future expenditures to be comprehended in the calculation of the amount of insurance required include the following.

- Need for immediate cash, such as for medical bills, funeral costs, emergency funds, etc.

- Need to pay off a mortgage, based on the status of the number of remaining mortgage payments, interest rate, etc.

- Living expenses, comprehending required adjustments for such items as food, health insurance, etc.

- Education costs for children

- Federal and state taxes.

Secondly, the income available from one or more of the following sources must be comprehended in the calculation of how much insurance is required.

- Investment assets

- Earnings of the surviving spouse

- Survivor pension benefits available

- Survivor's social security benefits, including social security benefits for children under 18 years of age.

- Trust and other annuity incomes that may be available.

If the projected expenditures exceed income, then additional income will have to be generated from available life insurance death benefits. If the living expenditures still exceed the income, then *additional life insurance* is required.

At the end of this chapter, a <u>worksheet</u> is provided for the purpose of calculating an individual's insurance needs. This worksheet is applicable for surviving spouses, 60 years of age or younger, that is, during the period of greatest need for life insurance.

Sample Family Life Insurance Needs

In the initial meetings with the Sample family, an evaluation was made relating to their *total life insurance* needs. The following issues were discussed.

➡ **Surviving Spouse's Living Expenses–**

In establishing the surviving spouse's living expenses, a decision was made to pay off the mortgage at the first death, in that approximately 85% of the current monthly payments were allocated to interest, and 15% to principal.

John's employer did not have provisions for continuing health insurance coverage; therefore, the current monthly employer health insurance coverage was to be continued under the federal law called *COBRA*. Under the COBRA regulations, the surviving spouse could participate under John's employer's group health plan for three years.

In as much as Mary's employer did not provide any health insurance coverage, private health insurance was scheduled to be purchased starting in the 4th year following the first death. The premiums for the private health insurance was included in the survivor's living expenses.

In the projection of living expenses, the variable living expenses were increased annually at the assumed inflation rate of 3.0%.

➡ **Savings and Income Resources–**

The Sample's balance sheet savings in year 2001 are as follows:

- Taxable savings $73,215
- College savings   27,000
- Retirement savings   98,666

In the evaluation of insurance needs, the retirement savings were not to be considered as available savings.

After extended discussion relating to Mary's continuing employment after John's death, there was a mutual agreement that the insurance needs calculation would include a projection of Mary's earnings, of $15,700 per year, being increased at 3% annually and Mary continue working until age 55.

In the evaluation of insurance requirements, any projection of a surviving spouse's earnings must take into consideration whether the spouse has worked or is working outside the home, the current job market, costs of any pre-employment education or training needed, etc.

Social security provides monthly benefits to the children of the deceased spouse, without regard to the age of the surviving parent, who is caring for at least one child under age 16, or for a disabled child under age 22.

A widow may start receiving social security benefits at age 60.

The projection of social security benefits, based on the above regulations, were comprehended in the calculation of insurance needs for the Sample family.

Table 7-1 provides a projection of the inflation adjusted expenditures and income resources for the surviving spouse.

Table 7-1 also provides the projected after-tax cash flow and the present value of savings required to offset years in which the expenditures exceed income, that is, years in which the cash flow is negative.

The projections in Table 7-1 are based on the following assumptions.

- After-tax investment rate of return on insurance death benefits of 5.0%.
- Living expenses increased annually at an assumed inflation rate of 3.0%.
- The surviving spouse has a life expectancy of 50 years.

Table 7-1
Surviving Spouse's Capital Needs

(1)	(2)	(3)	(4)	(5)	(6)	(7)	(8)	(9)	(10)
YEAR	AGE	LIVING EXP	EDUC COST	SOC.SEC	WAGES	TOTAL INCOME	CASH FLOW	START BAL	END BAL
2001	32	$29,500		$30,864	$15,687	$46,551	$17,051	$322,947	$356,998
2002	33	30,385		31,636	16,158	47,793	17,408	356,998	393,127
2003	34	31,297		32,426	16,642	49,069	17,772	393,127	431,444
2004	35	34,421		33,237	17,142	50,379	15,958	431,444	469,772
2005	36	35,454		34,068	17,656	51,724	16,270	469,772	510,344
2006	37	36,517		34,920	18,186	53,105	16,588	510,344	553,279
2007	38	37,613		35,793	18,731	54,524	16,911	553,279	598,700
2008	39	38,741		36,688	19,293	55,981	17,240	598,700	646,736
2009	40	39,903	$17,729	16,112	19,872	35,984	(21,648)	646,736	656,343
2010	41	41,100	18,616	16,515	20,468	36,983	(22,733)	656,343	665,290
2011	42	42,333	39,093		21,082	21,082	(60,344)	665,290	635,193
2012	43	43,603	41,048		21,714	21,714	(62,937)	635,193	600,868
2013	44	44,911	21,550		22,366	22,366	(44,096)	600,868	584,612
2014	45	46,259	22,628		23,037	23,037	(45,850)	584,612	565,700
2015	46	37,815			23,728	23,728	(14,087)	565,700	579,194
2016	47	38,949			24,440	24,440	(14,509)	579,194	592,918
2017	48	40,118			25,173	25,173	(14,945)	592,918	606,873
2018	49	41,321			25,928	25,928	(15,393)	606,873	621,054
2019	50	42,561			26,706	26,706	(15,855)	621,054	635,459
2020	51	43,838			27,507	27,507	(16,330)	635,459	650,085
2021	52	45,153			28,332	28,332	(16,820)	650,085	664,928
2022	53	46,507			29,182	29,182	(17,325)	664,928	679,983
2023	54	47,903			30,058	30,058	(17,845)	679,983	695,245
2024	55	49,340			30,960	30,960	(18,380)	695,245	710,708
2025	56	50,820					(50,820)	710,708	692,883
2026	57	52,344					(52,344)	692,883	672,565
2027	58	53,915					(53,915)	672,565	649,583
2028	59	55,532					(55,532)	649,583	623,753
2029	60	57,198		25,180		25,180	(32,018)	623,753	621,322
2030	61	58,914		25,809		25,809	(33,105)	621,322	617,628
2031	62	60,682		26,455		26,455	(34,227)	617,628	612,571
2032	63	62,502		27,116		27,116	(35,386)	612,571	606,044
2033	64	64,377		27,794		27,794	(36,583)	606,044	597,934
2034	65	66,308		28,489		28,489	(37,820)	597,934	588,120
2035	66	68,298		29,201		29,201	(39,097)	588,120	576,474
2036	67	70,347		29,931		29,931	(40,416)	576,474	562,861
2037	68	72,457		30,679		30,679	(41,778)	562,861	547,138
2038	69	74,631		31,446		31,446	(43,185)	547,138	529,151
2039	70	76,870		32,232		32,232	(44,637)	529,151	508,739
2040	71	79,176		33,038		33,038	(46,138)	508,739	485,731
2041	72	81,551		33,864		33,864	(47,687)	485,731	459,947
2042	73	83,997		34,711		34,711	(49,287)	459,947	431,193
2043	74	86,517		35,578		35,578	(50,939)	431,193	399,267
2044	75	89,113		36,468		36,468	(52,645)	399,267	363,953
2045	76	91,786		37,380		37,380	(54,407)	363,953	325,023
2046	77	94,540		38,314		38,314	(56,226)	325,023	282,237
2047	78	97,376		39,272		39,272	(58,104)	282,237	235,340
2048	79	100,297		40,254		40,254	(60,044)	235,340	184,061
2049	80	103,306		41,260		41,260	(62,046)	184,061	128,115
2050	81	106,405		42,292		42,292	(64,114)	128,115	67,201
2051	82	109,598		43,349		43,349	(66,249)	67,201	1,000

The interpretation of Table 7-1 is as follows:

Col (2):   At age 32 the life expectancy is 50 years

Col (3):   <u>Living expenses</u>: the Sample's base budget is adjusted for the payoff of the home mortgage and increase in health insurance costs. The living expenses are increased at the assumed inflation rate of 3.0%.

Col (4):   <u>Education costs</u>: the projected education costs for the two children is detailed in Chapter 2, **Financial Position and Goal Setting**.

Col (5):   <u>Social security</u>: the social security survivor's benefits are based on John's current earning base. The spouse receives social security benefits until the youngest child turns 16. Each child's social security benefits end when he or she reaches age 18.

     The surviving spouse does not receive any social security benefits from the time the youngest child turns 16 until age 60, the so-called *'black-out period.'*

Col (6):   <u>Wages</u>: the surviving spouse's current wages are increased annually at 3.0%. The spouse intends to continue working until age 55.

     The present value of the projected spouse's wages shown in Table 7-1 is approximately $230,000, based on an investment rate of return of 8.0%.

     Therefore, if, for whatever reason, the spouse does not fully realize the projected earnings, the insurance requirements can be significantly understated.

     When incorporating the surviving spouse's projected future earnings, these projections must be *realistic*.

Col (7):   <u>Total Income</u>: the total before-tax incomes, including social security benefits, Col (5), and wages, Col (6).

Col (8):   <u>Cash Flow</u>: the cash flow is equal to the total income, Col (7), minus the living expenses, Col (3), and education costs, Col (4).

Col (9):   Starting Balance: the initial entry in this column, of $322,947, represents the *capital needs* to offset the negative cash flows over the projected period.

The initial starting capital needs can be calculated using the 'back-solution' analysis which is available in computer spreadsheets.

Col (10):   Ending Balance: the annual ending balance calculation is as follows:

End Bal = (Starting balance + Cash flow) x (1 + After-tax investment rate of return)

The after-tax investment rate of return assumed in Table 7-1 projections, as previously stated, is 5.0%.

The calculation of the Sample's insurance requirements is, then, as follows:

	Home mortgage payoff	$156,500
Plus:	Projected capital needs, Table 7-1	322,947
Equals:	Total capital needs	$479,447
Less:	Taxable savings (1)	(72,710)
Less:	College savings (1)	(27,000)
Less:	John's life insurance (2)	(161,000)
Equals:	Additional insurance required	$218,737

(1) See Chapter 2, **Financial Position & Goal Setting**, Table 2-1.
(2) Life insurance with employer.

Based on the above calculations, $220,000 of additional insurance coverage is required. To provide a safety net, that is, if the spouse's estimated earnings are less than projected, or income taxes and non-recurring expenses are higher than projected, the required additional insurance was increased to $275,000.

At the end of 20 years the children education will be completed and the home mortgage, based on a pre-payment schedule (see Chapter 2, **Financial Position & Goal Setting**), will have been paid off. Consequently, a *20-year level premium term policy*, with $275,000 of additional insurance was purchased.

The premiums for the 20-year level term policy, of approximately $300 per year, was included in the Sample's base budget.

Employer defined benefit pension plans provide for various annuity payments, from single life annuities to joint-and-survivor annuities. Pension maximization is a strategy in which you select the single life annuity, which provides the *highest* monthly pension payments and then insure your life to protect your spouse, in that a single life annuity provides payments for your life only.

The amount of insurance coverage required must ensure your spouse's ability to purchase a lifetime annuity equivalent to the joint-and-survivor annuity, starting on "day one" of your retirement.

For example, a retiree's single life monthly annuity benefit is $2378 per month, whereas the 100% joint-and-survivor annuity is $1974 per month, reflecting a *before-tax difference* of $404 per month. Based on the spouse's life expectancy of 30 years, the required insurance coverage needed is approximately $300,000.

Pension maximization won't work unless the insurance premium is less than the *after-tax difference* between the single life annuity and the joint-and-survivor annuity.

It has been our experience, taking into consideration the time value of money and taxation, that insurance premiums based on the after-tax difference between a single life annuity and joint-and-survivor annuity *will not* provide the necessary insurance coverage in most cases.

Insurance Companies–Financial Stability

In that the death benefits to be received from a life insurance policy may be many years in the future, the financial strength of the insurance company must be such that it will be there at such time as death benefits are to be received.

As a consumer, there are several independent firms that rate insurance companies. The rating firms include *A. M. Best, Duffs & Phelps, Moody's Investor Services* and *Weiss Research*. All of these firms rate the insurance companies on the same financial and business strengths.

However, each rating firm has its own rating system, and they don't necessarily correlate with each other. Therefore, in evaluating an insurance company, it is recommended that the rating for several different firms be evaluated to determine the insurance companies financial strength.

> The rating companies rate the insurance *company* on their financial and business strengths, not on the company's *products*.
>
> Therefore, high ratings for companies do not necessarily imply good products, which are competitively priced.
>
> With the advent of the internet, there are many sites that provide comparative detail as it relates to the product features and costs of insurance carriers

Health Insurance

Overview:

Health insurance is a basic element of risk management. It is essential that a person have health care coverage, in that, even a relatively minor illness or accident can cost thousands of dollars.

Health insurance elections change depending on whether the coverage period is pre- or post- age 65.

Health Insurance–
- Pre- age 65
  - ➜ Individual health plans
  - ➜ Employer health plans
  - ➜ Disability plans

- Post- age 65
  - ➜ Medicare/medicaid
  - ➜ Medicare supplement
  - ➜ Long term care

The method of payment for a health plan is based on the following forms of coverage.

- Fee-for-service
- Health maintenance organizations, HMO's
- Preferred provider organizations, PPO's

The primary differences in the above health care coverages include the following.

- Constraints as to freedom of selecting physicians
- Conditions or treatments which will or won't be covered
- Expense coverage, with regards to deductibles, co-payments and stop-loss provisions

  - <u>Deductibles</u> are the amounts a person must pay-out-of-pocket before the health policy starts to make payments. The higher the deductible, the lower the insurance premium.
  - <u>Co-payments</u> are the percent of the bill a person must pay over and above the deductible, i.e. the percent of the total bill not covered by insurance.
  - <u>Stop-loss provisions</u> are the cut-off point for *annual* medical expenses, after which the insured individual pays nothing more.

The combination of deductibles, co-payments and stop-loss provisions determine how much an individual will pay of his/her medical expenses.

For example, if the deductible for a health policy is $500, with a 20% co-payment and a stop-loss limit of $3000, an individual's maximum out-of-pocket-expenses are as follows...

$$
\begin{aligned}
\text{Deductible} &= \$\ 500 \\
\text{Co-pmts} = 20\% \times 3000 &= \underline{\hspace{0.4em}600} \\
\text{Medical expense individual pays} &= \$1100
\end{aligned}
$$

Therefore, based on the above health insurance policy, the maximum annual out-of-pocket expenses is $1100.

Employer Based Health Insurance:

Employer group health plans most commonly offer insurance coverage under one or more options, such as fee-for-service, managed-care, flexible benefits, etc.

A federal law, COBRA, allows a person to continue his group health plan coverage for an extended period after leaving the employer or on death.

If an employee with coverage voluntarily or involuntarily leaves the company, the company must offer continuing coverage, if the employee elects same, for up to a period of 18 months. The employer may charge the employee a premium of up to 102% of the regular goup health premium.

Extended coverage may apply to disabled individuals for an extended period of 29 months. The maximum premium that can be charged is 150% of the regular group health premium.

Upon the death of a covered employee, continuing coverage is available to the surviving spouse and dependent children, who are beneficiaries under the plan, for a period of up to 36 months.

If a person is self-employed and not covered by an employer, the health insurance policies are more limited and more expensive.

Disability Insurance:

Disability insurance provides a source of income if you become disabled and are not able to work. The probability of becoming disabled at age 30 or 40 is much higher than that of dying.

The amount of disability coverage available is based on a percentage of the individual's income. Insurance providers will limit the coverage; however, a person should try to have at least 60% of his/her income covered.

The employer group disability insurance will provide the lowest cost coverage. However, there are various limitations.

The definition of disability under a group plan may be liberal for the first two years; however, after two years the definition of disability becomes much more restrictive.

Group disability insurance may also have "cap-out" features which limits the maximum monthly payment.

If an individual purchases private disability coverage, the following features are to be considered.

- **Definition of Disability**: this describes when a person is considered to be disabled, for the purpose of collecting benefits. There are two basic disability definitions:

  Any occupation defines a disability as the complete inability of the covered person to engage in any occupation whatsoever. This is a very strict approach.

  Own occupation defines disability so that the covered person is considered disabled if prevented from performing any and every duty pertaining to the employee's occupation. The 'own' occupation definition is the most liberal from the consumer's viewpoint.

- **Waiting period**: this defines the period a person must wait before disability benefits begin. The premium difference for a waiting period of 30 days, as compared to 120 days, is significant.

- **Benefit period**: this defines the period of time over which the policy will provide benefits.

- **Renewability and non-cancelability**: with such provisions in the policy, the insurance provider cannot cancel an individuals coverage if he/she continues to pay the premiums.

- **Waiver of premiums**: with this provision in the policy, the insurance premiums are waived during the period of disability.

Medicare:

Prior to age 65, your health coverage is provided either under an employer's group health plan, or if self-employed, under an individual health plan.

Medicare is the federal health insurance program for persons age 65 and over, and certain disabled persons.

The Medicare federal health insurance program has two parts:

- Part A – Hospital insurance
- Part B – Medical insurance

Medicare Part A pays some of the costs of hospitalization. Part B primarily covers doctor's fees and outpatient hospital services. Medicare *does not* cover long-term nursing home care or prescription drugs.

Medicare Part A is financed by payroll taxes and is premium free, whereas Medicare Part B is partially financed by monthly premiums which are deducted from the enrollee's social security benefits, and the balance is financed by the federal government.

Medicare is available at the beginning of the month a person turns age 65, whether he/she is retired or still working. Under the current regulations the retirement age of 65 is *not* scheduled to rise, even though the full retirement age for social security benefits is gradually increasing from age 65 to age 67. Medicare benefits also become available after a person has been entitled to social security disability benefits for two years, even though that person may be under age 65.

When a person enrolls in Medicare Part A, he/she also automatically enrolls in Part B. Part B, however, is elective, and therefore an individual does not have to participate in Part B.

If an employer does not provide post-retirement health coverage and a spouse is several years younger, COBRA benefits may not provide coverage until age 65.

For example, suppose a person retires at age 65 and is eligible for Medicare health coverage. If the spouse is more than three years younger, considering that COBRA provides a maximum continuation of coverage of three years, there will be a gap in coverage between the end of the COBRA continuation period and the spouse's age 65.

If the spouse is more than three years younger, and insurable, consideration should be given to the purchase of an individual health policy, as opposed to continuation of health coverage under COBRA.

Medigap Insurance:

Medicare provides health insurance coverage starting at age 65. Due to the various Medicare limitations in which a person is subjected to out-of-pocket expenses such as deductibles, co-payments and services that may not be covered, the need for a medigap health insurance policy should be considered.

To avoid the out-of-pocket expenses, it is necessary to purchase a *medigap insurance* policy, which is private health insurance designed specifically to protect against these out-ot-pocket expenses.

Currently, there are ten standard medigap plans, starting with a basic *Plan A*. The other nine plans, Plan B through Plan J, provide the basic Plan A coverage plus additional benefits. The additional benefits provide coverage for deductibles, co-insurance, prescription drugs, etc.

Long Term Care Insurance

Based on current statistics, approximately half of all women and a third of all men who are 65 will spend time in a nursing home. The cost of nursing home care varies by geographical location, and ranges from $30,000 to $70,000 per year or more.

Medicare and Medigap policies provide very little coverage for long term care in a nursing home. The inflation rate for nursing home care has been twice that of general inflation. Long Term Care, LTC, insurance provides for payment of such needs as nursing home care, home care, assisted living, etc., if a person is unable to care for himself due to a prolonged illness or disability. The annual premiums for LTC insurance may range from $500 to $2500 per year for an individual depending on age and type of coverage.

The decision to purchase a LTC insurance, or to self-insure, depends on the individual's financial status. If a person qualifies for *Medicaid*, then the purchase of LTC insurance is not recommended. If the financial situation is such that an expenditure of $160,000 to over $200,000 would not significantly reduce the life-style of the stay-at-home spouse, then LTC insurance is not recommended. For persons between these two extremes, the purchase of LTC insurance should be considered.

Purchasing of LTC insurance requires the evaluation of a multitude of factors. The costs can vary widely, depending on age, level of care coverage, etc.

The LTC insurance features that have a significant impact on LTC insurance costs include the following.

- Benefits: the amount the policy pays to cover daily nursing home care. The daily benefits election should be equivalent to 65% to 75% of the nursing home daily cost.

- Length of coverage: the length of time that benefits will be paid can be expressed in years or in dollar amounts. Coverage for three to five years is recommended; however, the decision as to length of coverage should take into consideration the unique family and health circumstances.

- Elimination period: the elimination period is the initial period of care for which the individual must pay the costs before the LTC policy begins to provide coverage. Long elimination periods, such as 90-100 days, are an effective strategy for reducing premium costs, as long as the individual can pay for the uncovered period.

- Inflation protection: to minimize the impact of inflation on the daily benefits' purchasing power, LTC policies offer simple or compound inflation riders.

  A simple interest rider automatically increases the daily benefits by 5% of the *original* benefit amount on an annual basis. The compound rider automatically increases the daily benefit by 5% of the *previous year's* benefit amount.

- Age: a person's age at the time of purchase of LTC insurance often has the biggest influence on the premium. The younger the age at the time of original purchase, the lower the base premium.

Table 7-2 illustrates the impact that the above features will have on an individual's LTC policy premiums.

Table 7-2
Comparing LTC Policy Alternatives

POLICY(1)	DAILY MAX BENEFITS,$	BENEFIT PERIOD,YRS	HOME CARE,%	WAITING PER. DAYS	INFLATION PROTECTION	ANNUAL PREMIUMS
Policy #1, Base						
@ Age 55	$100	4	100%	100	No	$609
@ Age 65	$100	4	100%	100	No	$1,133
Policy #2, Reduce benefitperiod to 3 yrs						
@Age 55	$100	3	100%	100	No	$556
@Age 65	$100	3	100%	100	No	$1,030
Policy #3, Reduce home care to 50%						
@ Age 55	$100	4	50%	100	No	$527
@ Age 65	$100	4	50%	100	No	$985
Policy #4, Reduce waitingperiod to 30 days						
@ Age 55	$100	4	100%	30	No	$683
@ Age 65	$100	4	100%	30	No	$1,299
Policy #5, Increase dailybenefit to $200						
@ Age 55	$200	4	100%	100	No	$1,218
@ Age 65	$200	4	100%	100	No	$2,265
Policy #6, Inflation Pro-tection = 5% simple						
@ Age 55	$100	4	100%	100	Yes	$950
@ Age 65	$100	4	100%	100	Yes	$1,702
Source: Prudential Financial, 8/2001						

The decision to purchase a LTC policy with lower daily benefits, but with inflation protection, vs starting with a higher daily benefit with no inflation protection must be based on the *age* of the insured.

For example, in comparing Policy #5 in Table 7-2, with $200 daily benefits but *without* inflation protection, with Policy #6 in Table 7-2, with $100 daily benefits and *with* inflation protection, the economics of benefits for Policy #5 is greater than for Policy #6 during years 1-18 of the policy if maximum benefits are paid at any time during this period.

Therefore, a recommended strategy is for individuals age 65 or younger to purchase a policy with *lower daily benefits*, and *with inflation protection*. However, for an individual over age 65 it would be more beneficial to consider a policy with 100% greater daily benefits but *without* any inflation protection.

The following policy features must be evaluated: (1) the conditions that must be satisfied to be eligible to receive benefits; (2) what levels of care are included, such as, skilled nursing care, intermediate care, custodial care and home care; (3) the company's financial rating, such that it will be able to pay claims 15 to 30 years in the future; (4) the terms of renewability, and (5) waiver of premiums, etc.

Summary

- Risk management is the financial planning process of protecting your family and assets against financial problems arising from unexpected events, such as death, disability, etc.

- The major vehicle for risk management is the use of insurance, which is a means of transferring the risk. Therefore, an individual must evaluate how much of the risk he/she is willing to retain and how much should be transferred.

- Life insurance is a way to *buy time* until a person or family wealth is such that they are self-insured.

- There are various "rules of thumb" used to determine how much life insurance is required. However, these evaluations overlook many factors that are unique to a specific individual or family. The evaluation of life insurance requirements is based on a cash flow analysis with detailed inputs relating to available financial resources and required spending rates over a designated time period.

- Health insurance is a basic element of risk management. Health insurance elections can change depending on whether the coverage is pre- or post- age 65.

Life Insurance Capital Needs Worksheet

The basic computational methodology in the determination of additional life insurance requirements is to express all outflows, that is, living expenses, college funding, debt, etc., as *present values* over the payout period. If the present value of outflows exceeds the *present value of inflows,* that is, pension incomes, social security benefits, savings, etc., then additional insurance is required.

The basic worksheet computation components and procedure are as follows:

Inflows: The present value of the survivor's pension, social security benefits, savings, life insurance, etc.

Outflows: The present value of living expenses, college funding and payment of debts.

Additional life insurance is required if the present value outflows are greater than the present value inflows. Referenced tables are on pages 197-199.

Worksheet Description:

Line #	Description	Example	Your Numbers
1	Enter age of surviving spouse.	45	
2	Enter the number of years for which insurance coverage is required.	30	
3	Enter after-tax investment rate of return.	5.5%	
4	Enter the ages of children requiring college funding.		
	Child 1	8	
	Child 2	10	
5	Enter survivor's pension, $/year	$24,000	
6	If pension is *adjusted* for cost-of-living, COLA, choose an annuity factor from Table A, corresponding to years of payout, Line 2, and after-tax investment rate of return, Line 3.		
7	If pension is *not adjusted* for cost-of-living, COLA, choose an annuity factor from Table B, corresponding to years of payout, Line 2 and after-tax investment rate of return, Line 3.	15.33	
8	Multiply Line 5, pension, by applicable annuity factor, Line 6 or Line 7. The entry in this line represents the present value of the pension payout.	$367,920	
9	Enter the social security annual benefits expected at age 60, $/yr.	$8,400	
10	Choose from Table A an annuity factor corresponding to the years of payout, Line 2, and investment rate of return, Line 3.	24.56	
11	Multiply the social security benefits, Line 9, by the annuity factor, Line 10. This entry represents the present value of social security benefits.	$206,304	

12 Enter the surviving spouse's years prior to age 60.   15

13 Choose from Table A an annuity factor corresponding to the years prior to age 60, Line 12, and the investment rate of return, Line 3.   13.60

14 Multiply the social security benefits, Line 9, by the annuity factor in Line 13. The entry in this line represents the loss of social security benefits during the *blackout period.** $114,240

15 Subtract Line 14 from Line 11. This entry represents the present value of social security benefits to be received from age 60 through the end of the payout period. $92,064

16 Enter the sum of the present value of social security, Line 15, plus the present value of the pension, Line 8. This entry represents the present value of incomes. $459,984

17 Enter the surviving spouse's current annual living expenses. $40,000

18 Multiply the annual living expenses, Line 17, by the annuity factor in Line 10. The entry in this line represents the present value of living expenses. $982,400

19 Enter for Child #1 the years prior to the start of college.   10

20 Enter the annual college tuition in *today's dollars.* $10,000

21 Choose from Table C a present value factor corresponding to the years prior to the start of college, Line 19.   3.807

22 Multiply the annual college tuition, Line 20, by the present value factor, Line 21. This represents the present value of college funding required for Child #1. $38,070

23 Enter for Child #2 the years prior to the start of college.   8

24 Enter the annual college tuition in *today's dollars.* $12,000

25 Choose from Table C a present value factor corresponding to the years prior to start of college, Line 23.   3.843

26 Multiply the annual college tuition, Line 24, by the present value factor, Line 25. This represents the present value of college costs for Child #2. $46,116

27 Add Line 22 and Line 26. This entry represents the present value of total college tuitions. $84,186

28 Sum up the present values of available resources:	$459,984	
Income resources, Line 16	225,000	
Current life insurance (input this number)	175,000	
Investment assets (input this number)		
Cumulative college savings available (input this number)	23,000	
Total available resources	$882,984	
29 Total current debt:		
Home mortgage (input this number)	$55,000	
Home equity loans (input this number)	10,000	
Other debt (input this number)	5,000	
Total debt	$70,000	
30 Additional insurance required:		
Present value of living expenses, Line 18	$982,400	
Plus: PV of college funding, Line 27	84,186	
Plus: Current debt, Line 29	70,000	
Less: Available resources	(882,984)	
Equals: Required *additional insurance*	$253,602	

* This worksheet does not include social security benefits for a surviving spouse with a child age 18 or younger. Under such circumstances, the additional insurance required would be overstated under the above conditions.

TABLE A
INFLATION ADJUSTED ANNUITY DUE FACTORS

AFTER TAX RATES OF RETURN

		4.50%	5.00%	5.50%	6.00%	6.50%	7.00%	7.50%	8.00%
	1	1.00	1.00	1.00	1.00	1.00	1.00	1.00	1.00
	2	2.00	1.99	1.99	1.98	1.98	1.97	1.97	1.96
	3	2.99	2.97	2.96	2.94	2.93	2.92	2.90	2.89
	4	3.97	3.94	3.92	3.89	3.86	3.83	3.81	3.78
	5	4.95	4.91	4.86	4.81	4.77	4.73	4.68	4.64
	6	5.93	5.86	5.79	5.72	5.66	5.59	5.53	5.47
	7	6.90	6.80	6.71	6.62	6.53	6.44	6.35	6.27
	8	7.87	7.74	7.61	7.49	7.37	7.26	7.15	7.04
	9	8.83	8.66	8.50	8.35	8.20	8.05	7.91	7.78
	10	9.79	9.58	9.38	9.19	9.01	8.83	8.66	8.49
	11	10.74	10.49	10.25	10.02	9.80	9.58	9.37	9.17
	12	11.69	11.39	11.10	10.83	10.57	10.31	10.07	9.83
	13	12.63	12.28	11.95	11.63	11.32	11.02	10.74	10.47
	14	13.57	13.17	12.78	12.41	12.05	11.71	11.39	11.08
	15	14.51	14.04	13.60	13.17	12.77	12.39	12.02	11.67
	16	15.44	14.91	14.40	13.92	13.47	13.04	12.63	12.24
	17	16.36	15.76	15.20	14.66	14.15	13.67	13.22	12.79
	18	17.29	16.61	15.98	15.38	14.82	14.29	13.79	13.31
YEARS OF PAYOUT	19	18.20	17.46	16.75	16.09	15.47	14.89	14.34	13.82
OR	20	19.12	18.29	17.52	16.79	16.11	15.47	14.87	14.31
YEARS TO AGE 60	21	20.03	19.12	18.27	17.47	16.73	16.04	15.39	14.78
	22	20.93	19.93	19.01	18.14	17.34	16.59	15.89	15.23
	23	21.83	20.74	19.74	18.80	17.93	17.12	16.37	15.67
	24	22.72	21.55	20.46	19.45	18.51	17.64	16.84	16.09
	25	23.62	22.34	21.17	20.08	19.08	18.15	17.29	16.49
	26	24.50	23.13	21.86	20.70	19.63	18.64	17.72	16.88
	27	25.39	23.91	22.55	21.31	20.17	19.12	18.15	17.25
	28	26.26	24.68	23.23	21.91	20.69	19.58	18.56	17.62
	29	27.14	25.45	23.90	22.49	21.21	20.03	18.95	17.96
	30	28.01	26.20	24.56	23.07	21.71	20.47	19.34	18.30
	31	28.87	26.95	25.21	23.64	22.20	20.90	19.71	18.62
	32	29.74	27.70	25.85	24.19	22.68	21.31	20.06	18.93
	33	30.59	28.43	26.49	24.73	23.15	21.71	20.41	19.23
	34	31.45	29.16	27.11	25.27	23.60	22.10	20.75	19.52
	35	32.30	29.88	27.73	25.79	24.05	22.48	21.07	19.79
	36	33.14	30.60	28.33	26.30	24.49	22.85	21.39	20.06
	37	33.98	31.31	28.93	26.81	24.91	23.21	21.69	20.32
	38	34.82	32.01	29.52	27.30	25.33	23.56	21.98	20.57
	39	35.66	32.71	30.10	27.79	25.73	23.90	22.27	20.80
	40	36.48	33.39	30.67	28.26	26.13	24.23	22.54	21.03

The entries in the cells of TABLE A represent the *present value* of $1.00 to be paidout over the designated payout period. The annual payments are made at the start of each year. The annual payments are adjusted each year at the assumed inflation rate of 4.0%. The PV values in the cells are based on the respective after-tax investment rates of return.

EXAMPLE: The *present value*, that is, the *lump sum investment* required to provide an inflation adjusted annual payment of $1,000 at the start of each year for ten years, assuming a 4.0% inflation rate and a 5.50% rate of return, is $9.380 ($1,000 x 9.38).

The inflation adjusted payout at the start of year 10 is $1,480. The account balance is depleted after the 10 annual payments.

TABLE B

ANNUITY DUE FACTORS
AFTER-TAX RATES OF RETURN

		4.50%	5.00%	5.50%	6.00%	6.50%	7.00%	7.50%	8.00%
	1	1.00	1.00	1.00	1.00	1.00	1.00	1.00	1.00
	2	1.96	1.95	1.95	1.94	1.94	1.93	1.93	1.93
	3	2.87	2.86	2.85	2.83	2.82	2.81	2.80	2.78
	4	3.75	3.72	3.70	3.67	3.65	3.62	3.60	3.58
	5	4.59	4.55	4.51	4.47	4.43	4.39	4.35	4.31
	6	5.39	5.33	5.27	5.21	5.16	5.10	5.05	4.99
	7	6.16	6.08	6.00	5.92	5.84	5.77	5.69	5.62
	8	6.89	6.79	6.68	6.58	6.48	6.39	6.30	6.21
	9	7.60	7.46	7.33	7.21	7.09	6.97	6.86	6.75
	10	8.27	8.11	7.95	7.80	7.66	7.52	7.38	7.25
	11	8.91	8.72	8.54	8.36	8.19	8.02	7.86	7.71
	12	9.53	9.31	9.09	8.89	8.69	8.50	8.32	8.14
	13	10.12	9.86	9.62	9.38	9.16	8.94	8.74	8.54
	14	10.68	10.39	10.12	9.85	9.60	9.36	9.13	8.90
	15	11.22	10.90	10.59	10.29	10.01	9.75	9.49	9.24
	16	11.74	11.38	11.04	10.71	10.40	10.11	9.83	9.56
	17	12.23	11.84	11.46	11.11	10.77	10.45	10.14	9.85
	18	12.71	12.27	11.86	11.48	11.11	10.76	10.43	10.12
YEARS OF PAYOUT	19	13.16	12.69	12.25	11.83	11.43	11.06	10.71	10.37
OR	20	13.59	13.09	12.61	12.16	11.73	11.34	10.96	10.60
YEARS TO AGE 60	21	14.01	13.46	12.95	12.47	12.02	11.59	11.19	10.82
	22	14.40	13.82	13.28	12.76	12.28	11.84	11.41	11.02
	23	14.78	14.16	13.58	13.04	12.54	12.06	11.62	11.20
	24	15.15	14.49	13.88	13.30	12.77	12.27	11.81	11.37
	25	15.50	14.80	14.15	13.55	12.99	12.47	11.98	11.53
	26	15.83	15.09	14.41	13.78	13.20	12.65	12.15	11.67
	27	16.15	15.38	14.66	14.00	13.39	12.83	12.30	11.81
	28	16.45	15.64	14.90	14.21	13.57	12.99	12.44	11.94
	29	16.74	15.90	15.12	14.41	13.75	13.14	12.57	12.05
	30	17.02	16.14	15.33	14.59	13.91	13.28	12.70	12.16
	31	17.29	16.37	15.53	14.76	14.06	13.41	12.81	12.26
	32	17.54	16.59	15.72	14.93	14.20	13.53	12.92	12.35
	33	17.79	16.80	15.90	15.08	14.33	13.65	13.02	12.43
	34	18.02	17.00	16.08	15.23	14.46	13.75	13.11	12.51
	35	18.25	17.19	16.24	15.37	14.58	13.85	13.19	12.59
	36	18.46	17.37	16.39	15.50	14.69	13.95	13.27	12.65
	37	18.67	17.55	16.54	15.62	14.79	14.04	13.35	12.72
	38	18.86	17.71	16.67	15.74	14.89	14.12	13.42	12.78
	39	19.05	17.87	16.80	15.85	14.98	14.19	13.48	12.83
	40	19.23	18.02	16.93	15.95	15.06	14.26	13.54	12.88

The entries in the cells of TABLE B represent the *present value* of $1.00 to be paid out over the designated payout period. The annual payments are at the start of each year. The annual payments are <u>not</u> adjusted for inflation. The *present values* in the cells are based on the respective *after-tax* investment rate of return.

EXAMPLE: The *present value*, that is, the *lump sum investment* required to provide an annual payment of $1,000 at the start of each year for 10 years, based on a 5.5% rate of return, is $7,950 ($1,000 x 7.95). The annual payment is fixed at $1,000. The account balance is depleted after the ten annual payments.

TABLE C

	PV FACTOR
1	3.972
2	3.953
3	3.935
4	3.916
5	3.898
6	3.880
7	3.861
8	3.843
9	3.825
10	3.807
11	3.789
12	3.772
13	3.754
14	3.736
15	3.719
16	3.701
17	3.684

YEARS PRIOR TO START OF COLLEGE

The entries in the "PV FACTOR" column represent the *present value* of an inflation adjusted payout of $1.00 over a four year period . The assumed inflation rate is 6.0%. The assumed investment rate of return is 6.5%. The *present value* of the college tuition is calculated by multiplying the current annual college tuition by the appropriate factor in TABLE C.

EXAMPLE: Current *college tuition* is $10,000 per year; *years to start* is 8 years (Child's age = 10). The *PV of college tuition* is equal to $10,000 x 3.843 = $38,430. If the *present value* , that is, *lump sum* of $38,430 earns 6.5%, at the start of college the market value of the *lump sum investment* is $59,720. The $59,720 will support annual college tuition payments of $15,036, $15,938, $16,894 and $17,908 at the start of each year.

—ESTATE PLANNING—

Overview:

Anyone who owns property–a home, a car, a bank account, investments, business interests, a retirement plan, personal belongings, etc., needs an estate plan.

An estate plan allows a person to direct how and to whom their properties will be distributed after their death.

Without an estate plan a person's properties will be distributed by the *state intestacy laws* of the state in which he/she resides.

Estate planning is an ongoing process which changes with marriage, arrival of children, accumulation of wealth, divorce, etc.

An estate plan may be as simple as a *Will*, or, as the need dictates, the estate plan may include various trusts, powers of attorney and other legal documents.

The primary estate planning objectives are the following.

- Transfer of assets to family members and others in accordance to the decedent's wishes.
- Designate appropriate guardians for minor children or disabled family members.
- Establish trusts as required.
- Minimize estate taxes, probate and administrative expenses.

Many people who carefully plan for income taxes do not give any thought to estate taxes. They assume that estate taxes, unlike income taxes, affect only people with large estates.

Table 8-1 is a tabulation of the total amount of estate taxes paid and the number of taxable returns, based on US Treasury Department 1999 returns. The estate tax data in Table 8-1 is categorized in accordance to estate size.

Table 8-1
Estate Tax Profile

ESTATE SIZE	TAXES PAID (Billions)	TAXABLE RETURNS
$600,000	$0.80	19,136
$1,000,000	$5.33	22,233
$2,500,000	$4.57	5,217
$5,000,000	$3.89	2,046
$10,000,000	$2.85	770
$20,000,000	$5.47	467

SOURCE: US TREASURY DEPARTMENT, BASED ON 1999 RETURNS

As illustrated in Table 8-1, for estate sizes ranging from $1,000,000 to $2,500,000, there were 22,233 taxable returns, the highest number of returns of any of the estate size brackets.

Also, the amount of estate taxes paid, $5.33 billion, was second only to the highest estate size bracket, which paid $5.47 billion in taxes, but which affected only 467 taxpayers.

Chart 8-1 is a graphic illustration of the data in Table 8-1.

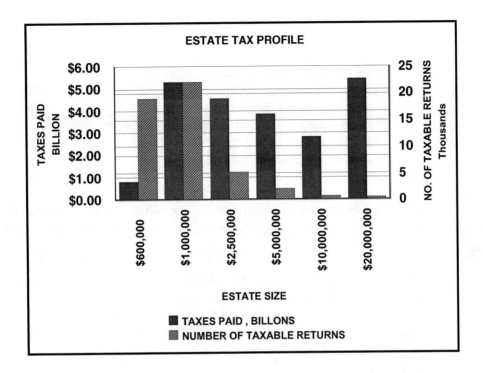

Chart 8-1

Based on year 2001 estate tax legislation, tax relief would be phased in slowly over the next decade. That is so far in the future that many lawyers and accountants assume that total repeal will never happen.

This chapter will discuss the estate planning tools and strategies available. However, individuals must consult with professional advisors before implementing any of the strategies discussed.

Wills

A Will is the cornerstone of estate planning. A Will is a legal document that allows a person to direct how the estate will be administered and distributed. Without a Will a state court will choose an administrator for the estate or, if needed, a guardian for any minor children of the decedent.

The primary reasons why a Will is the cornerstone of estate planning include the following:

- Avoids intestacy
- Designates an executor (administrator) for the estate
- Designates a guardian for minor children or disabled individuals
- Establishes various testamentary trusts
- Provides for distribution of assets to the surviving spouse or other heirs
- Provides for specific bequests
- Provides for charitable distributions
- Etc.

Property which is *owned outright*, that is, the owner can use the property as collateral, give it away, pass it on to heirs as he/she wishes, etc., will be distributed by the Will.

Property which is transferred by operation of law, such as contractual agreements, designated beneficiaries, etc., are *not* distributed via the Will.

All assets that have designated beneficiaries, such as

- Insurance policies
- IRA accounts
- Qualified retirement plans
- Annuities
- Etc.

will be transferred directly to the designated beneficiary at the death of the owner.

Property jointly held, such as the personal residence, with right of survivorship will pass directly to the surviving tenant or spouse on the death of the first tenant or spouse.

All property which is transferred by a Will is subject to probate. Probate is the legal process required to transfer title to property and to distribute assets from the decedent's estate to his or her survivors. To accomplish such transfers, the probate court will ascertain the validity of the decedent's Will, ensure that claims of creditors are satisfied and that all income and estate taxes are paid. Once these steps are taken, the court will authorize the final distribution of assets.

The probate process is often time-consuming and can be expensive, depending of the size and complexity of the estate, as well as the state of residence. When the Will is probated, its terms generally become public record.

Use of a living trust is a strategy to avoid probate and protect a person's financial privacy. A living trust is a legal document under which a person *transfers* assets to a trust.

The transferring of assets to a living trust requires changing title from the owner's name to the name of the trust. *Remember one thing—only those assets titled in the trust's name avoid probate. Upon the creation of the trust, a person must make sure he/she changes the title of the assets to be transferred to the trust.*

It has been our experience that many individuals with living trusts fail to retitle assets, resulting in an expensive legal document which is ineffective.

During a person's lifetime he/she controls the assets in the living trust. If he/she is their own trustee, no tax returns need to be filed. Taxes are paid on any income earned by the trust, the same as if he/she had never created the trust. In other words, the owner can do anything he/she wishes with the assets—he/she retains control.

In that a living trust is revocable, it can be terminated by the owner at any time.

Chart 8-2 is a graphic illustration of assets that are subjected to probate and assets that are not subjected to probate at the time of death.

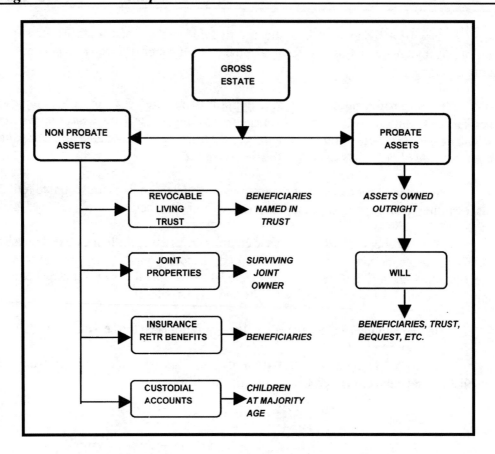

Chart 8-2

The naming of an *executor* or *personal representative* for the Will is a very important estate planning decision.

The primary function of the executor is to administer the estate and distribute the assets in accordance to the instructions in the Will. A person may choose anyone who is an adult and is legally competent to serve as an executor.

The executor appointed under the decedent's Will has the following basic duties.

- Collects assets and information
- Determines debts and claims against the estate
- Manages the estate assets
- Determines and pays all taxes
- Distributes the estate assets

The duties of an executor may be overwhelming; therefore, a person may want to give serious consideration to naming a professional as the executor or naming a professional to serve as a co-executor with a family member or a friend.

Estate Planning–Use of Trusts

Overview:

The primary objectives for using trusts in estate planning include the following.

- Asset management
- Minimize estate and income taxes

A trust is a document involving the following parties:

➡ **Trustor:** the person who transfers assets to the trust and sets up the terms under which the trust will operate, such as designated beneficiaries, distribution of trust assets, etc.

➡ **Trustee:** the trustee has legal title to the trust assets and has the fiduciary responsibility for the management of the trust assets and to carry out the terms of the trust, i.e. distribute income, etc.

➡ **Beneficiary:** the parties who are entitled to receive distributions of the trust assets.

The primary trusts used in estate planning are as follows:

- Marital trust, Trust A
- Credit shelter trust
- Qualified Terminable Interest Property trust, QTIP
- Charitable trust

Estate planning may comprehend one or more trusts, such that the estate planning goals are realized.

Marital Trust, Trust A:

At death assets may pass either outright or in trust to the surviving spouse. Assets that pass to the surviving spouse, at death, are not subjected to federal estate taxes, in that the federal estate tax law provides for unlimited marital deductions. However, on the death of the surviving spouse, the assets are subject to estate taxes.

If asset management is an objective for the surviving spouse, then a marital trust is established. Marital trusts are established solely for asset management purposes. The marital deduction trusts are referred to as *"Trust A"*.

Under a marital trust, the surviving spouse must be entitled to receive the entire net income if the trust is to qualify as a marital trust.

Under the marital trust, excluding the QTIP trust, the surviving spouse has a general power of attorney to distribute the trust property. The spouse may be given a lifetime power to distribute trust property, or the spouse can be given power to distribute property only by a Will.

The assets in the marital trust are subjected to estate taxes.

Credit Shelter Trust, Trust B:

While the benefit of professional management and investment should be the primary motive for establishing a trust, other benefits include estate tax and income tax savings. These potential taxes can become significant as the value of an estate increases in size.

Since the federal estate tax law provides for an unlimited marital deduction, it would seem sufficient for a married individual to leave the entire estate outright to his or her spouse, or put it in a marital trust if asset management were an important objective.

However, this strategy could potentially result in a federal estate tax liability upon the death of the surviving spouse, since that spouse becomes the owner of the assets inherited from the first spouse, and only the allowable exclusion for the surviving spouse can be sheltered from estate tax liability on his/her death.

Every individual is allowed a unified credit that permits a certain amount of assets to pass free of estate and gift tax.

The Economic Growth and Tax Relief Reconciliation Act of 2001 (EGTRRA) will significantly impact all future estate planning, in that both the income tax marginal rate and the allowable estate exemption amount are increased through 2009, and the estate and top gift tax rate is reduced.

The bill repeals the estate and generation skipping transfer taxes, beginning in 2010.

The following table shows the scheduled increase in the estate tax exemption and highest estate and gift tax rates.

Year	Estate Exemption	Top Tax Rates, % Estate	Income
2002	$1 million	50.0%	38.6%
2003	1 million	49.0	38.6
2004	1.5 million	48.0	37.6
2005	1.5 million	47.0	37.6
2006	2 million	46.0	35.0
2007	2 million	45.0	35.0
2008	2 million	45.0	35.0
2009	3.5 million	45.0	35.0
2010	Repealed		

After the repeal in year 2010, the bill replaces *step up in basis* with *carryover basis* for transfers at death for assets in excess of $1.3 million and spousal transfers in excess of $4.3 million.

Due to the gradual phase-in of the exemption amount, individuals who are potentially liable for estate taxes will need to review their estate planning every two or three years.

If the asset passed to the surviving spouse exceed the allowable exemption amount, to avoid or minimize the estate taxes for the surviving spouse, a portion of the "first-to-die" estate assets should be transferred to a credit shelter trust, Trust B, at the first death.

The assets transferred to the credit shelter trust do not qualify for the marital deduction on the first death. The credit shelter trust may be funded with an amount of assets equaling the allowable exemption, and the estate taxes on the first-to-die estate could be reduced to zero due to the unified estate tax credit.

The above estate planning strategy removes the assets from the second-to-die estate and the trust can pay the surviving spouse a lifetime income and then pass the credit trust assets tax free to the trust named beneficiaries upon the death of the spouse.

Upon the death of the surviving spouse, the estate taxes will be reduced by the unified tax credit. Therefore, under the 2001 tax reduction legislation, maximizing the use of the allowable exemption amount, in 2002 an estate of $2,000,000 will be free of federal estate tax, and by year 2009, an estate of $7,000,000 will be free of federal estate taxes.

The proposed estate tax exemption amounts should be put into proper perspective, in that, between 2001 and 2010 there will be two presidential and four congressional elections. Therefore, proper estate planning should not be neglected.

The estate planning strategy presented above, utilizing the exemption amount, is graphically illustrated in Chart 8-3.

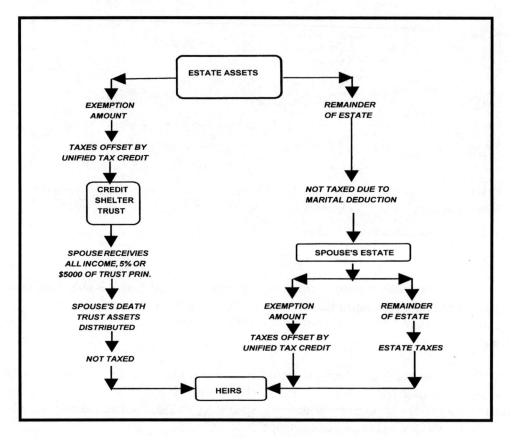

Chart 8-3

Qualified Terminable Interest Property, QTIP:

Where there is a need to limit the power of appointment for the surviving spouse, for example couples with children from a previous marriage, the QTIP trust provides income for the surviving spouse, but the underlying assets will go to the children of the previous marriage upon the death of the surviving spouse.

The QTIP trust is a marital trust; however, for the assets passing to the QTIP trust to qualify for the marital deduction, the following conditions must be satisfied.

- The trust must provide income to the spouse for life.
- The spouse may not transfer the trust income to anyone else during life or at death.

The QTIP trust assets will be included in the spouse's estate. If estate taxes are incurred, the spouse's estate may have to pay the estate taxes on the trust assets.

The QTIP trust assets must be distributed on the death of the surviving spouse, in accordance to the trust agreement, in that the QTIP trust retains the control over the distribution of the trust assets.

The Two-Trust Estate Plan:

The trusts which have been briefly described are the primary trusts used in the development of a basic estate plan.

There are many other trusts that are in the estate planning tool kit, such as, personal residence trusts, charitable trusts, irrevocable insurance trusts, trusts for minor children, etc., which have not been discussed.

Chart 8-4 is a graphic illustration of the application of the credit trust "B" and the marital trust "A" in the estate planning process and the resulting estate tax liability.

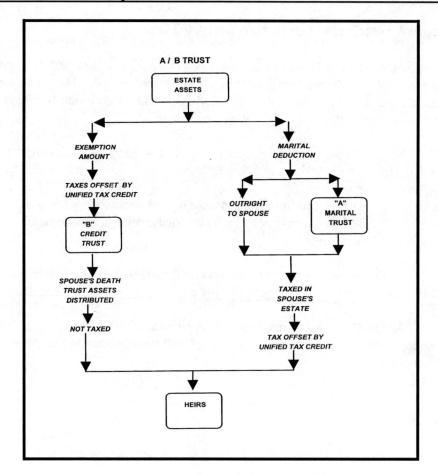

Chart 8-4

Trustee:

A trustee is the person or institution entrusted with the duty of managing property placed in the trust.

The selection process and decision criteria for selecting a trustee is similar to that of choosing an estate executor. However, there are several significant differences. The role of the executor is concluded upon the distribution of the estate assets, whereas, the trustee's responsibility may last for one or more generations. This fact has a significant impact on the selection of the trustee, co-trustee and successor trustees.

The primary duties of the trustee are as follows.

- To accept trusteeship and assume control of trust assets,
- To adhere strictly to the code of trust ethics,
- To manage investment assets and make required distributions,
- To be responsible for matters of trust taxation, and
- To distribute the trust assets when the trust terminates.

The above trustee duties require a trustee with various attributes, such as, integrity, decision making ability, investment management skills, accounting and tax planning knowledge, etc.

In selecting a trustee it may be that a team approach be considered, that is, the combining of both the professional and non-professional trustees by naming a co-trustee. The co-trustees are often family members, whereas the professional is usually a corporate fiduciary.

Lifetime Gifting:

Each year a person can give any number of people up to $10,000 each in assets ($20,000 if both spouses join in the gift) without triggering any federal transfer tax, that is, gift, estate or generation skipping taxes. This annual tax exclusion is available in addition to the unified credit.

If a person's annual gifting is in excess of the above limits, which are adjusted annually for inflation, the excess gifting is required to be reported and the excess gifting reduces the unified credit amount available at death.

Power of Attorney:

There are times in the lives of many individuals when they must turn over their authority to someone else. In fact, there are plenty of good reasons for entrusting another person with the authority to act on their behalf, should he/she be unable or unavailable to act for himself. To do so, a person is given a *power of attorney.*

The most obvious reason for giving a power of attorney is that the individual may become incapacitated, but there are many other reasons why it may be given.

The ordinary power of attorney is a written agreement under which an individual (the "principal") nominates another person (the "attorney in fact" or "agent") to act in the principal's place and on the principal's behalf. There can be more than one agent, but the document should specify whether those named are authorized to act separately or must act jointly. In addition, the agent can be permitted to delegate any or all of this authority to a third party.

If you have set up a traditional power of attorney, it can be revoked at any time while you are competent. In addition, the agent's authority is terminated upon the principal's death.

Proper planning, using a special type of power of attorney, will ensure that the power to carry out the principal's wishes remains should the principal become incompetent. This is known as a *durable power of attorney*. It is the type of power of attorney that has generated considerable interest among older individuals, particularly retirees. For purposes of this presentation, we will concentrate on the *durable* power of attorney.

The powers that should be enumerated in a durable power of attorney include the following.

- Funding trusts
- Borrowing funds
- Making retirement plan elections
- Preparing and filing tax returns
- Executing disclaimers
- Purchasing insurance
- Making gifts
- Executing trust agreements

The most important factor in drafting this versatile instrument is the selection of a capable person as the attorney in fact. Ordinarily, a spouse will be most familiar with family needs. However, care must be taken to carefully evaluate the person to whom power is given over personal affairs.

Providing for health care is an essential goal of many individuals when granting durable powers of attorney. If this is a concern, make certain a power of attorney is drawn to meet your state's requirements. Most states will accept health care decisions through a power of attorney if the power of attorney document begins with a statement of general authority to the agent. In addition, a person should detail his/her wishes on medical treatment, drugs and medicines, and artificial means of sustaining life. The agent should also be empowered to obtain medical records, sign waivers and releases, and consent to disclosures about the person's medical history.

The scope of a durable power of attorney for health care goes beyond that of a living will. While a living will usually is concerned with the withholding of life support in the event a person becomes terminally ill, a durable power of attorney for health care can address nearly any health decision.

Disclaimers:

A disclaimer is the refusal by a beneficiary to accept inherited assets.

The reason a person makes a disclaimer may be tax related, or they may disclaim for the benefit of others, etc.

Legally, when someone disclaims inherited property the property passes as if the disclaimant had died before the property owner. In other words, the property is inherited by the next beneficiary in the property owner's Will.

It should be noted that, if the owner of the property did not designate a secondary beneficiary, the disclaimed property will become part of the residual estate and be distributed in accordance with the local law. Therefore, the Will should have provisions that specifically direct where the disclaimed property will go.

Disclaimers can be valuable in financial and estate planning. The most common use may be in adjusting marital deductions. To deal with this uncertainty, the estate plan Wills should provide for the husband and wife to leave all their property to each other outright, but provide that if the surviving spouse may disclaim any or all inherited property, up to the amount of the deceased spouse's applicable exclusion amount, the disclaimed funds can be used to fund a credit trust for the surviving spouse's benefit.

In the above scenario there are no taxes, as the assets pass to the surviving spouse as a result of the marital deduction. However, upon the death of the surviving spouse, substantial estate taxes may be incurred if the disclaimer is not implemented.

Through the use of the disclaimer, the credit trust can be funded up to the allowable exclusion; therefore, these assets are removed from the surviving spouse's estate and are not taxed in the first-to-die estate due to the allowable unified tax credit.

In that the disclaimant *cannot direct* who will inherit the disclaimed property, the Will must include language directing who would receive the property.

The IRS regulations specifies that disclaimers must meet the following requirements to be valid.

- There must be a statement that identifies the property, signed by the person who is disclaiming, and delivered to the estate's executor.

- The person who is disclaiming must demonstrate that he/she has not accepted any of the benefits of the property.

- A disclaimer must be filed within nine months of the date of death of the property owner.

It should be pointed out that, effective 1/1/98, the IRS regulations pertaining to disclaimers was changed such that a surviving spouse may disclaim a deceased spouse's fifty percent interest in jointly owned property.

In that married couples usually hold title to their home, bank and brokerage accounts as joint tenants, this IRS ruling greatly expanded the opportunity to use disclaimers.

Estate Planning: Regular IRA's and Qualified Savings Plans

Tax-deferred retirement savings, such as regular IRA's and qualified corporate savings plans may represent a significant portion of a retiree's estate. Therefore, such issues as *maximizing* the deferral period and ultimate taxation must be comprehended in the estate planning process.

Tax-deferred savings remaining in the estate are subjected to income taxes and estate taxes if the estate exceeds the exclusion amount.

In April, 2002, the IRS released new regulations regarding how minimum required distributions, MRD, are to be calculated. These regulations apply to regular IRA's and all qualified retirement plans and custodial accounts.

The new MRD regulations greatly simplified the calculation, in that a *uniform table* for determining lifetime required distributions will be used by all IRA and qualified plan owners, regardless of the designated beneficiaries.

The effect of the new legislation will be to *reduce* the MRD required to be withdrawn each year by owners 70½ and older.

A single exception exists for IRA owners whose sole beneficiaries are spouses who are more than ten years younger than the owner, in that these IRA owners may choose a MRD factor using a *joint life expectancy factor*, which would be more favorable than the uniform table factor.

The uniform table minimum required distribution divisors for retirees, starting in 2002, are tabulated below in Table 8-2.

Table 8-2
Minimum Required Distribution Factors

Uniform Table for Determining Applicable Factors											
Age	Divisor	Age	Divisor	Age	Divisor	Age	Divisor	Age	Divisor	Age	Divisor
70	27.4	78	20.3	86	14.1	94	9.1	102	5.5	110	3.1
71	26.5	79	19.5	87	13.4	95	8.6	103	5.2	111	2.9
72	25.6	80	18.7	88	12.7	96	8.1	104	4.9	112	2.6
73	24.7	81	17.9	89	12.0	97	7.6	105	4.5	113	2.4
74	23.8	82	17.1	90	11.4	98	7.1	106	4.2	114	2.1
75	22.9	83	16.3	91	10.8	99	6.7	107	3.9	115	1.9
76	22.0	84	15.5	92	10.2	100	6.2	108	3.7		
77	21.2	85	14.8	93	9.6	101	5.9	109	3.4		

The minimum required distributions, MRD, are calculated by dividing the prior year's ending tax-deferred savings account balance by the appropriate factor from the uniform table.

For example, if the prior year ending tax-deferred savings account balance was $100,000 and the owner's age is 75, the MRD is $4367 ($100,000/22.9).

After the death of the account owner, the MRD will generally be based on each beneficiary's individual life expectancy, if the assets are in separate IRA accounts.

If the account is an IRA account and the spouse is the sole beneficiary of the owner's IRA, the spouse may roll over the IRA into her name and the MRD will be based on the surviving spouse's age using the uniform table factors as tabulated in Table 8-2.

If the beneficiary is a non-spouse, the minimum required distributions will be based on a single-life table.

The single-life factors are tabulated in Table 8-3.

Table 8-3
Single-Life MRD Factors

Age	Divisor	Age	Divisor	Age	Divisor	Age	Divisor	Age	Divisor	Age	Divisor
20	63.0	31	52.4	42	41.7	53	31.4	64	21.8	75	13.4
21	62.1	32	51.4	43	40.7	54	30.5	65	21.0	76	12.7
22	61.1	33	50.4	44	39.8	55	29.6	66	20.2	77	12.1
23	60.1	34	49.4	45	38.8	56	28.7	67	19.4	78	11.4
24	59.1	35	48.5	46	37.9	57	27.9	68	18.6	79	10.8
25	58.2	36	47.5	47	37.0	58	27.0	69	17.8	80	10.2
26	57.2	37	46.5	48	36.0	59	26.1	70	17.0	81	9.7
27	56.2	38	45.6	49	35.1	60	25.2	71	16.3	82	9.1
28	55.3	39	44.6	50	34.2	61	24.4	72	15.5	83	8.6
29	54.3	40	43.6	51	33.3	62	23.5	73	14.8	84	8.1
30	53.3	41	42.7	52	32.3	63	22.7	74	14.1	85	7.6

The use of the factors in Table 8-3, in determining the MRD for a non-spouse beneficiary is best illustrated by the following example.

If we assume an IRA owner dies at age 80 and the non-spouse beneficiary is age 35 in the year following the death of the owner, the starting factor from Table 8-3 is 48.5. Therefore, if the account balance of the inherited IRA is $100,000, the *MRD* is $2062 ($100,000/48.5).

The 48.5 factor from Table 8-3 is applicable only to the first year minimum required distribution for the non-spouse beneficiary, in that the factor for the following year is obtained by subtracting 1.0 for each year, i.e. fixed term. For example, the factors for the 2nd, 3rd, 4th year, etc., are as follows.

Year	Factor	Comment
1	48.5	Table 3, age 35
2	47.5	Year 1 factor minus one
3	46.5	Year 2 factor minus one
4	45.5	Year 3 factor minus one
Etc	Etc	Etc

The factors shown in Table 8-3 provide only the *starting* factor for the non-spousal beneficiary for the first year of distributions.

The computational procedure described is referred to as "fixed term."

In our example, the MRD factor for the owner in the year of death at age 80, assuming a $100,000 balance, and using the uniform table factor from Table 8-2, is 18.7, resulting in a MRD of $5348 ($100,000/18.7).

The MRD of $2062 for the non-spouse beneficiary at age 35, as compared to the MRD for the owner, whose MRD at age 80 would be $5348, is 61% less. This illustrates the planning opportunities in selecting appropriate beneficiaries and thereby extending the deferral of taxation on the earnings of the inherited IRA.

If the IRA owner dies *without* designating a beneficiary, the remaining balance of the IRA distributions are based on the owner's remaining life expectancy in the year of death, using the fixed term computational procedure.

In our example, the owner was 80 years old in the year of death. Therefore, the distribution factor for the first year after death, from Table 8-3, is 10.2; the following year it would be 9.7, etc.

Taking into consideration the estate taxes paid on the IRA at the death of the owner plus the income taxes paid as the IRA is distributed to the beneficiary, the total taxes on an IRA could be very significant.

Upon the death of an IRA owner, the tax-deferred savings are subjected to income tax as distributions are made. Withdrawals from tax-deferred savings after the owner's death are considered *income in respect of a decedent*, or IRD, meaning income that wasn't taxed before the owner's death. The beneficiary withdrawing money from tax-deferred savings, after the owner's death, must pay income tax on it. However, when distributions or withdrawals are made from the IRA after the owner's death, the government allows the beneficiary to take a deduction for the estate taxes paid on the IRA.

In that a charity is tax-exempt organization, distributions to a charity are not subject to income tax on the *income in respect of a decedent*. In addition, the estate can take a charitable deduction for the amount left to the charity.

Table 8-4 is a brief summary of the minimum required distributions, MRD, for beneficiaries after the IRA owner's death after the required beginning date, RBD.

Table 8-4
Summary of Beneficiary Minimum Required Distributions

Beneficiary	Distribution Rules at Death of Owner
Spouse	• Rollover
	♦ Minimum required distribution, MRD, based on the *uniform* table life expectancy, starting no later than spouse's age 70½ or at attained age.
	♦ Spouse may designate new beneficiaries.
	♦ If beneficiary accounts are separate, the MRD is based on the respective *single life* expectancy (less one each year); otherwise based on the single life expectancy of the oldest beneficiary (less one each year).
	♦ Beneficiary must start MRD in the year following the death of the owner.
	• No rollover
	♦ Spouse's MRD is based on *single life* expectancy table, starting no later than age 70½ or at attained age.
	♦ Cannot designate new beneficiaries.
Non-Spouse	• No rollover available
	• If the beneficiary accounts are separate, the MRD is based on the respective *single life* expectancies (less one each year); otherwise based on the single life expectancy of the oldest beneficiary (less one each year)
	• Must start MRD in the year following the death of the IRA account owner
Trust	• If trust is a qualified trust, and beneficiary accounts are separate, MRD is based on the respective *single life* expectancies of the beneficiaries (less one each year); otherwise based on the single life expectancy of the oldest beneficiary (less one each year).
	• Must start MRD in year following the death of the IRA account owner.
No Beneficiary	• MRD is based on the IRA account owner's remaining single life expectancy.

Federal Estate Taxes

Figuring estate taxes is complex. However, to effectively plan an estate, an individual needs at lease a basic understanding of how the estate tax is calculated.

Estates are subjected to a federal estate tax if the total *taxable* estate exceeds the unified credit exemption. The basic computational procedure used in the termination of the taxable estate is as follows.

Gross Estate
Less: Deductions
Equals: Adjusted Gross Estate

Less: Marital Deduction
Less: Charitable Deductions
Equals: Taxable Estate

Times: Federal Estate Tax Rate
Equals: Total Estate Taxes

Less: Unified Tax Credit
Less: State Tax Credit
Equals: Net Payable Estate Tax

The gross estate includes all investment assets, personal assets, life insurance, etc.

The allowable deductions include estate administration fees, funeral expenses, valid debts, etc.

The marital deductions represent the value of assets that pass from a person to his/her spouse in a qualified manner during their lifetime or at the owner's death. The assets may pass outright or in trust.

The assets passed to the surviving spouse are not subject to taxes in the owner's estate. While the idea of passing all assets to the surviving spouse tax-free may sound attractive, this planning strategy is not good tax planning strategy if the second-to-die's taxable estate will exceed the allowable exclusion.

If a person makes a charitable gift in his/her Will, the estate can claim an estate-tax deduction for the value of that gift.

The total estate tax is based on the application of the Federal estate tax rates to the taxable estate.

The total estate taxes are adjusted by deducting the applicable unified tax credit and the state tax credit to arrive at the net estate taxes payable.

As previously mentioned, on receiving a distribution from inherited IRA's, or other such retirement plans, income tax is incurred on withdrawal, that is, income in respect of a decedent, IRD, meaning income that wasn't taxed before the owner's death.

In that IRA's or other such retirement plans that are inherited are subject to estate taxes and, subsequently, income taxes when the beneficiary makes withdrawals, the IRS has provided for a tax deduction for "income in respect of a decedent," IRD.

To calculate the total income tax deduction that the heirs of an IRA can claim over time, the estate is recalculated without the inclusion of the IRA assets. This amount of federal estate tax is subtracted from the actual federal estate tax paid to arrive at the deduction that can be claimed.

The IRD deductions are taken at such time as the IRA assets are withdrawn or distributed and are subjected to income tax.

The following example illustrates the IRD tax deduction concepts. If the actual estate tax paid was $80,000 with the inclusion of the IRA assets and the estate tax calculation without the IRA assets was $65,000, then $15,000 ($80,000 - $65,000) of the federal estate tax is allocable to the inclusion of the IRA in the estate.

If the inherited IRA value is $100,000 and a beneficiary withdraws $20,000, which is 20% of the IRA, he/she is entitled to claim a deduction of $3000 ($15,000 x .20) against the taxable income. The deduction is claimed as a miscellaneous deduction that is not subject to the 2% AGI floor. As additional withdrawals are made, the individual may claim a proportional part of the remaining $12,000 ($15,000 - $3,000). This continues until the federal estate taxes paid on the IRA are consumed. After that, all further withdrawals are fully taxed.

It should be noted that income tax form do not emphasize this tax break, nor is it comprehended in most personal income tax-preparation software.

In fact, most heirs, not knowing of this opportunity, can pay significantly more taxes than necessary on their inherited IRA's or other tax-deferred retirement plans.

Summary

- Estate planning is not only for the wealthy.

- A Will is the cornerstone of estate planning. All property that is transferred by Will is subjected to probate.

- Properties that are transferred by operation of law, such as contractual agreements, designated beneficiaries, joint ownership, etc., are not subjected to probate.

- The primary objectives for using trusts in estate planning are 1) minimize estate taxes and 2) asset management.

- The criteria to be used in selecting a trustee should be based on the individual's integrity, decision making ability, investment and tax management skills, etc.

- The continuation of the deferral of taxation on tax-deferred savings, on death of the owner, may be significantly increased by the proper selection of beneficiaries.

- In addition to the Will and trusts, estate planning comprehends powers of attorney, living wills, gifting, charitable giving, use of disclaimers, etc.

- Estate planning is complex; therefore, individuals must consult with professional advisors before implementing any of the strategies discussed.

–TIME VALUE OF MONEY–

Overview

There is no area of understanding that is more important to personal financial planning than the *time value of money.*

An incredible amount of money and human energy are expended in the interest of achieving financial security and yet most people do not have a clear understanding of the intricacies of the financial planning process and the time value of money.

The establishment of goals relative to the various financial planning elements, such as Risk Management, Investment Planning and Retirement Planning, etc., all require the use of the time value of money computational procedures.

The *internet* provides an array of "tools" that are available to perform the complex mathematical computations as they relate to the financial planning process.

However, without the proper understanding of concepts and input requirements, you may be solving the *wrong* problem.

Only with proper understanding of the required input variables and the interpretation of results can the planning tools available on the *internet* be used with the *highest level of confidence.*

The following are examples of issues and financial goals common to the development of a financial plan, requiring the application of time value of money concepts.

These examples provide a statement of the financial planning goals or issues, and delineate the data inputs that must be comprehended.

Issue: Future Value of a lump sum investment

➜ *Data Inputs required–*
  » Initial investment amount, that is, the present value
  » Length of accumulation period
  » Investment rate of return, expressed as pre-tax or after-tax
  » Frequency of investment compounding: monthly, quarterly, annually, etc.

➜ *Time Value of Money concept–*
  » Calculation of the future value of an initial investment

Issue: The Future Value of periodic savings contributions

➜ *Data Inputs required–*
  » Amount of each savings contribution
  » Frequency of savings contributions: monthly, quarterly, annually, etc.
  » Is contribution made at the <u>start</u> or <u>end</u> of each period
  » Investment rates of return, expressed as pre-tax or after-tax
  » Frequency of investment compounding

➜ *Time Value of Money concept–*
  » Calculation of the future value of a series of equal savings contributions

Goal: What is the <u>initial</u> investment required such that, at the end of a stated planning period, an accumulation of a stated number of dollars is realized?

➜ *Data Inputs required–*
  » Required future savings
  » Length of accumulation period
  » Investment rate of return, expressed as pre-tax or after-tax
  » Frequency of investment compounding

➜ *Time Value of Money concept–*
  » The calculation of the initial investment required to achieve required future savings.

Goal: Determine the periodic savings contributions required such that at the end of a stated planning period an accumulation of a stated number of dollars is realized.

➜ ***Data Inputs required–***
  » Required future savings
  » Length of accumulation period
  » Investment rate of return, expressed as pre-tax or after-tax
  » Frequency of investment compounding: monthly, quarterly, annually, etc.
  » Frequency of savings contributions: monthly, quarterly, annually, etc.
  » Whether savings contributions are made at the start or end of each contribution period

➜ ***Time Value of Money concepts–***
  » Calculation of the periodic savings contributions required to accumulate the required savings at the end of the planning period

Goal: ***Determine the investment rate of return required to achieve the stated dollar savings at the end of a designated planning period.***

➜ ***Data Inputs required–***
  » Required savings
  » Contributions:
    ▪ Lump sum
    ▪ Periodic savings contributions
  » Duration of planning period
  » Frequency of periodic savings contributions: monthly, quarterly, annually, etc.
  » Frequency of investment compounding: monthly, quarterly, annually, etc.

➜ ***Time Value of Money concepts–***
  » Calculation of the investment rate of return needed to accumulate a stated dollar savings over a given period of time.

Issue: ***What is the inflation adjusted annuity payment, constant purchasing power, that the cumulative retirement savings will generate over a stated retirement period?***

➜ ***Data Inputs required–***
» Savings at start of retirement
» Duration of the retirement period
» Frequency of annuity payments: monthly, quarterly, annually, etc.
» Investment rate of return, expressed as pre-tax or after-tax
» Frequency of investment compounding: monthly, quarterly, annually, etc.
» Inflation rate
» Are payments made at start or end of each period

➜ ***Time Value of Money concepts–***
» Calculation of the inflation adjusted payments that can be generated from the accumulated retirement savings over a stated retirement period.

Goal: ***Retirement Savings required to support a stated inflation adjusted life style during the retirement years***

➜ ***Data Inputs required–***
» Required annuity payment
» Length of retirement period
» Frequency of payments and are they made at the start or end of each period
» Investment rate of return, expressed as pre-tax or after-tax
» Investment compounding frequency: monthly, quarterly, annually, etc.
» Inflation rate

➜ ***Time Value of Money concept–***
» Calculation of the required savings at the start of retirement that will support *constant purchasing power* over the retirement period

Goal: ***College Tuition funding***

➜ ***Data Inputs required–***
» Number and age of children
» Years of education to be provided

- » College tuition in today's dollars
- » Tuition inflation adjustment
- » Current college savings already accumulated
- » Contribution frequency
- » Investment rate of return, expressed as pre-tax or after-tax
- » Investment compounding frequency: monthly, quarterly, annually, etc.

→ *Time Value of Money concept–*
- » Calculation of the periodic savings required to achieve the stated tuition funding at the start of college for each of the respective children

Issue: *Life Insurance requirements*

→ *Data Inputs required–*
- » Age of surviving spouse
- » Number of children and current ages
- » College tuition requirements
- » Current savings available, survivor's pension benefits, social security benefits, etc.
- » Spouse's income from work
- » Social security benefits
  - ▪ Benefits for children under 18 years of age
  - ▪ Benefits for surviving spouse
- » Current life insurance coverage
- » Outstanding liabilities, such as home mortgage, etc.
- » Living expenses
  - ▪ While children at home
  - ▪ After children are gone
- » Planning period for survivors

→ *Time Value of Money concepts–*
- » The calculation of the life insurance requirements requires multiple time value of money calculations, with the integration of these results into a cash flow plan that takes into consideration all asset inflows and outflows.

Issue: **Return on an Investment over a given investment period**

➜ *Data Inputs required–*
» Share price and number of shares purchased
» Dividends per share
» Distribution of dividends or reinvestment of dividends
» Share price and number of shares at the end of the investment period
» Duration of investment period

➜ *Time Value of Money concepts–*
» Calculation of the return on the investments, expressed as the annualized rate of return, takes into consideration the initial investment amount, the periodic payment of dividends, the investment period and the ending market value.

Issue: **Annual Effective Rate: two different banks offer a one-year certificate of deposit with a 5.0% _nominal_ interest rate. Which certificate provides the highest _annual effective rate_?**

➜ *Data Input required–*
» Nominal investment rate of return
» Compounding period per year: daily, monthly, quarterly, etc.

➜ *Time Value of Money concept–*
» The calculation of the annual effective rate takes into consideration the nominal rate and the compounding periods in the year.

Although the time value of money concepts seem rather complex, they are actually not difficult to understand. It is not necessary to memorize equations, but it is necessary to understand the mathematical relationships.

Solutions can be obtained using financial calculators, spreadsheet @ financial functions and internet tools.

Cash Flow Diagrams

An invaluable aid in the analysis of time value of money is the use of cash flow diagrams. This is simply a pictorial representation of the timing and direction of financial transactions.

The diagram begins with an horizontal line, called a time line. It represents the duration of a financial planning period, and is divided into compounding periods. For example, a financial problem that transpires over 6 years, with annual compounding, would be diagramed like this.

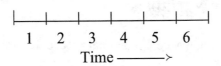

The exchange of money in a problem is depicted by vertical arrows. Money you receive is represented by an arrow pointing up from the point in the time line when the transaction occurs; money you pay out is represented by an arrow pointing down.

Every completed cash flow diagram must include at least one cash flow in each direction.

One more bit of information must be specified for our cash flow diagram for problems involving periodic payments. Such payments can be made either at the beginning of a compounding period (payments in advance, or annuities due) or at the end of the period (payments in arrears, or ordinary annuities).

Calculations involving payments in advance yield different results than calculations involving payment in arrears. Illustrated below are portions of cash flow diagrams showing payments in advance, or at the beginning of a time period, and payments at the end of the time period.

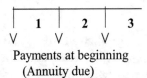

Payments at beginning
(Annuity due)

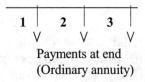

Payments at end
(Ordinary annuity)

Time Value of Money Variables

The time value of money computational procedures are based on five different variables.

➜ <u>Present Value, PV</u>;   this represents the current value of one or more savings contributions over a designated planning period.

➜ <u>Future Value, FV</u>:   the cumulative savings value based on one or more savings contributions over the designated planning period.

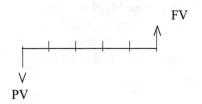

→ <u>Payments, Pmt</u>:   these are periodic savings contributions or distributions over the designated planning period.

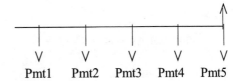

Pmt1   Pmt2   Pmt3   Pmt4   Pmt5

If the payments are equal, the payments are called annuity payments.

→ <u>Investment Rate, I</u>:   the investment rate of return, expressed as a yearly nominal rate.

If the interest earned on the principal is compounded, i.e. earned semi-annually, quarterly, monthly, etc., the nominal rate must be converted to represent the rate applicable to the compounding time interval.

In the calculation of the future value of an initial investment, or a series of contributions or payments, the interest rate is referred to as simple "interest rate."

However, in the calculation of the present value of a future value, or of a series of future contributions or payments, the interest rate used is referred to as the "discount rate."

→ <u>Time Interval, N</u>:   the time interval, N, represents the number of time periods over the designated planning period.

The time intervals may be expressed as annual, quarterly, monthly, etc.

Simple and Compound Interest Concepts

Bank A has an advertisement that they offer a three-year CD with a 5.0% rate of return.

Bank B advertises a three-year CD with a 4.91% rate of return.

These stated rates of return are the 'nominal' rates. The actual rates of return earned by an investment may be quite different, as will be illustrated.

As an investor it would appear that the first bank with the CD that earns 5.0% is the bank where he/she would invest their savings. Is this a correct decision?

To determine if this decision is correct we need to know if the interest is simple or compounding. The differentiation between simple interest and compound interest is as follows.

➡ Simple interest–interest earned *only* on the initial principal.

➡ Compound interest–interest earned on the initial principal plus *interest earned on the interest*.

We can best illustrate this with an example. Suppose we invest $1000 in a money market account that earns 5.0% *simple* interest and another $1000 in a money market that earns 5.0% *compound* interest. What will the difference in earnings be at the end of five years? Lets first calculate the interest earned in the simple interest account.

Table 9-1

	SIMPLE INTEREST INCOME		
	Interest Rate 5.0%		
Year	Starting Balance	Interest Income	Ending Balance
1	$1,000	$50.00	$1,050
2	1,050	50.00	1,100
3	1,100	50.00	1,150
4	1,150	50.00	1,200
5	1,200	50.00	1,250

As illustrated above, the interest earned at the end of five years on $1000, at a 5.0% simple interest rate was $250 ($1250 - $1000).

It should be noted that no interest was earned on interest.

Using annual compounding, the interest earned is as follows.

Table 9-2

	COMPOUND INTEREST INCOME		
	Interest Rate 5.0%, Annual Compounding		
Year	Starting Balance	Interest Income	Ending Balance
1	$1,000	$50.00	$1,050
2	1,050	52.50	1,103
3	1,103	55.13	1,158
4	1,158	57.88	1,216
5	1,216	60.78	1,276

As illustrated above, the interest earned at the end of five years on $1000 at a 5.0% rate, compounded annually, is $276 ($1276 - $1000).

Therefore, the increase in interest earnings is $26 ($276 - $250) using annual compounding, as compared to simple interest, a difference of approximately 10.0%.

This difference of $26 is the result of earning *interest on interest.*

It is significant to note that the frequency of compounding will also increase the interest earnings. In our examples the compounding was done at the end of each year. The following table illustrates the effect on interest earnings by increasing the frequency of compounding, using the above example.

If we assume that the compounding is quarterly, then, in the second quarter interest is earned on the interest earned in the first quarter, and in the third quarter interest is earned on the interest earned in the first two quarters, etc.

The interest rate applicable to each quarter is the nominal rate divided by the number of compounding periods. Therefore, the interest rate for the quarterly compounding periods for our example is 1.25% per quarter (5.0% ÷ 4).

The table below illustrates the interest earned on $1000, based on quarterly compounding for five years.

Table 9-3

COMPOUND INTEREST INCOME			
Interest Rate, 5.0%, Quarterly Compounding			
Quarter	Starting Balance	Interest Income	Ending Balance
1	$1,000	$12.50	$1,013
2	1,013	12.66	1,025
3	1,025	12.81	1,038
4	1,038	12.97	1,051
5	1,051	13.14	1,064
6	1,064	13.30	1,077
7	1,077	13.47	1,091
8	1,091	13.64	1,104
9	1,104	13.81	1,118
10	1,118	13.98	1,132
11	1,132	14.15	1,146
12	1,146	14.33	1,161
13	1,161	14.51	1,175
14	1,175	14.69	1,190
15	1,190	14.87	1,205
16	1,205	15.06	1,220
17	1,220	15.25	1,235
18	1,235	15.44	1,251
19	1,251	15.63	1,266
20	1,266	15.83	1,282

As illustrated above, the interest earned at the end of five years on $1000, at a 5.0% rate, compounding quarterly, is $282 ($1282 - $1000).

Therefore, the increase in interest earnings of $32 ($282 - $250), using quarterly compounding, as compared to simple interest, is approximately 13.0%.

As illustrated, when comparing different investment rates of return a person should compare the *annual effective rate*, AER, which comprehends the number of compounding periods, not the nominal rates.

The following formula converts the nominal interest rate to the effective rate.

$$\textbf{AER} \quad = \quad (1.0 + I/C)^{\,C} - 1.0 \qquad\qquad [1]$$

Where   I = nominal interest rate, expressed as a decimal
                 C = number of compounding periods

The "^" implies that C is an exponent.

For example, the AER for the quarterly compounding is calculated as follows, based on a nominal interest rate of 5.0%:

$$
\begin{aligned}
AER &= (1 + 0.05/4)^{^4} - 1 \\
&= (1 + 0.0125)^{^4} - 1 \\
&= (1.0125)^{^4} - 1 \\
&= 1.05094 - 1 \\
&= 0.05094 \text{ or } 5.094\%
\end{aligned}
$$

Using the AER, as calculated above, the future value of the $1000 at the end of five years is calculated as follows.

Table 9-4

ANNUAL EFFECTIVE RATE INTEREST INCOME			
AER = 5.0945 %			
Year	Starting Balance	Interest Income	Ending Balance
1	$1,000	$51	$1,051
2	1,051	54	1,104
3	1,104	56	1,161
4	1,161	59	1,220
5	1,220	62	1,282

Note that the ending balance of $1282 in Table 9-4 is the same as the ending balance in Table 9-3.

The AER is also referred to as the annualized or compounding rate of return.

Because a person has learned that compounding more often increases the effective interest rate, he/she might think that continuous compounding would quickly double, triple or quadruple an investment in a dizzying geometric progression.

Unfortunately, continuous compounding produces an annual effective rate only slightly higher than the rate earned with monthly compounding.

The mathematical process of continuous compounding is, nevertheless, intriguing. In experimenting with pushing compounding to its limit, mathematicians and financial experts discovered that if $1.00 is invested for one year and if the frequency of compounding periods increases indefinitely, the sum of the principal and interest eventually reach a limiting value of $2.718282. This number is the natural "e" that has long fascinated mathematicians.

To convert nominal rates to the effective rates in a continuous compounding setting, the following formula is used.

$$AER \quad = \quad e^{\wedge I} - 1.0 \qquad\qquad [2]$$

$$\text{Where} \quad e \quad = \quad \text{natural number } 2.718282$$
$$I \quad = \quad \text{nominal rate}$$

The above formula is based on a 365 day year.

For example, the AER, using the nominal rate of 5.0%, is calculated as follows.

$$AER \quad = \quad e^{\wedge.05} - 1$$
$$= \quad 5.13\%$$

Table 9-5 illustrates the impact resulting from the frequency of compounding. The AER is also displayed for the respective compound periods.

The future values in Table 9-5 are based on investing $1000 at a 5.0% investment rate of return over a five year period.

Table 9-5

Future Value of $1000, Interest Rate ,5.0%					
Compounding=>	Simple	Annual	Quarterly	Monthly	Continuous
Years ⇓					
1	$1,050.00	$1,050.00	$1,050.95	$1,051.16	$1,051.27
2	1,100.00	1,102.50	1,104.49	1,104.94	1,105.17
3	1,150.00	1,157.63	1,160.75	1,161.47	1,161.83
4	1,200.00	1,215.51	1,219.89	1,220.90	1,221.40
5	1,250.00	1,276.28	1,282.04	1,283.36	1,284.03
AER=>	NA	5.00%	5.09%	5.12%	5.13%

Let's go back to the original bank decision as to where to purchase the three year certificate of deposit.

Bank A advertised the 5.0% nominal rate, compounded annually, whereas Bank B advertised the 4.91% rate, compounded quarterly.

The AER for Bank B, which compounded quarterly, is 5.0%. Therefore the interest earned at Bank B is equivalent to the interest earned at Bank A.

The Magic of Compound Interest

Financial independence is a function of 1) Time, 2) Dollars Invested, 3) Rate of Return and 4) Compounding.

Most people think a few extra percentage points of interest will not significantly impact the end results. Just one or two percent of interest compounded over a number of years can be the difference of thousands and thousands of additional dollars.

For example, if a person invested a lump sum of $1000 at three different rates of interest, 5%, 10% and 12%, compounded annually, the difference in the growth of your money is tabulated below.

Table 9-6

FUTURE VALUE OF $1000			
YEARS	5%	10%	12%
5	$1,276	$1,611	$1,762
10	1,629	2,594	3,106
15	2,079	4,177	5,474
20	2,653	6,727	9,646
25	3,386	10,835	17,000
30	4,322	17,449	29,960
35	5,516	28,102	52,800
40	7,040	45,259	93,051
45	8,985	72,890	163,988
50	11,467	117,391	289,002

As illustrated in Table 9-6, the future value of $1000 at the end of 20 years, earning 10%, and compounded annually, is $6727, whereas, the future value of $1000 at the end of 20 years, compounded annually, earning 12% is $9646. The 2.0% difference in rates of return resulted in approximately 43% more earnings.

The future value of $1000, earning 10%, at the end of 25 years is $10,835, as compared to earning 12%, a value of $17,000, representing an increase of 57%.

Chart 9-1 provides a graphic illustration of the future value over time for the respective investments tabulated in Table 9-6.

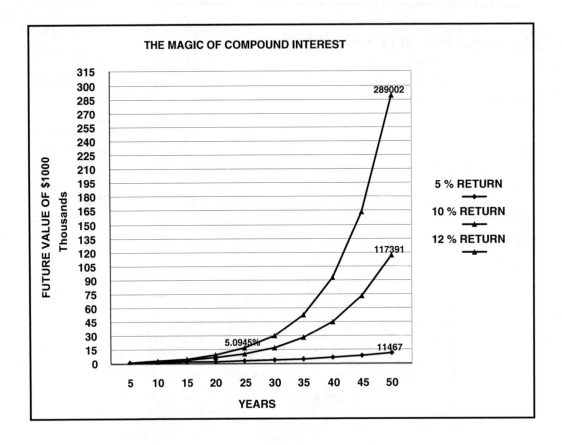

Chart 9-1

Present Value, PV, to Future Value, FV

In the development of a personal financial plan, the need to know the future value, FV, of a lump sum investment, or the present value, PV, of some future investment, is a very common question.

The cash flow diagram for a future value is represented as follows.

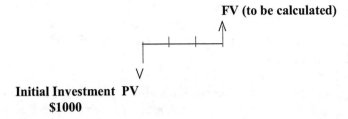

FV (to be calculated)

Initial Investment PV
$1000

The question illustrated above is, *"What is the future value, FV, of $1000 invested today, PV, with after-tax earnings of 6.5%, at the end of three years?"*

In our example, we assume that our investment is compounded annually; therefore, the annual effective rate, AER, and the nominal rate are equivalent, that is, 6.5%.

The following is a conceptual presentation of the calculation of the future value, FV.

The value of our investment at the end of the first year is the initial investment plus the interest earned.

$$
\begin{array}{lcl}
\text{Initial investment} & = & \$1000 \\
\text{Interest earned (1000 x 6.5\%)} & = & \$65 \\
\text{Future value, end Yr 1, FV1} & = & \$1065 \\
\end{array}
$$

The future value of our investment at the end of the second year, FV2, is the investment value at the end of the first year, FV1, plus interest earned in the second year.

$$
\begin{array}{lcl}
\text{FV 1} & = & \$1065 \\
\text{Interest earned (1065 x 6.5\%)} & = & \$69 \\
\text{Future value, end Yr 2, FV2} & = & \$1134 \\
\end{array}
$$

(Note: values are rounded)

The future value of our investment at the end of the third year, FV3, is the investment value at the end of the second year, FV2, plus the interest earned in the third year.

$$
\begin{array}{lcl}
\text{FV2} & = & \$1134 \\
\text{Interest earned (1134 x 6.5\%)} & = & \$74 \\
\text{FV3} & = & \$1208 \\
\end{array}
$$

(Note: Values are rounded)

We could continue this procedure for any number of years and find the value of the deposit in the Nth year, but this would require 'N' of the above computations. Instead, we will go to an alternate method which gives us a general formula. To get this formula, we start by defining the following terms.

PV	=	Present Value, the value of a sum of money today
FV1, FV2,..... FVN	=	the Future Value of a sum of money at the end of periods 1, 2, ... N
I	=	the interest rate per period
N	=	the number of periods

The above computation of the future value at the end of year 3 may be expressed as follows.

$$FV3 \quad = \quad FV2 \times (1 + I)$$

("x" implies multiplication)

In that FV2 is equal to FV1 x (1 + I), we can substitute this term in the above equation, as follows.

$$FV3 \quad = \quad FV1 \times (1 + I) \times (1 + I)$$

In examining the above formula we note that we lost sight of the initial deposit, PV. To correct this problem, since FV1 is equal to PV x (1 + I), further substitution yields

$$FV3 \quad = \quad PV \times (1 + I) \times (1 + I) \times (1 + I)$$

Notice that we have multiplied the expression (1 + I) three times, once for each year. Instead of writing it three times we could use an exponent of 3 and write it only once:

$$FV3 \quad = \quad PV \times (1 + I)^{3}$$

Finally, since we don't want to limit ourselves to three year problems, we can generalize to N time periods. This gives us the general formula for the determination of Future Value, FV.

$$FV_{N} \quad = \quad PV \times (1 + I)^{N} \qquad\qquad [3]$$

Where FV_{N}	=	Future value of a sum of money at the end of N periods of time
PV	=	Present value, the value of a sum of money today

$$\text{I} \quad = \quad \text{interest rate per period}$$
$$\text{N} \quad = \quad \text{number of time periods}$$

Substituting the values for our problem, we have—

$$\text{PV} \quad = \quad \$1000$$
$$\text{I} \quad = \quad 6.5\%$$
$$\text{N} \quad = \quad 3$$

into formula [3], the future value at the end of three years is calculated as follows:

$$
\begin{aligned}
\text{FV} \quad &= \quad \text{PV x } (1 + \text{I})^{\wedge\text{N}} \\
&= \quad 1000 \text{ x } (1 + 0.065)^{\wedge 3} \\
&= \quad \$1208
\end{aligned}
$$

In that the various time value of money computations are mathematically complex, it is necessary to use a *financial calculator* or *computer spreadsheet @* functions to make this calculation.

The computation of the future value of a present value for our example, using a financial calculator requires the following inputs.

$\boxed{\text{PV}}$ present value   = $1000

$\boxed{\text{I}}$ interest rate   =   6.5%

$\boxed{\text{N}}$ time periods   =   3

With the above data inputs, the $\boxed{\text{FV}}$ key will calculate the future value.

Formula [3] assumes annual compounding; therefore, if compounding occurs 'C' times a year, the formula must be modified to comprehend the compounding periods as follows.

$$\text{FV}_\text{N} \quad = \quad \text{PV x } (1 + \text{I/C})^{\wedge\text{N*C}} \qquad\qquad [4]$$

For example, if the compounding for our example is each quarter, the calculation of the future value, using formula [4] is as follows.

$$FV \quad = \quad 1000 \times (1 + 0.065/4)^{\wedge 3 \times 4}$$
$$\quad = \quad \$1213$$

The quarterly compounding increased the future value at the end of the three year period by $5.00 ($1213 - $1208), as compared to annual compounding.

The computation of the future value of a present value compounding quarterly, using a financial calculator, requires the following inputs.

$$\boxed{PV} \quad = \quad \text{present value} \quad = \quad 1000$$

$$\boxed{I} \quad = \quad \text{interest rate} \quad = \quad 1.625\% \ (6.5\%/4)$$

$$\boxed{N} \quad = \quad \text{time periods} \quad = \quad 12 \ (3 \times 4)$$

With the above inputs the $\boxed{FV}$ key will calculate the future value.

The internet provides many sites that will provide calculation of future values when given the required inputs.

Future Value, FV, to Present Value, PV

Converting a "Future Value, FV, to a Present Value, PV," is the reverse of the "Present Value, PV, to Future Value, FV" computation.

For example, you require a stated number of dollars in the future, such as scheduled major home improvements.

The issue is to determine what is the lump sum investment that you need today, PV, to achieve the target future value over a designated planning period and with know investment rates of return.

The unknown variable to be solved for is the present value, PV, as a lump sum.

The cash flow diagram for the Present Value computation is the same as the cash flow diagram for the Future Value computation.

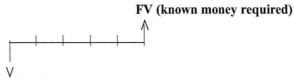

Unknown Investment PV

In the determination of Present Values we move backwards along the time axis, which is a technique generally know as discounting. When we are computing a Future Value, FV, we are moving ahead in time which is a technique generally known as compounding.

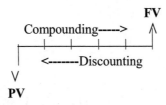

When converting from a future value to a present value, the following variables are known.

Future Value, <u>FV</u>
Number of Time Periods, <u>N</u>
Investment Rate of Return, <u>I</u>

Since all of these variables are in our general formula [3] for Future Value computation, and all are known except the Present Value, PV, we can rearrange the Future Value formula to solve for the Present Value as follows.

If   **FV**   =   **PV x (1.0 + I)** $^{\wedge N}$

Then   **PV**   = $\left(\dfrac{FV}{(1.0+I)^{\wedge N}} \right)$

PV   =   **FV** $\times \left(\dfrac{1.0}{(1.0+I)^{\wedge N}} \right)$ [5]

If we have a stated future value goal of $10,000 at the end of five years, what is the present value, or lump sum investment, required at the start of the five year planning period, on the assumption that our after-tax rate of return is 7.0%?

The PV factor used to multiply the FV by is...

$$\left(\frac{1.0}{(1.0+I)^{\wedge}N}\right)$$

Using the input variable for our example, where I = 7.0% and N = 5, we can solve for the PV for the various time periods.

The present value factor is .....

$$\text{PVfactor} = \left(\frac{1.0}{(1.0+I)}\right) = \left(\frac{1.0}{1.07}\right) = 0.9346$$

The conceptual computational procedure to determine the required PV is as follows.

$$
\begin{array}{lcl}
\text{FV5 x PV factor} & = & \text{PV4} \\
\text{FV4 x PV factor} & = & \text{PV3} \\
\text{FV3 x PV factor} & = & \text{FV2} \\
\text{FV2 x PV factor} & = & \text{FV1} \\
\text{FV1 x PV factor} & = & \text{PV}
\end{array}
$$

Where   FV(N) = future value at the end of the Nth time period.

              PV(N) = the present value at the beginning time period.

The computational procedure is tabulated in Table 9-7.

Table 9-7

	FV	FV	PV
YEAR	BALANCE	FACTOR	BALANCE
5	$10,000	0.9346	$9,346
4	9,346	0.9346	8,734
3	8,734	0.9346	8,163
2	8,163	0.9346	7,629
1	7,629	0.9346	7,130

FUTURE VALUE TO PRESENT VALUE CALCULATION

The interpretation of Table 9-7 is as follows:

A present value investment of $7130 is required if a future value of $10,000 is to be accumulated at the end of five years, based on a 7.0% rate of return and compounded annually.

Using the present value formula [5], the calculation of the required present value is as follows.

$$PV = FV \times \left(\frac{1.0}{(1.0 + I)^{\wedge}N} \right) \qquad [5]$$

$$= 10,000 \times \left(\frac{1.0}{(1.0 + 0.07)^{\wedge}5} \right)$$

$$= \left(\frac{1.0}{1.4026} \right)$$

$$= \quad \$7130$$

The present value, PV, of a future value, FV, can be calculated using a financial calculator that requires the following inputs.

FV   Future value   = $10,000

I   Interest rate   =   7.0%

N   Time periods   =   5

With input of the above data, the $\boxed{\text{PV}}$ key will calculate the present value.

The relationships between the four variables of FV, PV, I and N in the Present Value and the Future Value formulas are delineated below. Given any three of the four variables, we can solve for the unknown fourth variable.

Unknown Variable	Future Value FV	Present Value PV	Compounding/ Discount Rate I	Time Period N
Value of sum in future	?	known	known	known
Value of sum in present	known	?	known	known
Compounding/ Discount Rate	known	known	?	known
Time Period	known	known	known	?

Annuity Computations

An annuity is a series of equal payments made at regular intervals. Your paycheck is an example of an annuity, also your monthly rent or mortgage payments, the premiums on an insurance policy, the installments on a car loan, or regular deposits into a savings account.

The annuity computational procedures to be described are only applicable if the annuity payments are of *equal amounts* each time period.

If payments are not equal or paid at regular time intervals, the solution to these problems requires the use of a computer spreadsheet in conjunction with the use of various financial @ functions.

The time interval between annuity payments is called the payment period. If your payment is due at the end of each payment period, it is called an *ordinary* annuity. Examples of ordinary annuities are a car loan or a mortgage. The cash flow diagram for an ordinary annuity is as follows.

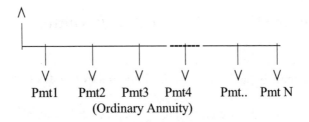

(Ordinary Annuity)

The arrow pointing up is the loan money received at the start of the financial transaction. The down arrows represent the payments made on the loan at the *end* of each time period.

But with some annuities, like insurance premiums or a lease, the payment is due at the beginning of the month. This is called an *annuity due*. The cash flow diagram for an annuity due is as follows.

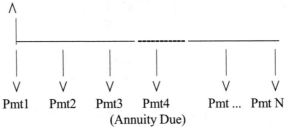

(Annuity Due)

The arrow pointing up is the loan money received at the start of the financial transaction. The down arrows represent the payments made on the loan at the *beginning* of each time period.

There are four different types of annuity calculations that are encountered in the development of a personal financial plan. The development of the formulas for annuity calculations involve the same concepts used in the development of our Present Value and Future Value formulas. The four types of annuity computations are...

- Future value of an <u>ordinary</u> annuity
- Future value of an annuity <u>due</u>
- Present value of an <u>ordinary</u> annuity
- Present value of an annuity <u>due</u>

Future Value of an Ordinary Annuity

We are interested in the calculation of the future value of a series of equal payments or savings at regular intervals over a designated planning period.

Example: What is the Future Value of an IRA account for which annual payments of $2000 are made at the end of each year for ten years, earning 8.0% compounded annually?

The cash flow diagram for this problem is as follows.

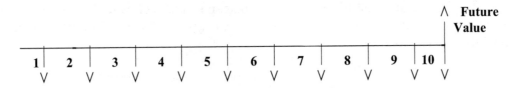

The concepts of the calculation of the future value of annuity payments can be illustrated using formula [3], that is, converting present values to future values.

For each annual IRA contribution of $2000 the future value of the contribution is calculated.

For example, the $2000 contributed at the end of the first year, earning 8.0%, has a future value of $3998, as illustrated in Table 9-8.

Whereas the $2000 contributed at the end of the 10th year has no earnings. Its future value is $2000.

Therefore, the future value of ordinary annuity payments is the sum of the individual future values, or $28,973, as illustrated in Table 9-8.

The computational procedure is illustrated in Table 9-8.

Table 9-8

CONTRIBUTION PERIOD	CONTRIBUTION DOLLARS	COMPOUNDING PERIODS	FUTURE VALUE
	FUTURE VALUE OF ORDINARY ANNUITY		
1	$2,000	9	$3,998
2	2,000	8	3,702
3	2,000	7	3,428
4	2,000	6	3,174
5	2,000	5	2,939
6	2,000	4	2,721
7	2,000	3	2,519
8	2,000	2	2,333
9	2,000	1	2,160
10	2,000	0	2,000
		FUTURE VALUE=>	$28,973

The above computational procedure is given to illustrate the basic concepts involved in the computation of the future value of an ordinary annuity.

This procedure is very time consuming and cumbersome. However, the series of future value computations shown in Table 9-8 can be represented by the following factor.

Ordinary annuity--

$$FVfactor = \left(\frac{(1.0+I)^{\wedge N} - 1.0}{I} \right) \qquad [6]$$

Substituting the interest rate, I, of 8.0%, and time periods, N, of 10, the future value factor for an ordinary annuity in our example, is .....

$$FVfactor = \left(\frac{(1.0+0.08)^{\wedge 10} - 1.0}{0.08} \right) = 14.4866$$

The future value of our example is then calculated as follows.

$$
\begin{aligned}
FV &= \text{Pmt x FV Factor (ordinary)} \\
&= 2000 \times 14.49 \\
&= \$28,973
\end{aligned}
$$

The future value of $28,973 is the same future value as computed in Table 9-8.

In that the various time value of money computations are mathematically complex it is necessary to use a financial calculator or a computer spreadsheet @ financial function.

The computation of the future value of ordinary annuity payments using a financial calculator requires the following inputs for our problem.

Pmt	=	Annuity payment	=	$2000
I	=	Interest rate	=	8.0%
N	=	Time periods	=	10
End	=	Computational mode		

With input of the above data the FV key will calculate the future value for our problem.

The internet provides many web sites that can provide calculation of the future value of an ordinary annuity.

Future Value of an Annuity Due

The calculation of the future value of an annuity due is the same procedure as the calculation of the future value of an ordinary annuity, with the exception that payments are made at the *start* of each time period, as opposed to at the end.

The cash flow diagram for the future value of an annuity due is as follows.

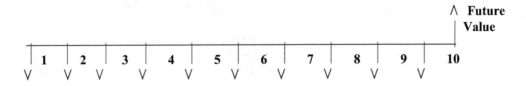

Beginning of year payments

If we compare this cash flow diagram to the Future Value of the individual payments are calculated using our present value to future value formula [3].

Table 9-9

	FUTURE VALUE OF ANNUITY DUE		
CONTRIBUTION PERIOD	CONTRIBUTION DOLLARS	COMPOUNDING PERIODS	FUTURE VALUE
1	$2,000	10	$4,318
2	2,000	9	3,998
3	2,000	8	3,702
4	2,000	7	3,428
5	2,000	6	3,174
6	2,000	5	2,939
7	2,000	4	2,721
8	2,000	3	2,519
9	2,000	2	2,333
10	2,000	1	2,160
		FUTURE VALUE=>	$31,291

In comparing Table 9-9 with Table 9-10 we note that the future value of the contribution in the first year is $4318 as compared to $3998 resulting from the increase in compounding periods from nine for the ordinary annuity to ten for the annuity due.

The above computational procedure illustrates the basic concepts involved in the computation of the future value of an annuity due.

The above series of future value calculations for an annuity due may be represented by the following factor.

Annuity Due:

$$\textbf{FVfactor} = \left(\frac{(1.0+I)^{\wedge N} - 1.0}{I} \right) \times (1.0 + I) \qquad [7]$$

Substituting the interest rate, I, of 8.0%, and the time periods, N, of 10, the future value factor for an annuity due in our example is.....

$$\textbf{FVfactor} = \left(\frac{(1.0+0.08)^{\wedge 10} - 1.0}{0.08} \right) \times (1.0 + 0.08)$$

$$= 14.4866 \times 1.08$$
$$= 15.65$$

The future value for our example is then calculated as follows:

$$
\begin{aligned}
\text{FV} \quad &= \quad \text{Pmt x FV factor(due)} \\
&= \quad 2000 \times 15.64 \\
&= \quad \$31{,}291
\end{aligned}
$$

The future value of $31,291 is the same future value as computed in Table 9-9.

The calculation of the future value on an annuity due requires the use of a financial calculator or a computer spreadsheet and @ financial functions.

The computation of the future value of annuity due payments using a financial calculator requires the following inputs.

| Pmt | Annuity payment | = | $2000 |

| I | Interest rate | = | 8.0% |

| N | Time periods | = | 10 |

| Begin | | Computational mode |

With the above inputs the FV key will calculate the future value of an annuity due.

The internet provides many web sites that will calculate the future value of annuity payments, both ordinary and annuity due.

Present Value of an Ordinary Annuity

In the calculation of the present value of an annuity, we are asking the question as to what is the present value of savings required to provide a series of annuity payments over a designated planning period.

For example, suppose your retirement life style requires annual supplemental payments of $25,000 per year at the end of each year for 20 years from your retirement savings, assuming your savings earn 8.0%, compounded annually.

What are the savings you need at the start of retirement, PV, that will provide an annual distribution of $25,000, based on the above assumptions?

The cash flow diagram for this problem is .....

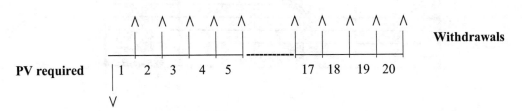

The computational procedure concepts require that each individual future annuity payments be discounted back to its equivalent present value, and the resulting present value is the sum of the respective individual present values.

The discounting of the respective annuity payments to their present values is accomplished using formula [5].

Table 9-10 illustrates the calculation procedure for the determination of the present values for the individual annuity payments.

Table 9-10

	PRESENT VALUE OF AN ORDINARY ANNUITY		
PERIOD	DISTRIBUTION DOLLARS	DISCOUNT PERIODS	PRESENT VALUE
1	$25,000	20	$5,364
2	25,000	19	5,793
3	25,000	18	6,256
4	25,000	17	6,757
5	25,000	16	7,297
6	25,000	15	7,881
7	25,000	14	8,512
8	25,000	13	9,192
9	25,000	12	9,928
10	25,000	11	10,722
11	25,000	10	11,580
12	25,000	9	12,506
13	25,000	8	13,507
14	25,000	7	14,587
15	25,000	6	15,754
16	25,000	5	17,015
17	25,000	4	18,376
18	25,000	3	19,846
19	25,000	2	21,433
20	$25,000	1	23,148
	PRESENT VALUE =>		$245,454

As illustrated in Table 9-10, the present value of the annuity payment of $25,000 to be received at the end of the 20th year, based on an 8.0% investment rate of return, is $5364. The present value of the $25,000 to be received at the end of the 19th year is $5793, etc.

The sum of the individual present values is $245,454. Therefore, if we are to achieve our retirement goal of an annuity payment of $25,000 at the end of each year for 20 years, a lump sum retirement savings of $245,454 is required at the start of retirement.

Table 9-10 provides a conceptual computational procedure to calculate the present value of an ordinary annuity.

The above series of present value calculations can be represented by the following ordinary annuity factor.

Ordinary Annuity:

$$PVfactor = \left(\frac{1.0 - \dfrac{1.0}{(1.0+I)^{\wedge N}}}{I} \right) \qquad [8]$$

Substituting the interest rate, I, of 8.0%, and the time period, N, of 20, the present value factor for an ordinary annuity is calculated as follows.

$$PVfactor = \left(\frac{1.0 - \dfrac{1.0}{(1.0+I)^{\wedge N}}}{I} \right)$$

$$= \left(\frac{1.0 - \dfrac{1.0}{(1.0+0.08)^{\wedge 20}}}{0.08} \right)$$

$$= \quad 9.818$$

The present value for our example is calculated as follows.

$$
\begin{aligned}
PV \quad &= \quad \text{Pmt x PV factor (ordinary annuity)} \\
&= \quad 25{,}000 \text{ x } 9.818 \\
&= \quad \$245{,}454
\end{aligned}
$$

As illustrated in Table 9-10, the necessary PV of $245,454 is required if a payment of $25,000 is to be made at the end of each year for 20 years, based on an 8.0% investment rate of return.

In that the annuity factor is mathematically complex, the use of a financial calculator or computer spreadsheet with financial @ functions is required.

The computation of the present value of ordinary annuity payments using a financial calculator requires the following inputs for our problem.

PV	Annuity payments	= $25,000
I	Interest rate	= 8.0%
N	Time periods	= 20
End	Computation mode	

With the input of the above data, the PV key will calculate the present value for our problem.

Present Value of an Annuity Due

We shall use the same data used in the Present Value ordinary annuity problem. However, the withdrawals for an annuity due are made at the *beginning* of the year as opposed to the end of the year. The cash flow diagram for this problem is as follows.

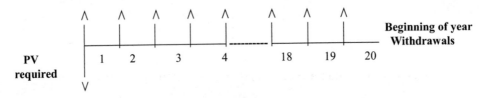

In comparing the above cash flow diagram for an annuity due with the cash flow diagram for the ordinary annuity, it should be noted that each payment has one less period of compounding, in that, the payment is made at the start of each year, as opposed to the end.

Therefore, the present value of the annuity due will be greater than that of the ordinary annuity.

Table 9-11 illustrates the calculation procedure for the determination of the present value for the individual annuity payments.

Table 9-11

	DISTRIBUTION	DISCOUNTING	PRESENT
PERIOD	DOLLARS	PERIODS	VALUE
1	$25,000	19	$5,793
2	25,000	18	6,256
3	25,000	17	6,757
4	25,000	16	7,297
5	25,000	15	7,881
6	25,000	14	8,512
7	25,000	13	9,192
8	25,000	12	9,928
9	25,000	11	10,722
10	25,000	10	11,580
11	25,000	9	12,506
12	25,000	8	13,507
13	25,000	7	14,587
14	25,000	6	15,754
15	25,000	5	17,015
16	25,000	4	18,376
17	25,000	3	19,846
18	25,000	2	21,433
19	25,000	1	23,148
20	25,000	0	25,000
		PRESENT VALUE=>	$265,090

PRESENT VALUE OF AN ANNUITY DUE

The interpretation of Table 9-11 is the same as for Table 9-10.

The present value of our annuity due is $265,090, as compared to $245,454 for the ordinary annuity, reflecting the impact of the compounding periods.

The above series of present value calculations can be represented by the following annuity due factor.

Annuity Due:

$$\text{PVfactor} = \left(\frac{1.0 - \dfrac{1.0}{(1.0+I)^{\wedge N}}}{I} \right) \times (1.0+I) \qquad [9]$$

Substituting the interest rate, I, of 8.0%, and the time periods, N, of 20, the present value factor for an annuity due is calculated as follows.

$$PVfactor = \left(\frac{1.0 - \dfrac{1.0}{(1.0+I)^{\wedge N}}}{I} \right) \times (1.0+I)$$

$$= \left(\frac{1.0 - \dfrac{1.0}{(1.0+0.08)^{\wedge 20}}}{0.08} \right) \times (1.0+0.08)$$

$$= \quad 9.818 \times 1.08$$
$$= \quad 10.604$$

The present value for our example is calculated as follows.

$$
\begin{aligned}
PV \quad &= \quad \text{Pmt x PV factor (annuity due)} \\
&= \quad \$25,000 \ \times \ 10.604 \\
&= \quad \$265,090
\end{aligned}
$$

As illustrated in Table 9-11, the necessary present value of $265,090 is required if payments of $25,000 are made at the start of each year, based on an 8.0% investment rate of return.

Annuity Calculation Variables

The relationship between the five variables in the annuity problems are delineated below.

Unknown Variable	Future Value FV	Present Value PV	Period Payment Pmt	Compounding/ Discount Rate I	Time Period N
Value of sum in future	?	NA	known	known	known
Value of sum in present	NA	?	known	known	known
Period Pmt	**	**	?	known	known
Compounding/ Discount Rate	**	**	known	?	known
Time Period	**	**	known	known	?

NA   =   not applicable
**   =   either FC or PV known

Inflation

The development of a personal financial plan must take into consideration inflation if the projection of college costs, retirement purchasing power, etc., are to be realistic.

To get an insight into the impact of inflation it is necessary to review historical inflation data.

Chart 9-2 is a graphic profile of inflation rates over the last 30 years, 1970 through 1999.

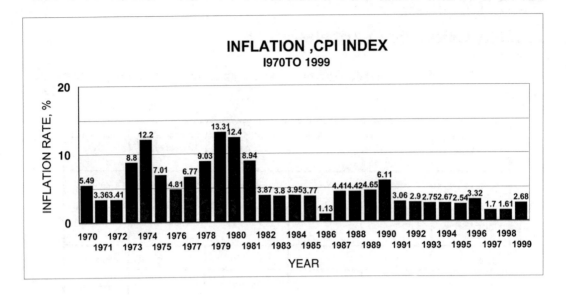

Chart 9-2

During the 30 year period of 1970 through 1999 inflation ranged from a low of 1.13% in 1986 to a high of 13.31% in 1979, averaging 5.16% over the 30 year period.

Inflation erodes the purchasing power of the dollar. For example, at a 4.0% inflation rate the reduction in purchasing power is illustrated in Table 12, Col (2) and Col (3).

Column (4) of Table 9-12 illustrates the future dollars required to provide the same purchasing power as today's dollars, based on a 4.0% inflation rate.

Table 9-12

(1) YEAR	(2) PURCHASING POWER, $	(3) % REDUCTION IN PURCHASE POWER	(4) CONSTANT PUR. POWER
1	$1,000	0.00%	$1,000
5	815	18.46%	1,217
10	665	33.52%	1,480
15	542	45.79%	1,801
20	442	55.80%	2,191
25	360	63.96%	2,666
30	294	70.61%	3,243
NOTE: PROJECTIONS BASED ON 4.0 % INFLATION			

Real Rates of Return

The *real rate* of return for an investment is defined as the difference between the *inflation rate* and the *rate of return* on the investment.

Table 9-13 provides a profile of the real rate of return for the S&P 500 Index, which is a measure of stock performance and inflation for the 30 year period from 1970 through 1999.

Table 9-13

(1) YEAR	(2) S&P 500, %	(3) CPI, %	(4) REAL % RETURN
1970	4.01%	5.49%	-1.48%
1971	14.31	3.36	10.95
1972	18.98	3.41	15.57
1973	-14.66	8.80	-23.46
1974	-26.47	12.20	-38.67
1975	37.20	7.01	30.19
1976	23.84	4.81	19.03
1977	-7.18	6.77	-13.95
1978	6.56	9.03	-2.47
1979	18.44	13.31	5.13
1980	32.42	12.40	20.02
1981	-4.91	8.94	-13.85
1982	21.41	3.87	17.54
1983	22.51	3.80	18.71
1984	6.27	3.95	2.32
1985	32.16	3.77	28.39
1986	18.47	1.13	17.34
1987	5.23	4.41	0.82
1988	16.81	4.42	12.39
1989	31.49	4.65	26.84
1990	-3.17	6.11	-9.28
1991	30.55	3.06	27.49
1992	7.67	2.90	4.77
1993	9.99	2.75	7.24
1994	1.31	2.67	-1.36
1995	37.43	2.54	34.89
1996	23.07	3.32	19.75
1997	33.36	1.70	31.66
1998	28.58	1.61	26.97
1999	21.04	2.68	18.36
==============	===============	===============	=============
AVG=>	14.89	5.16	9.73

The average rate of return for the S&P 500 Index, for the 1970 through 1999 period, was 14.9%, whereas the average inflation rate was 5.2%, resulting in an average real rate of return of 9.70% over the 30 year period.

As illustrated in Table 9-13, the real rates of return for 1973 and 1974 were a -23.5% and a -38.7%, respectively.

The real rates of return in Table 9-13 are defined as the S&P 500 Index returns adjusted for inflation. For example, in 1970 the S&P 500 Index return was 4.0%, whereas inflation was 5.5%, resulting in a real rate of return of -1.5% (4.0% - 5.5%).

In the application of the time value of money concepts, the use of the real rate of return, as defined above, will result in inaccuracies. Therefore, the following equation is used in the development of the real rate of return.

$$d = \left(\frac{1.0 + I}{1.0 + R} - 1.0 \right) \times 100 \qquad [10]$$

Where   I = Interest rate
             R = Inflation rate

In the development of the present value of required savings, as shown in Table 9-11, the annual payments are *not adjusted* for inflation, that is, they are constant over the 20 year retirement period.

Therefore, the calculation of the present value of retirement savings did not provide for the protection of purchasing power.

If we assume an inflation rate of 4.0% and an investment rate of 8.0%, and apply formula [10], the *real* rate of return is .....

$$d = \left(\frac{1.0 + I}{1.0 + R} - 1.0 \right) \times 100$$

$$= \left(\frac{1.0 + 0.08}{1.0 + 0.04} \right) \times 100$$

$$= \quad 3.846$$

Using formula [9] to calculate the present value for a series of annuity due payments, and substituting the real rate of return, of 3.8% for the interest rate, the annuity due factor becomes...

$$\text{PVfactor} = \left(\frac{1.0 - \dfrac{1.0}{(1.0+d)^{\wedge N}}}{d} \right) \times (1.0+d)$$

$$= \left(\frac{1.0 - \dfrac{1.0}{(1.0+0.03846)^{\wedge 20}}}{0.03846} \right) \times (1.0+0.03846)$$

$$= \quad 14.307$$

Therefore, if we are to maintain a constant purchasing power over the 20 year retirement period, the lump sum of savings required, PV, is calculated as follows.

$$
\begin{aligned}
\text{PV} \quad &= \quad \text{Pmt} \ \ \text{x} \ \ \text{PV factor (annuity due)} \\
&= \quad \$25,000 \ \ \text{x} \ \ 14.307 \\
&= \quad \$357,685
\end{aligned}
$$

The retirement savings of $357,685 will provide an inflation adjusted payment of $25,000 over a 20 year period, assuming a 4.0% inflation rate and an 8.0% investment rate of return.

Table 9-14 illustrates the cash flow profile.

Table 9-14

(1) YEAR	(2) START BALANCE	(3) INFL ADJ. DISTRIBUTION	(4) END BALANCE
1	$357,685	$25,000	$359,300
2	359,300	26,000	359,964
3	359,964	27,040	359,558
4	359,558	28,122	357,951
5	357,951	29,246	355,001
6	355,001	30,416	350,551
7	350,551	31,633	344,432
8	344,432	32,898	336,456
9	336,456	34,214	326,421
10	326,421	35,583	314,106
11	314,106	37,006	299,267
12	299,267	38,486	281,644
13	281,644	40,026	260,947
14	260,947	41,627	236,866
15	236,866	43,292	209,060
16	209,060	45,024	177,159
17	177,159	46,825	140,762
18	140,762	48,698	99,429
19	99,429	50,645	52,687
20	52,687	52,687	0

Column (3) depicts the 4.0% inflation adjusted annual distributions. At the end of the 20 year period the retirement savings have been depleted, Col (4).

In the development of the cash flow profile in Table 9-11, there is no adjustment for inflation. The required lump sum was $265,090 in Table 9-11, as compared to a lump sum requirement of $357,685 in Table 9-14, needed to maintain a constant purchasing power, representing a difference of approximately $92,600.

In the development of a personal financial plan, the assumptions used in the selection of 1) investment rate of return, 2) inflation rate and 3) number of retirement years can have a significant impact on establishing your retirement savings goals.

Summary

- There is no area of understanding that is more important in the development of a personal financial plan than the *time value of money*.

- Only with proper understanding of the required time value of money input variables and the interpretation of results can the planning tools available, using financial calculators, computer spreadsheets or internet tools, be used with the highest level of confidence.

- Although the time value of money concepts seem rather complex, they are actually not difficult to understand. It is not necessary to memorize formula, but it is necessary to understand the mathematical relationships.

- It is important to understand the difference between nominal investment rates of return and annual effective rates of return in selecting an investment option.

- Financial independence is a function of 1) Time, 2) Dollars Invested, 3) Rate of Return and 4) Compounding Intervals.

- The basic time value of money computational procedures are as follows...

  → Present Value to Future Value
  → Future Value to Present Value
  → Future Value of an Ordinary Annuity
  → Future Value of an Annuity Due
  → Present Value of an Ordinary Annuity
  → Present Value of an Annuity Due

- The development of a personal financial plan must also take inflation into consideration if projections of such goals as college costs, retirement savings, etc., are to be realistic.

INDEX

HIGHLIGHTED BOXES

CHARTS & FLOWCHARTS

WORKSHEETS